SAM WHITES PA

SAM WHITE'S
PARIS

NEW ENGLISH LIBRARY

For Ronald Hyde. My news editor for most of my time on The *Standard*, who was not only responsible for my being sent to Paris in the first place – but with whom these pieces were part of our continuing dialogue over the years.

First published in Great Britain in 1983 by
New English Library, Mill Road, Dunton Green, Sevenoaks, Kent.
Editorial office: 47 Bedford Square, London WC1B 3DP.

Photoset by Rowland Phototypesetting Ltd,
Bury St Edmunds, Suffolk.

Printed and bound in Great Britain by Biddles Ltd,
Guildford, Surrey

British Library Cataloguing in Publication Data

White, Sam
  Sam White's Paris.
  1. Paris (France)—History—1945–
  l. Title
  944′.36′0924   D707

ISBN: 0 450 06015 2

CONTENTS

ACKNOWLEDGEMENTS

Grateful acknowledgment is made to Mr Louis Kirby of the *Standard* and Mr Alexander Chancellor of the *Spectator* for their kind permission to reproduce the articles in this collection.

PREFACE

The Paris that I stepped into from the warm luxury of a Golden Arrow Pullman that January evening in 1947 was as cold and as hungry as it had been at any time during the German occupation. Against this dismal background of penury and disenchantment the city's psychological scars left by defeat and humiliation showed up more glaringly than ever. I had been present at the liberation of Paris and left it three months later with a sour taste in my mouth. Now, returning to it nearly three years later, the sourness gave place to something akin to nausea.

The black market flourished; and in a city where people bore the visible marks of under-nourishment one could eat magnificently in furtive black-market restaurants behind heavily curtained windows; and with the £ in illegal transactions fetching four times the official rate it was tempting to do so if one could overcome repugnance for one's fellow diners.

Most of the major collaborationist trials were mercifully over, but there was still the steady drumbeat of minor ones with the victims consisting mainly of journalists, writers and stage and screen stars. The rationing system had broken down and many people could not even obtain the meagre rations to which they were entitled. Scandals, mostly to do with the distribution of food and wine, abounded. The Communist Party remained as it did immediately after the liberation, the strongest single political force in the country, with a commanding position in every sector of French life.

One problem, however, had been solved satisfactorily, from the politicians' point of view anyway, and that was how to get rid of de Gaulle. He had solved it for them, to their great astonishment, by resigning in protest against a constitution which was a replica of the one which had brought France to its present pass.

Meanwhile, I too was having pressing if more personal problems, the chief one being how to acquire quickly sufficient knowledge of the language to be able at least to read the newspapers. Oddly enough, in despatching me to Paris, no one had thought of asking me if I spoke French. The subject only cropped up two months later when Lord Beaverbrook asked me that fateful question, to which I gave a breathtakingly honest reply. He was greatly amused and commented: 'At last we will have someone in Paris who won't let himself be bamboozled by the French.'

Fortunately, however, there were in Paris at the time any number of distractions which did not require even a primitive knowledge of the language, and among them were the activities of some spectacular crooks who quickly began making frontpage news in England.

The first of them to hit the headlines was a man with the almost comically melodramatic name of Max Intrator, an Egyptian-born Jew who was making a fortune by helping English visitors contravene the £50 currency restrictions by advancing francs in exchange for cheques on English banks. At the time the better bars in Paris were haunted by a Detective Inspector Tarr, who made a point of noting down the names of Englishmen who were clearly living beyond the official spending limits, and it was in no time that he stumbled on the activities of Black Max, as he quickly became known in the Press.

No sooner was the chief villain identified than the story was put about that Intrator really worked for the most notorious of the Jewish terrorist organisations of Palestine, the Stern Gang, and that therefore any cheques cashed with him helped to provide bullets to kill British soldiers. Intrator was quickly bundled out of France, but I had become chummy with him and before leaving he sent me a present. It was a precious gift at the time, a bottle of whisky labelled Black and White, and the accompanying note read: 'From Black Max to White Sam'.

Another was George Dawson, an operator of sound cockney stock, who had mysteriously acquired a fortune from scrap-metal deals. He went everywhere with a bodyguard (a former public-school man), lived lavishly in the best hotels and even had an ocean-going yacht harboured in Cannes. Then the astonishing Sydney Stanley took refuge in Paris after nearly bringing down the first Labour Government by lavishing gifts and hospitality on a junior minister called Belcher. Stanley was the archetypal con-man, who had gone to seed by the time he came here and whose main line of patter consisted of claiming that he was working for MI5, who wanted him to find out if the Russians really had the atom bomb.

With such assistance I survived my first year and acquired

some French into the bargain. Meanwhile, political crisis followed political crisis, governments fell with clockwork regularity and it was difficult for even well-informed foreigners to recall the name of the current French Prime Minister. In those circumstances, writing about politics became an abstruse art of interest to the initiated and other distractions had to be found to justify one's job in Paris.

I had by this time developed a distinct taste for levity and as Fleet Street appeared to be intent on restoring the image of Gay Paree, I decided to make my own contribution to this worthy cause.

This was the period of spectacular parties mostly given by rich foreigners. There was thus a succession of Bestigui balls, Lopez balls, Elsa Maxwell balls, and with some wedding spectaculars thrown in such as the famous Aly Khan/Rita Hayworth one. And there was, of course, an all-time epic, the Prince Rainier/Grace Kelly nuptials. All these events could have provided material for a string of Marx Brothers comedies. Then there were the high jinks at the British Embassy under the Duff Coopers, which at one time resembled the kind of revolving bedroom farce. I see that in a recent publication Lady Diana Cooper blames me for recording each of her various face-lifts. This is not so – the information was communicated direct to the *Evening Standard* by one of her closest women friends.

I was interested in more earthy matters – an interest, incidentally, which led me to my greatest scoop – the discovery that Lady Diana's successor, Lady Jebb, had ordered the removal of the bidets in the British Embassy residence. It was about this time that Jimmy (now Sir James) Goldsmith crossed my path and he guided me unwittingly to the secret of his impending elopement with Isobel Patino. When the couple finally disappeared from view, I wrote the story which was killed on legal advice. It broke two weeks later with headlines worthy of a declaration of war.

And so the merry round continued while all the time the storm clouds gathered over a regime not only unable to control events but more dangerously unable even to control the apparatus of State and especially its army. There had been a disastrous colonial war in Indo-China and no sooner had that been lost than a fresh one started in Algeria.

Not that all the news was bad, for the country had already begun to make a remarkable industrial recovery. I recall, for example, the piece I wrote in 1954 which was appropriately headlined: 'Don't feel sorry for the French'. Then there was the brief Mendès-France interlude during which he not only ended the Indo-Chinese war but gave independence to the two French protectorates Tunisia and Morocco. However, he too was stuck with the intractable Algerian problem, insisting that the country was and would remain an integral part of France. Then came the army mutiny in Algiers, the evident inability of the Paris Government to cope with it and the return of de Gaulle.

I stuck my neck out on the General, not only tipping his return but insisting that far from destroying French democracy he would put it on a sound footing (an unpopular view at the time). I went even further by claiming that he was determined to give independence to Algeria, a view which made many of my friends doubt my sanity.

Today, if a man's greatness is to be judged by the survival of his legacy, then de Gaulle was a very great man indeed for it survives intact. His constitution, for example, is now accepted by those who once so bitterly opposed it, and his independent atomic striking force, once so derided, remains the cornerstone of French defence policy.

I also took an unpopular line on de Gaulle's veto on Britain's entry into the Common Market, arguing that the fault was more ours than his, and rendered myself unpopular at the British Embassy by revealing some highly dubious anti-de Gaulle plotting. It all ended happily with the arrival of Sir Christopher Soames as Ambassador when he went to the heart of the matter, which was to seek an Anglo-French understanding; and although his first effort to do so was sabotaged by the Foreign Office in the so-called Soames Affair he finally succeeded in his aim with Pompidou.

The student riots of 1968 took me completely by surprise and caught me off balance; and for a brief couple of hours on that famous afternoon when de Gaulle 'disappeared' I thought along with Pompidou himself, that he had decided to quit. Now a new and exciting chapter has opened with the election of Mitterrand as President. I wish him well in his search for a new kind of Socialism different both from Soviet Communism and traditional western Social Democracy. I am, however, sceptical as to the outcome.

Although I feel myself deeply involved in what happens in this country (it could hardly be otherwise after living in it for 35 years), I have never become 'assimilated' and I still look on France with the eyes of a foreigner, which has its advantages to a reporter.

Professionally, these have been very happy years. Despite Lord Beaverbrook's awesome reputation in such matters neither he nor any of his editors have ever interfered with my copy or suggested a particular line, either as regards politics or people. I have enjoyed a remarkable freedom and independence and this remains my great bond with the *Standard*.

I was fortunate in having Charles Wintour as my editor for most of my years with the *Standard*. He was the most independent of Beaverbrook's editors and he conferred a similar independence on his writers. He gave me my head especially in the matter of de Gaulle, and this was particularly exhilarating during that period when the General was under fierce attack from the entire British press. I was fortunate too in Wintour's successor, Louis Kirby, who after an unsettling period following a change of proprietors, re-settled me, as it were, on the *Standard*.

The selection for this volume was made entirely by Simon Scott of New English Library and I did not question his choice – which includes pieces I would rather forget.

SAM WHITE, Paris 1983

1947

THE PEASANTS HOLD PARIS
TO RANSOM

Paris, facing a food crisis, is today hungrier than it ever was during the occupation or since.

The Government edict that countryfolk must not sell food above certain fixed prices has caused a new wave of hoarding, with the peasantry holding the city to ransom.

Most Parisians are on a diet almost entirely of vegetables. And there are very little of those. In the shops there is no meat, no offal, no fish, no potatoes, no cauliflower – except at black market prices, well out of reach of the low-salaried or wage-earning Parisian.

So there are queues of working-class women outside shop windows containing nothing more than the notice saying that all prices have been reduced five per cent.

For the average tourist or wealthy Frenchman, however, menus in smart restaurants differ little from pre-war luxury.

And it seems certain that the peasants will win and that the price edict will be withdrawn.

Thursday, January 23, 1947

COLONEL ARRIVES WITH HIS SECOND

Communiqué No. 1 – Swords or pistols?

Parisians who awakened today eager to hear the result of a dawn duel between a famous criminal lawyer and a colonel were disappointed.

1

Sam White's Paris

Instead, a communiqué was issued on behalf of the pair. It said that their seconds were still arguing over the choice of weapons – swords or pistols?

The lawyer is Maître Maurice Garçon, and his challenger is Colonel Henri Groussard, whom Garçon accused, during a recent treason trial, of having arrested patriots while serving as inspector of police under the Vichy Government.

Originally the duel was to have been fought with pistols. The colonel is a crack shot.

Tuesday, January 28, 1947

PUT YOUR MONEY INTO A NIGHT CLUB FOR SAFETY

Prodded by the big fashion houses, Paris society (or what is left of it) has been busy for the past month in trying to revive the ancient splendours of the pre-war Paris season.

Beginning with the Prix de Diane, the French Ascot – which was ruined by a strike of stable boys – the season stalked with magnificent disdain through every obstacle that weather and current discontents could place before it. The triumphal finale came last week with a revival of the pre-war charity ball, 'Le Bal des Petits Lits Blancs'.

Now, everybody who is anybody is going off to Deauville, leaving Paris empty – to use the quaint pre-war phrase. Empty, that is, except for four million Parisians sweltering in midsummer heat.

The Ball of the Little White Beds was a charity affair in aid of children's hospitals. It was attended by about 7,000 guests who paid £6 each for admission.

It took place in the floodlit Opera, in the presence of the President, with scarlet-coated Gardes Republicaines lining the staircase, and with many beautiful women, beautifully dressed. But profitable as it undoubtedly was, the whole affair seemed stale and flat.

'Out of tune with the times,' seems to be the verdict on it.

The gathering included the Aga Khan, the Maharanee of

2

Hyderabad, Miss Paulette Goddard, Baron de Rothschild, and a host of French film stars, some of whom paid as much as £100 for dinner and a box.

President Auriol entered the ballroom to the strains of the Marseillaise – and was promptly offered a programme, which cost £2 10s. a copy. The President rummaged through his wallet, and then confessed that he did not have the money.

Meanwhile the franc continues its runaway course.

The cost of living has increased by over a hundred per cent in the past year, and a new Budget has been introduced which will increase it by yet another twenty per cent.

It seems unnecessary to look for sinister plots as an explanation for the present wave of strikes. When the price of a pocket handkerchief – to say nothing of a good meal – is almost equal to half a workman's weekly wage, it is a mystery how ordinary people have borne their hardships for so long.

How on earth do workers and civil servants earning between £14 and £20 a month manage to survive in this inflationary jungle?

The answer is by nation-wide 'fiddling'; by every adult or near-adult member of the family being set to doing some kind of work to supplement the family income: or by a break-up of the family so that children and parents are scattered throughout France each trying to subsist independently.

Paris continues to delight tourists – especially from Britain – by its lavish stage shows, its superb food and its apparent gaiety.

Dozens of *nouveau-riche* black marketeers have sought safe investments for their fortunes in financing new night clubs.

Some of the traditional Paris pleasure haunts have, however, changed considerably. Montparnasse has lost its artists, who have moved down into the St Germain des Près area. Famous cafés like the Dome and the Coupole, which before the war bulged with Bohemia, are now semi-deserted, and patronised only by respectable middle-class families, with their children and dogs.

A mild night club boom, however, has restarted in the area. Night clubs like 'Jimmy's', just off the Boulevard Montparnasse, with what must surely be one of the finest Cuban bands in the world, are now fashionable enough for visiting film stars to patronise.

In the Boulevard St Germain the famous Alsatian restaurant

'Lips' is enjoying a revival after a post-war slump due to its popularity with German officers.

Jean Paul Sartre, the founder of the new French philosophy of existentialism (incidentally, he is giving support to the Jewish terrorists in Palestine), has moved from the Café Flore in the Boulevard St Germain and established his headquarters in the bar of the Hotel Pont Royal – quite one of the best and most expensive bars in Paris. As a result of Sartre's patronage, the bar is now the fashionable centre for successful Left Bank intellectuals.

Montmartre is as shady, shoddy and garish as ever except for the traditional attractions like the Folies Bergère and the Bal Tabarin which continue to provide the best spectacles and music-hall performances in Paris.

Night Club Corner   The three smartest night clubs in Paris are the Club de Champs Elysées, where a British accent is as good as a membership card; the Drap d'Or, also off the Champs Elysées, where you drink champagne out of gold goblets and the prices suggest that the management is insuring itself against possible theft; and the Monseigneur, in Montmartre, with a horde of perambulating violinists.

Distinguished house hunters   The de Gaulles (General and his wife) are flat hunting in Paris but are faced with a more than usually difficult problem. A benevolent French Government refuse to permit them to rent a flat unless it also provides accommodation for the permanent police guard which the authorities insist on his having.

Book of the Month   *The Pest* by Albert Camus. Won the French Critics' Prize without any member of the selection committee having read it.

The book was published only a few hours before the prize was awarded; but the critics voted for Camus on his reputation for a previous book, *The Outsider*.

The Pest deals with an outbreak of cholera in Oran but is actually a philosophical treatment of the effects of the German occupation on France.

Play of the month   Still drawing the biggest crowds in Paris is '*L'Immacule*', by Philipe Herriot – a clumsy, pretentious dramatic treatment of artificial insemination.

Thursday, July 3, 1947

1950

'NO NIGHT CLUBS' AFTER THE VISCOUNT'S PARTY

It was almost like old times at Maxim's in Paris last night. The Edwardian splendour of the famous restaurant looked down on a scene which it had not witnessed since the war – an Englishman entertaining on a scale which made it seem as though Cripps did not even exist.

Viscount Furness, heir to a £3 million fortune, was celebrating his twenty-first birthday with a dinner party for forty guests. Sixteen had travelled over with him on the Golden Arrow.

Said Albert, Maxim's head waiter, 'It's just like old times – we dreamed of the day when the English "milords" would be back with us again; now here they are to show that Britain is not down and out.'

The dinner included steaks, foie gras, truffles, oysters, caviare. The drinks consisted of choice Bordeaux and Burgundies, 1890 Cognac, and champagne. Estimated cost for the forty guests – £400. After dinner there was dancing to Maxim's rumba band.

Asked about the cost of the evening, Lady Furness, the Viscount's mother, explained: 'This party has not been given by my son. It is being given by me and by my sister, Mrs Gloria Vanderbilt, for him.

'Both of us are American citizens. We are not bound by any currency restrictions. This has nothing to do with the British Treasury. It is our party for my son, and we are paying for it.'

The party began to break up after midnight. 'We are not going on to any night clubs,' said Lady Furness firmly. 'The girls and boys have to be in bed early.'

Viscount Furness and his guests are remaining in Paris over the weekend. Tomorrow they will picnic at Fontainebleau.

Hotel accommodation for the guests over the weekend will cost Lady Furness £300. Total cost of the weekend is likely to be nearly £3,000.

Saturday, April 1, 1950

THE BOOMING CULT OF ST TROPEZ

To the cynical, St Tropez is little more than a cult dedicated to the worship of the nymphet.

It is, of course, much more than a mere mecca for lechers. It is also a phenomenon of our times which has already set its stamp on this decade as surely as the Charleston put its stamp on the 20s.

From two or three small shops employing local needlewomen it decrees beach fashion styles the world over.

It alone, for example, holds aloft the flag of the bikini, and by so doing has ensured its survival.

The resort flourishes without a single large hotel and attracts the rich without a casino.

It defies the law of the land by publicly flaunting nudism on three-quarters of its principal beach, and it defies the economics of success by remaining topographically almost exactly as it was twenty years ago.

It provides an unrivalled social comedy of contrast, with the yacht-owning rich apeing the dress and manners of Parisian Left Bank Bohemians.

This year St Tropez has reached the paroxysm of its success. Seventy thousand holidaymakers this weekend invaded the tiny Mediterranean fishing village with an all-the-year round population of 4,000.

The narrow streets of the village teemed with Ferraris, Mercedes and Aston Martins honking their way through swarms of weekenders from nearby Toulon and Marseilles.

In horror at the invasion, distinguished villa owners such as the twin patron saints of the new St Tropez, Brigitte Bardot and Françoise Sagan, fled north.

It all started only about five years ago and the boom here is an

6

exact replica of what has happened in Paris. Just as the artists' and writers' quarter of St Germain has become fashionable in Paris, so St Tropez, which is a kind of St Germain-by-the-sea, has become the target for the rich and not-so-rich sightseers and sensation-seekers.

Nevertheless, its overwhelming characteristic is that of youth, with the average age between eighteen and twenty.

Despite the presence of the rich it remains, as one bar proprietor put it to me: 'Strictly a beer and soft-drink crowd and not a whisky and soda crowd.'

It has also by a combination of circumstances retained an authentic flavour of carefree Bohemianism.

One factor in this has been the stolid, peasant obstinacy of the original inhabitants.

They refuse to sell land which has shot up in value from 2s. a square yard five years ago, to £5 a square yard today.

Similarly, a municipal council composed of local tradesmen and farmers does its best to hamstring any invasion by 'foreign' capital.

The result is that the front remains unchanged and the town offers only about 1,000 hotel rooms, most of them in dilapidated third-grade hotels.

The startling aspects of the St Tropez way of life is, of course, the nudism which now flourishes on its magnificent sandy beach.

This has grown to such a scale that even the most casual visitor who only ventures 100 yards from the nearest café cannot fail to notice it.

Most of the nudists are Parisians of the professional classes, and it is a disconcerting experience to exchange greetings with an acquaintance from Paris under these unconventional circumstances.

There is almost a total absence of gawpers and even provincial visitors in family groups show a splendid French capacity for minding their own business.

A few of the tourists are patently exhibitionists, and some of the visitors, especially foreign ones, are, equally plainly, sensation-seekers. But, on the whole, there is an almost total absence of prurience.

There are a few fascinating incongruities, however.

Like the elderly Englishman who strolled the beach naked, then solemnly wrapped a huge towel around himself when it was time to put on his trousers and leave.

Sam White's Paris

The only unpleasant sight I saw was provided by two Americans wearing Florida-style clothes, one of whom was enmeshed in camera equipment. The other acted as his spotter.

'Quick, look, over there!' he shouted hoarsely.

Both were nearly lynched and had to beat a hasty retreat.

The ritual at St Tropez, involving as it does a constant round of some eight exceptionally-gay night clubs until dawn, is a strict one.

Breakfast is at eleven at Senequier, a former pastry shop whose owner, Mme Senequier, has become with another woman, Mme Vachon, the town's fashion dictator, and the richest of the St Tropez inhabitants.

Lunch is taken on the beach and a café L'Escale provides the recognised evening rendezvous.

After that comes dinner and the heavy work of the evening begins with visits to St Tropez's blaringly noisy *caves*.

Fashions are also rigorously controlled. In fact, St Tropez is the only resort I know which imposes its own fashions.

FOR MEN, shorts are out and only linen slacks and rope-soled shoes are worn.

Ties and dark glasses are strictly out as are silk shirts, especially patterned ones.

FOR WOMEN, if they wear anything on the beach, it is bikinis and in the evening gingham trousers and straw hats accompanied by muslin scarves worn under the hat and low over the ears.

The Baby Doll look is observed studiously, especially in the manner of embroidered smocks.

Jeans are out and so is the so-called Greco or 'sordid' look. Make-up is worn but is kept to a minimum.

The Charleston, the fast foxtrot and the cha-cha-cha are in but rock 'n' roll is out.

In matters of drink, whisky is out as being so ostentatious and Americanos and Pastis are in.

The life is dizzy to a point that makes a stay of longer than three or four days almost unbearable to the over-thirties.

What is astonishing in a place of such cosmopolitanism and youth is the total absence of drunkenness or hooliganism.

Only the French, one feels, could carry off a phenomenon like St Tropez without lapsing into vulgarity.

St Tropez, Friday, August 21, 1950

8

COLETTE'S HUSBAND IS MARRIED AGAIN – AT 70

A marriage which touched me deeply occurred in Paris this week. It was between 70-year-old Maurice Goudeket, former husband of the famous French novelist Colette, and Mme Lelong, widow of the late dress designer Lucien Lelong.

Goudeket, a handsome man with gallant manners, is one of the most attractive, talented and sensitive men in present-day Paris.

He is a notable link with pre-1914–18 war Paris glories.

A member of a highly cosmopolitan, French-Jewish family, Goudeket fell in love with Colette when he was thirty-five and she fifty.

They were married ten years later and were never separated, except for a brief period of imprisonment which he underwent during the war, until her death in 1954.

It was an extraordinary attachment between people of superficially different tastes and completely different backgrounds.

Under Colette's influence Goudeket, city sophisticate and polished man of the world, began to share in her almost peasant-like sensual pleasures in cooking and the countryside.

When Goudeket was imprisoned by the Gestapo she stooped to even seeing Germans and collaborators in order to save him.

Then a French collaborator told her Goudeket could be saved from certain death if he were prepared to turn informer on his fellow prisoners.

'In that case,' Colette replied, 'we both choose death.'

On the day of the liberation of Paris, Colette refused to believe in the news unless a British soldier wearing a kilt was produced for her.

Goudeket promptly went out in search of one and finally delivered him to their flat where lunch was served in his honour.

They lived in a first-floor flat overlooking the gardens of Palais-Royal.

In the latter years of her life, Colette was unable to go out and her flat became one of the most noted intellectual meeting-places in Paris.

Goudeket still uses her flat as an office, but will now live in his new wife's sumptuous flat in the West End of Paris. The new Mme Goudeket is some thirty years his junior.

She was Lelong's second wife; he married her while she was working for him as a saleswoman.

Although Lelong retired during the war his perfume business continued to flourish, with the result that his widow is a very rich woman. It is a marriage which would have pleased and amused Colette.

Friday, December 27, 1950

1951

BLACK MAX 'MADE £13,000 IN A YEAR'

'Black' Max Intrator, dapper in a well-cut grey suit, white silk shirt and grey tie, appeared in the Paris High Court, today, to answer four-year-old charges of illegally cashing £170,000 worth of British tourists' cheques, in a one-year period between 1946 and 1947.

Five others were in the dock with Intrator, accused of similar offences.

Among them was elegant, 52-year-old Turkish-born Helda Carmona, alleged to have helped Intrator in transactions involving £50,000 worth of tourists cheques.

Twenty-eight names were called to appear on currency charges with Intrator. Of these, one has since died, sixteen have settled their cases with a payment of fines and two were represented by their lawyers.

The president of the court, M. Cosse-Maniere, said Intrator's black market operations started in 1945 and were based on complicated financial transfers, centring on Egypt, where his brother Erwin was his representative.

With Sterling, legally acquired in Britain, Intrator bought dollars in Egypt and changed them in New York, where they brought a much higher price.

Intrator, who was born in Berlin, but had spent the war years in Egypt, settled in France in March 1946, and became associated with a German, Karol Bitter.

He fled shortly after Intrator's arrest and is now accused of being Intrator's partner in illegal deals.

Intrator pleaded guilty to unauthorised currency deals, but said that many of the deals were carried out by Bitter, unknown to him.

The judge said: 'You only say that because Bitter is not here to give his version.'

Intrator replied: 'What I claim is true. My chief function was only to introduce British clients to Bitter. Unfortunately my name is the one that has received all the publicity.'

Intrator denied engaging in illegal deals in gold. But the prosecution produced evidence alleging that his gold deals amounted to £26,000.

Evidence was given that Intrator paid a visit to London in July 1946 and stayed at the Savoy Hotel.

During his stay, it was alleged, he made arrangements for 'representatives' to act for him in Britain.

A French Treasury expert, giving evidence, said he estimated Intrator's profits from illegal currency deals in the one-year period under examination at £13,000.

The expert said that Madame Carmona worked for a separate currency ring to that organised by Intrator.

Four large stacks of documents, 4ft high, were brought into court before the case commenced and placed on the President's desk.

Tuesday, January 16, 1951

WHY HAVE THEY BANNED CHEVALIER?

The refusal of the United States Government to grant a visa to Maurice Chevalier has caused little surprise in Paris.

Chevalier was said to have signed the Communist-sponsored Stockholm 'Peace' Appeal, to have sung at Communist fêtes, and to have supported the Party in other ways.

His case is not exceptional. The singer Yves Montand was refused a visa some time ago. A score of French screen and stage stars are known to figure in the American Embassy's 'Black Book' of 'Café Communists' likely to apply for visas in the future.

As for appearances on Communist platforms – purely as entertainers, of course – stars of such stature as Edith Piaf and a hundred others readily and regularly accept invitations to do so.

Why? Most of them are without any political convictions and many could look forward to profitable dollar contracts in the U.S.A. Why should they risk misunderstanding about their political sympathies?

The answer makes a curious story of blackmail, crude Press-agentry and cupidity. It adds up to an impressive tribute to the power of the Communist Party in France.

In some cases the support given to the Party by French stage and screen stars is the result of blackmail and nothing more.

After the Liberation many French stars found themselves in the embarrassing position of being open to collaboration charges. At the time the Communists were the best organised and most farseeing of Resistance groups. Just as they went about seizing printing-presses and the best office buildings, so they went about seizing names.

To the compromised stars they offered in best gangster fashion their 'Protection' if they made certain declarations, agreed to lend their talents to Party causes, and made cash donations to Party funds.

A majority of those approached in this way yielded. Some did not. Among them was the ballet star Serge Lifar.

What happened to Lifar? For nearly four years after the Liberation he remained jobless because any appearance of his on a public stage threatened a Communist riot.

Lifar has only recently been able to resume his professional career, but his appearances are still interrupted by demonstrations and occasional strikes of Communist stage-hands.

Those not directly threatened were suborned by more subtle means. The Communist Party in France are a great national force. They are the largest single party in the French Parliament, and polled 6,000,000 votes at the last elections.

They control a powerful Press Trust. It runs two big circulation morning papers in Paris, a popular Paris evening paper, a dozen provincial dailies and several big circulation weeklies and monthlies, including stage and screen reviews. The powerful Communist Press will flatter only those who support the Party, and attack those who don't. In short, a popular French star who does not 'play ball' with the Party risks getting bad notices in a large section of the French Press.

Finally, there are those stars – a small minority – who are convinced Communists. Among them is the singer Yves Montand.

He sets an example by singing songs with a strong propagandist flavour. Montand's most popular song at the moment is a ballad telling the sad story of a singer who refuses to sing the kind of songs 'that please the rich'.

The ballad ends with Montand broken, unemployed.

Montand is a long way from the breadline yet. He is among the three top-paid music hall and cabaret stars in France.

Other popular themes with fellow-travelling singers deal with anti-American or anti-war themes.

A Communist film magazine recently published a list of French stars who have signed the Stockholm appeal. They numbered sixty-four.

Tuesday, April 24, 1951

1952

MATISSE

*The unbeliever's chapel starts an argument –
why did he do it . . . ?*

Tourists on the Riviera are flocking to look at a religious
curiosity – a chapel designed and built by painter Henri
Matisse for the Dominican convent at Vence.

Matisse, eighty-two years old now, is an unbeliever, a
freethinker, a passionate anti-clerical. For such a man to build a
Roman Catholic place of worship is astonishing. The reasons are
as puzzling as the chapel itself.

Matisse, bedridden most of the time now, lives in a big
five-roomed flat in a semi-derelict building on the outskirts of
Nice: the building used to be a hotel.

He is separated from his wife who is Communist mayor of a
South of France village. His constant companion is his youthful
blonde Russian-born secretary, Mme Lydia Delectorskaya – a
tight-lipped woman with a dedicated air.

Matisse spends the greater part of the day drawing on the walls
and ceilings of his studio bedroom from his bed with a piece of
charcoal attached to a long cane. Mme Delectorskaya stands by
to erase anything with which he may be dissatisfied and the
completed drawing is then reproduced in colour.

Apart from his work, Matisse goes for brief drives occasionally and tries to visit his chapel at least once a month.

The chapel is a small, round, whitewashed building in a
suburban street which has been renamed Avenue Henri Matisse.
When you get there you find cars and tourists' buses jammed on
the road, and a long queue waiting to go in. A tall golden
wrought iron and highly stylised cross studded with crescents and
rising from an open scroll base encloses a bell. Slowly the queue,

chattering and giggling, makes its way gazing on the chapel's vivid blue tiled roof, past the narrow, small entrance, down a small flight of steps, past the blue-patterned font, and into the chilling austerity of the chapel itself.

Chilling it indeed is – one's first impression is of having strayed into a more than usually spacious modernistic bathroom. The bleak shiny whiteness of the interior is relieved by pagan-patterned stained glass, frosted bulbous lighting, phony-rustic doors, pews, and confessional, and a beige pink slab of an altar with candles which look as though they must be electrically lit. It all suggests an architectural style somewhere between Osbert Lancaster's Stockbroker Tudor and Hollywood Spanish Mission.

The white tiled walls are decorated with black line drawings of St Dominic, the Virgin and Child, and, crowded into one panel, the Stations of the Cross.

Matisse designed it all. It took him four years. He considers it his greatest single work and the crowning glory of an artistic lifetime.

Why did Matisse do it?

Well, Matisse himself says that vanity – 'I wanted to create a complete work of art and a monument to my work' – was the driving force which impelled him to undertake it.

The French Roman Catholic newspaper *La Croix* says that Matisse was nursed ten years ago, after a major operation, by a Dominican nun, Sister Jacques, who is now in the convent at Vence. He decided to build the chapel as a mark of gratitude to her and her Order.

But Mme Delectorskaya has a somewhat different version. She told me: 'Matisse knew Sister Jacques before she became a nun. One day, hearing that she was at the convent at Vence, he visited her. She told him of the convent's need for a chapel, and he immediately offered to design and decorate one for the nuns.'

Matisse's friends say that Sister Jacques, daughter of a retired French regular army officer, was a close friend of Matisse before she took the veil.

My own verdict on it all: Matisse has used a religion in which he does not believe as a means of self-glorification.

It is as though George Bernard Shaw, on the invitation of the Church of England, had written a Shavian version of the Anglican prayerbook.

Nice, Saturday, February 2, 1952

THE SQUIRE OF MARNE-LA-COQUETTE

A soldier and his wife settle down among the prefabs.
The name is . . . EISENHOWER

A mong the 850 inhabitants of the village of Marne-La-Coquette nestling in the Seine valley ten miles west of Paris, is a man who many people consider may be the next President of the United States. This is General Eisenhower, the Supreme Commander of the North Atlantic Treaty Organisation. He lives in squire-like style with his wife Mamie in the forty-room white-painted Villa St Pierre.

The villa, an early 19th-century building, two storeys high, stands in park overlooking the village square. It is one of eighteen villas within the park's boundaries.

Eisenhower's house is easy to find for its gates are guarded by United States and French troops and by United States and French plain clothes detectives.

The house, gleaming white, stands in the shadow of oak and chestnut trees. It is a prize won by Mrs Eisenhower by dint of hard house-hunting which revealed her as an unpretentious woman true to her Middle West background. She prefers solid comfort to glitter and splendour.

She was offered the late Lady Mendl's house, the Villa Trianon. She took one look at the priceless Louis XV and XVI furniture which crowded its rooms and exclaimed: 'Oh, my, I could never live among all those things. Why, there would be nowhere to sit down of an evening.' Later she saw the Villa St Pierre, which was in a considerable state of disrepair. She liked it, and she decided that this was where she would set up home in the latest of countless house-moves in her thirty-five years as an army wife.

The French Government have spent £25,000 on renovating the villa. They have discreetly pressed on the Eisenhowers an Aubusson carpet, Gobelin tapestries, paintings and period furniture from a national collection of *objets d'art*.

The house stands in six acres of ground. Mrs Eisenhower has laid down a vegetable plot and a putting green to cater for two of her husband's favourite hobbies, gardening and golf. She has also installed a small kitchen on the ground floor away from the main one in the basement where Eisenhower can practise another of his hobbies – cooking. (Ike likes to grill his own steaks and bake an occasional lemon pie.)

Only fifteen minutes' walk from the villa live Eisenhower's best friends in France – his Chief of Staff, General Gruenther and Mrs Gruenther. His personal physician, Major-General Howard Snyder, also lives near by. Other neighbours include a personal aide, Colonel Schultz, and Mrs Schultz, and his batman Sergeant Dry.

Eisenhower's office is in the vast spread of prefabs on the outskirts of Paris, which is Supreme Headquarters of the Allied Powers in Europe. It is fifteen minutes' drive from the villa.

He gets to the office at 7.30 each morning, usually at least an hour before his secretary. He lunches with up to a dozen fellow officers in his private dining-room each weekday. His diet is carefully watched by his physician and the food is cooked by a Negro GI.

He rarely takes wine with his meals and if he does it is usually with his evening meal. Regularly at 5.30 p.m. he leaves the office with a briefcase full of 'homework'.

The Eisenhowers never accept invitations to cocktail parties and never give any themselves. Nor do they dine out. The only Paris social occasions at which they are to be seen are receptions given by the French President.

Mrs Eisenhower is fifty-five – seven years younger than Ike. She is slim, carefully and conservatively dressed, with brown wavy hair, dressed in a fringe, visits Paris often for a day's shopping with Mrs Gruenther. Rarely photographed, she can wander through Paris without being recognised.

At home she looks forward to occasional bridge parties with the Gruenthers – General Gruenther being one of the most expert bridge players in the world.

The Eisenhowers are a devoted couple. A close friend once said: 'To Ike, Mamie is always twenty years old.' Another has described them cryptically as a 'formidable team'.

Is Mrs Eisenhower attracted by the idea of becoming America's First Lady? The only comment she allows herself on the matter is: 'What American woman wouldn't want her husband to be President?'

Saturday, March 15, 1952

1953

THE DUKE OF WINDSOR PLANS HIS HOME

Decorations await the Duchess

For the first time since the abdication the Duke of Windsor was reluctant to leave Europe this winter for his annual visit to the United States. The reason: he is designing a home for himself in France.

While the Duke and Duchess are in the United States they are in touch with two architects in France who are converting the 18th-century Moulin Aubert, in the beautiful valley of the Chevreuse near Paris, into a home for them.

The two architects – American Barry Dierks, a close friend of the Duke and Duchess, and former de Gaullist intelligence officer Franz Jourdain – are working from a mass of carefully drawn scale sketches done by the Duke, and detailed instructions given them by the Duchess.

Ever since the abdication the Windsors have lived in rented houses and rented villas among other people's furniture. The unpretentious Moulin Aubert, with its tiled roof, Georgian porch and solid rural architecture, is leased by them for nine years with an option of buying it outright after or during that period.

It is a house the Duke has long wanted; he took it instantly when its owner, the portrait painter, Driand, a personal friend, told the Duke he was prepared to lease it. Just how strong is the Duke's desire to recreate a home may be gathered from the fact that a great deal of the furniture from Fort Belvedere, and many of the Duke's personal possessions and mementoes, will be shipped to France early in the spring.

And to perfecting the Moulin, the Duke is devoting all the enthusiasm and skilled knowledge which he brought to the modernising of Fort Belvedere.

The outer aspect of the house will remain as it is, but the interior of the Z-shaped building is being carefully remodelled to provide a reception hall, large dining-room and quarters for the Duke and Duchess. The furthest wing of the house will provide two guest rooms and a new building in the grounds will provide two more.

A barn is being converted into a summer dining-room. An outhouse will be made into a study and 'gardening headquarters' for the Duke. Eight bathrooms will be installed.

Before he left France the Duke visited the house almost every day, supervising details of the plans. The layout of the gardens has been planned entirely by him. In the words of one of the local gardeners employed: 'He was just like a head gardener to us. He knew exactly what he wanted and the best way of getting it.'

Details of the decorations are being planned by the Duchess and will not be started until her return.

Footnote   The house is only ten minutes' drive from France's oldest, most beautiful golf course, La Boulie. The Duke's golf scores, incidentally, have dropped from the high 90s to the low 80s.

Wednesday, January 21, 1953

M. DASSAULT MAKES A FORTUNE FROM HIS PLANE 'AS GOOD AS MIG'

From the ashes of the French aircraft industry, ruined by enemy occupation and nationalisation, there has at last arisen an airplane to talk about. The airplane is the Mystère 4 and its manufacturer, 60-year-old Marcel Dassault, is one of the most remarkable public figures in France today.

This week, to M. Dassault's drab Avenue Kleber offices went a U.S. order for 85 million dollars' worth of Mystère 4s for the North Atlantic Treaty forces. This was followed by 42 million dollars' worth of orders from Belgium and Holland.

The deal came after a year of intensive U.S. testing of this jet fighter, still in the prototype stage, for which claims are made that it is as good as the Hunter and the MiG 15.

Dassault – real name Bloche – comes from a distinguished French Jewish family and spent a greater part of the war in Buchenwald concentration camp. He adopted the name of Dassault because his brother, a general, had used it in the Resistance. They both decided to retain it.

He returned from Buchenwald to find his own aircraft factory, dating back to the 1914–18 war, pillaged by the Germans, and the rest of the industry nationalised and under a Communist Minister for Air.

With money paid him by the French Government as compensation for German pillaging Dassault began work immediately with his own company, of which he remains chief engineer and sole proprietor. His first success came with the Ouragon fighter in 1949, followed by the Mystère 2, and now the Mystère 4. Dassault is one of the most powerful men in France and one of the richest.

In addition to his aircraft factories he owns a bank and a newspaper. Yet he remains astonishingly little-known. In newspaper libraries his file consists of three meagre cuttings. Dassault looks like a taller edition of Robertson Hare, but he is a shy man who is entirely absorbed in his work.

Married, he has two sons, one of whom is an engineer in one of his factories. The family live in a large flat overlooking the Bois de Boulogne and own a villa in Cannes which Dassault represents in Parliament as a de Gaullist.

He rarely attends Parliament and even more rarely speaks in debates. Both he and his wife shun social life.

His overcoats are tartan-lined and he uses the squares of the lining as an improvised tape-measure on his visits to factories or air shows.

Having perfected three prototypes, his great problem is now one of production. So far he is unique among aircraft manufacturers in having made money out of prototypes alone.

It remains to be seen whether he can get the Mystère 4 into effective service before Britain and the U.S.A. render it out of date.

Wednesday, April 29, 1953

1954

GENERAL DE GAULLE LAUNCHES HIS THUNDERBOLT

In a little less than three weeks the long-gathering storm of General de Gaulle's war memoirs will have broken over France.

Then the first 400-page volume of his memoirs, *The Call*, will be published. It will be followed at brief intervals by two other volumes.

De Gaulle has devoted himself to his memoirs for four years, to the almost total exclusion of political activity. Publication of them is the most eagerly awaited literary event in Paris since the war. And a first printing of 20,000 copies (at 24s. each) has been ordered.

At de Gaulle's request, the first edition will be followed by cheaper editions to ensure a maximum reading public for his work.

The book begins by recalling his pre-war struggle to revolutionise French military thinking, which was then based on 1914–18 concepts of trench warfare.

Villain of the first volume is Marshal Weygand; de Gaulle is surprisingly gentle in his treatment of Pétain.

He holds Weygand chiefly responsible for the French surrender of 1940, and describes him as 'this general who is so adept at scoring brilliant victories – on paper'.

After the collapse, defeatism was so general, says de Gaulle, that even Churchill 'seemed reconciled to France making a separate peace'.

De Gaulle was so disgusted that he wished to resign his post as Under-Secretary of State for Defence, but was dissuaded.

The night before his secret departure for England, de Gaulle dined in the same Bordeaux restaurant as Pétain, and as he passed the Marshal, 'I gravely saluted the man I no longer recognised as my chief'.

Of his stormy wartime relations with Churchill, de Gaulle writes: 'We at times appeared to be agreed on only three things: that Britain was an island, France was the nearest Continental point to Britain, and that America was another world.'

He speaks repeatedly and with great bitterness of 'English double-dealing, the intrigues of the Foreign Office and the Intelligence Service', and explains how, as a result, he established closer relations with the Russians.

At one time when relations with Sir Winston were at their worst, 'I suggested to the Russians that I might transfer my headquarters to Moscow'.

Friday, October 1, 1954

LADY JEBB DECLARES WAR ON THE BIDET

Lady Jebb, wife of the British Ambassador, Sir Gladwyn Jebb, has declared war on an estimable French institution, the crowning glory of French plumbing and an age-old mystifier to Anglo-Saxon tourists staying in a French hotel for the first time.

I refer, of course, to the bidet or hip-bath, which is a permanent feature of every French bathroom.

With the approval of the Minister of Works Lady Jebb has entered with enthusiasm upon the task of modernising the British Embassy here.

After the famous £7,000 improvements to the Embassy kitchens, Lady Jebb has turned her attention to the bathrooms.

There were only four bathrooms in the Embassy's residence and none at all for the servants. So Lady Jebb planned and supervised the installation of three new bathrooms and the remodelling of another. She also installed showers in the servants' quarters.

She then pondered the problem of the bidets in the existing

bathrooms. No doubt finding them unsightly, she ordered that they be uprooted.

Uprooted they were.

One can imagine the horror of the French plumbers as they went about their almost sacrilegious task.

This is not the limit of Lady Jebb's enterprise. Earlier she found there were too many trees in the Embassy garden. She ordered seven trees to be felled and had two rose and dahlia beds laid down. (Bill for garden improvements: £900.)

Prize winner

Before their traditionally excellent lunch in one of Paris's best restaurants, the ten-man jury which each year awards France's top literary prize, the Goncourt, had to tackle a delicate political task.

They had just elected as one of their members to replace the late Colette, a Right-wing author, thereby making it imperative that this year's prize winner should be a Left-wing one.

They promptly voted for 46-year-old Simone de Beauvoir, long-time friend of existentialist philosopher Jean-Paul Sartre, for her novel about disillusioned Left-wing intellectuals, *The Mandarins*.

The Goncourt prize, although small in itself, bestows a rich financial windfall in extra royalties. *The Mandarins* is expected to sell at least 200,000 copies netting its author £25,000 in royalties.

Until this prize came along Mlle de Beauvoir, though she had an established reputation, was only modestly prosperous.

She lives in a one-room studio which she rents furnished in a slum quarter near Notre-Dame. When she had to buy a car this year her publisher advanced her the money.

She will bank her royalties on her prize-winning novel with her publisher, drawing from him a £30-a-week allowance. Despite her somewhat schoolmistress-ish appearance she is a lively person and with her good features, blue eyes and chestnut hair she would be even more attractive if she did not deliberately strive after a 'severe' appearance.

She is a chain smoker and works a steady six-hour day for eight months of the year. The other four months she spends travelling abroad. She comes from a landowning, aristocratic family of extreme Right-wing views against which she had been in revolt most of her adult life. Despite this she has never been estranged from her family. She had a brilliant university career and was second only to Sartre in her philosophy class at the Sorbonne. A close friend describes her as 'a wonderfully balanced person'.

Wednesday, December 15, 1954

1955

PICASSO MOVES OUT . . .

Mlle Gilot gains a villa and a village loses its trade

The 2,000 inhabitants of the picturesque village of Vallauris overlooking Golfe-Juan on the Riviera have received some worrying news. Pablo Picasso is leaving.

To Vallauris, painter Picasso has been something more than its most distinguished citizen and a great tourist attraction in himself; he has also been a reanimator of the village's major industry.

When Picasso first went to Vallauris in 1946 he found an ancient pottery works in almost complete disuse. Only a handful of 'arty-crafty' shops kept alive the memory of what had once been Vallauris's great occupation.

Picasso fell in love with the medium, producing in ceramics some of his most brilliant work. Dozens of pottery workers who had drifted to other industries soon returned to their ancient craft. Picasso's studio, a converted garage, became a centre of instruction in the craft.

Why is Picasso leaving Vallauris? The reason lies in his recent separation from his 33-year-old common-law wife, Françoise Gilot, mother of two of his children. Picasso's simple three-storeyed house in Vallauris was bought by him in her name and now she has claimed it.

Picasso is not moving far. For £15,000 he has bought a villa, The California, on the outskirts of Cannes. His furniture and canvases are already being moved into it.

The California is an imposing property, in large grounds, and the villa itself contains some twenty rooms with four large salons, one of which will be converted into Picasso's studio.

It is in a part of Cannes in which are some of the Riviera's most

sumptuous villas. Among Picasso's near neighbours will be the
Aga Khan and Communist leader Maurice Thorez, for whom
the party has recently bought a villa.

Hopes in Vallauris of a reconciliation between Picasso and
Mlle Gilot are going to prove groundless. She plans to marry a
Paris painter.

One object of value which Picasso has left to the village and
which is a great tourist attraction is his statue *Man with a Sheep*,
which is in the village square opposite the 14th-century church.

French test

Recently I saw a group of English schoolgirls consulting their
dictionaries in puzzlement outside a Champs Elysées cinema.
They had reason to be puzzled. The cinema they were standing
outside advertised a film with the title *Razzia sur la Chnouf*.
Opposite, another cinema was showing *De Rififi Chez Les
Hommes*. Further along there was a film with yet another
baffling title: *Ne Touchez Pas le Grisbi*. All three films were
adapted from gangster thrillers written by a 40-year-old ex-
convict, Auguste le Breton.

Le Breton's works, written in almost incomprehensible gangster slang, are best-sellers in Paris now. For those who are
brushing up on their French here are rough translations of the
three titles in the order I have mentioned them:

Narcotics Raid; A Spot of Disagreement; Hands off the
Dough.

Wednesday, April 27, 1955

1956

BITTERNESS BEGAN FOR MISTINGUETT THE DAY CHEVALIER LEFT

The village girl made fabulous propaganda
out of her age . . .

Mistinguett, who died today, was so sensitive about her age that once she abruptly ended a telephone interview by hanging up on me. In an unguarded moment I had asked her if some incident had occurred before the First or the Second World War.

She was a completely feminine creature and that is what endeared her to generations of Parisians. She was also the symbol of a period which Frenchmen remember with nostalgia: the gay uninhibited 'ragtime' 20s when Paris was the gayest and one of the cheapest capitals in the world.

She was always associated in the public mind with another genius of the French music hall, Maurice Chevalier, whom she launched. She and Chevalier were partners in a song and dance act for ten years and these were probably the happiest years of her life. She was deeply in love with Chevalier, then at the beginning of his career.

Her salty, catty remarks after the partnership broke up and which she continued making to the end of her life were probably due – again utter femininity – to the bitterness of a woman over the younger man who had left her.

In his memoirs Chevalier wrote of her: 'She is professionally artful like a genial monkey of which she has the sad eyes and face.'

Back came the devastatingly feminine reply: 'I forgive him. I love him too much. He shows in his book that he never had much of a memory.'

As a music hall performer she had something more than mere talent as a singer or dancer: she had a compelling personality which could almost outshine the dazzling nudes who flanked her at the Folies Bergère or the Moulin Rouge. Extravagant in her attire and stage mannerisms she always courted ridicule. In her last few pathetic attempts at a comeback in London and Paris she always triumphed over it.

In an age before publicity agents she had discovered two key attractions for endless publicity: her legs, which she insured for three million dollars at the height of her career, and the mystery of her age, about which she told outrageous lies.

Her favourite year of birth was 1908, but in her memoirs she records that she was singing in Paris in 1895. It is generally believed that she was born in 1875 in a small village near Paris. Her father was an upholsterer and she was christened Jeanne-Marie Bourgeois.

Bourgeois she was born and bourgeois she remained in character, if not in name. Like Chevalier, she had the reputation of watching her francs carefully. She had a country house and a villa at Antibes in addition to a large flat in the centre of Paris, but she thought the price of petrol so outrageous that she visited her other homes rarely and usually only if she could inveigle a friend into giving her a lift.

How she came to get the name Mistinguett is another riddle. Apparently the prefix 'Miss' was considered smart on the music hall stage of Edwardian Paris, bathed in the glow of the *entente cordiale*, and after being 'Miss Elliott' for a time she became 'Miss Vertinguette' (acrobatic) and then 'Miss Tinguette'.

To the end of her life she retained her pride in her figure and did gymnastics regularly. Presents of chocolates she fed to her pomeranian. One early photo showed her in a Mack Sennett bathing costume on the beach at Cannes, her face contorted with pain as a muscular physical culture instructor twisted her ankles about.

She had a son by an early marriage to a former attaché in the Brazilian Embassy. Their son, now 59, Leopold de Lima, is a prosperous Paris doctor, father of two daughters.

Since 1946 she was believed secretly married to a handsome 40-year-old, little-known Italian singer and dancer, Lino Carenzio.

Her best songs were My Man, I Am Looking for a Millionaire, Valencia, and the startling song which made her famous: I Am the Torpedo Woman.

The best comment on her is that made by poet and playwright Jean Cocteau: 'If I were ever exiled from Paris the thing I would miss most is the sound of her voice, which recalls to me all the street cries of a city.'

Thursday, January 5, 1956

PRINCE RAINIER QUARRELS WITH FATHER TUCKER

A cold wind blows over the Royal Wedding

All is not well in Monte Carlo on the eve of Prince Rainier's wedding to film star Grace Kelly. This is a pity; it would be pleasant to report the occasion in a more appropriate manner, yet the fact remains that the atmosphere here among palace officials is as chilly as the weather.

The chill set in with Prince Rainier's return from America. Almost immediately he reverted, from the smiling, approachable young Prince of his American tour, to the unapproachable, unpredictable autocrat his ministers and advisers know so well.

He had scarcely unpacked when he quarrelled with his only really close adviser – his American chaplain, Father Tucker, who has figured so prominently in his romance with Miss Kelly.

The quarrel has not healed, and Father Tucker has not seen the Prince since their return to the principality.

This blow has saddened the normally jovial chaplain greatly. He has been the only person in the Prince's entourage who has never quarrelled with his master, who saw him daily, and whose influence has been considerable. Now that he is not seeing the Prince, an intermediary between the Prince and his officials has been removed.

Ministers who hitherto sought to influence the Prince by having a word with Father Tucker are now reduced to writing enormously fulsome highly stylised 'petitions' which go unanswered and are probably unread.

Father Tucker hopes that this climate will change with Miss Kelly's arrival, and that she will effect a reconciliation between himself and Prince Rainier.

Meanwhile, Rainier remains shut up in his palace, leaving it only on very rare occasions.

It is not fully realised abroad to what extent Rainier is a complete autocrat; he can ruin a man's career in Monaco and even revoke his Monégasque citizenship by a stroke of the pen. This power, which inspires considerable fear among his officials, is combined with an extremely suspicious and shy nature.

Has Metro-Goldwyn-Mayer carved out something of a new empire for itself with Miss Kelly's marriage to Rainier? It is an intriguing question. While Rainier was in America some of his Ministers opened negotiations with a Paris bank to finance a colour film of the marriage.

When the prince returned he killed this deal. The reason Rainier gave was this:

While in the United States he said he had been approached by MGM officials, who had pointed out to him that Miss Kelly's contract still had four years to run. While not wishing to be tough about this, they pointed out to the Prince a way in which Miss Kelly's obligations to the company could be squared with her proposed early retirement from the screen.

MGM proposed therefore that they should be given the exclusive rights to make the thirty-minute colour-film of the wedding. They also pointed out that by an odd coincidence they had almost completed a full version of the life of Miss Kelly, and all they needed for a final happy fade out were some shots of the wedding.

It is this which is behind the terrific row which has broken out this week between the U.S. television companies and the palace.

U.S. television cameras will not be allowed to photograph either the religious or civil ceremonies. With the facilities so far allotted them, they will be able to make films of only two or three minutes' duration.

In short, everything possible seems to have been done to make their task virtually impossible. There is talk that American TV may have to resort to a boycott of the wedding, but perhaps a boycott is just what some people want.

Monte Carlo, Friday, April 6, 1956

PICASSO KICKS THE WALL

See how solid my new house is, he says

At seventy-five, painter Pablo Picasso continues to flourish like some Biblical patriarch.

A Noah's Ark of children and dependants have followed him to his home near Cannes – only a few miles from the pottery town of Vallauris, which cashed in on him so heavily that it even had a Communist mayor elected in his honour.

The house is a hideous Victorian mansion built for a champagne millionaire. It confirms both externally and internally the sincerity with which Picasso clings to one of his favourite maxims: 'There is no such thing as ugliness.'

The house has a new mistress – a lovely, 36-year-old native of Vallauris, formerly the wife of a minor French colonial official.

Here in an atmosphere of almost farcical chaos Picasso is entirely happy. He had come to loathe Vallauris and the commercialism that had been built around his name. He had been a tourist attraction for whom busloads of tourists would wait to see him take his scheduled walk from his modern villa to his studio. Here in Cannes his studio is in its own grounds, which are protected by a caretaker's lodge.

The house is barely furnished and sparsely carpeted.

A house-proud Picasso, bronzed and dressed in shorts, can think of no better manner of showing off his new home to visitors than by kicking the walls hard and explaining, 'See, they're solid.'

At this point his more alert visitors stand clear from a downpour of plaster.

Stacks of canvases and newspapers litter each room, often serving as improvised tableclothes.

The key to the chaos is held only by Picasso, and he darts unerringly from pile to pile to show off whichever canvas he wants to.

Of Communism, which he claims as his political faith, he talks little and reluctantly, while Communists he discusses with an amused condescension of someone who is conscious of being a Stalin in his own right.

'Why should they try to talk to me about art?' he will say. 'I do not try to teach them economics.'

He is fundamentally not a Communist but a Spanish anarchist with one ruling political passion – a hatred of Franco.

Occasionally he drives over to Perpignan on the Spanish frontier. Friends who have accompanied him on these trips say that he is often overcome with emotion at being so near to his native Spain.

No doubt he could return, but he refuses to do so while Franco is in power.

His fortune which is one of the biggest personal fortunes in the world today is administered by a Paris banker, who has had charge of his investments since 1912.

What its fate will be after his death is a matter of considerable speculation.

At the moment Picasso is back in the news with a remarkable film, which he has made in collaboration with the French director, Clouzot.

The film lasts ninety minutes, and will have its première at the current Cannes Film Festival.

In this film, Picasso, who remains unseen throughout, draws fifteen sketches on a special paper with a special ink which reproduces the drawings on the other side.

Thus the spectator will see the evolution of a Picasso picture including corrections from the beginning to the end.

Clouzot who has made his reputation as a master of suspense in films says that all his previous efforts to create suspense are feeble compared to the excitement of watching a Picasso work in progress.

Saturday, April 28, 1956

NOW EVERYONE GOES TO SEE
DE GAULLE

*The stream of visitors to the wartime leader has almost
created a traffic problem. Does this mean that he will
return to power?*

The smartest thing to do among important French politicians
these days is to pay a regular pilgrimage to the hamlet of
Colombey-les-deux-Églises, where General Charles de Gaulle
lives in retirement.

There, in Freudian terms, they undergo a kind of political
psycho-analysis and they confess their fears, doubts and hope to
the Father Image.

The streams of visitors from Paris has been so considerable
that it has almost created a traffic problem in the normally sleepy
Colombey.

A man so occupied, for example, as the Socialist governor of
Algeria, M. Robert Lacoste, thinks nothing of driving 200 miles
to see de Gaulle before he attends important Cabinet meetings.

A dozen other political figures, including Ministers like M.
Mendès-France, see the general regularly.

What do they tell him and what does he tell them?

Roughly, they all tell de Gaulle that they are now convinced
that the present parliamentary system in France is unworkable,
that it cannot cope with the increasing worsening situation in
Algeria, and that it could not possibly survive Algeria's loss.

They add that they are now supporters of the kind of radical
constitutional reform long advocated by de Gaulle, which would
give France a form of government modelled on the American
Presidential system.

These confessions must be highly pleasing to de Gaulle's ears.

After all, he resigned from power ten years ago on this very
issue of constitutional reform, and he still remembers the relief
with which the politicians saw him go and reverted undisturbed
to the traditional French political game.

Now politicians on the right and left are vying with each other in denouncing the present system.

The former Premier and leader of the right, M. Pinay, is now for de Gaulle. The Socialist Premier, M. Mollet, anticipates competition by devoting a major speech to the needs of constitutional reform.

Even Pierre Poujade swells the chorus with a surprise declaration that he would support de Gaulle's return to power.

De Gaulle's answer is clear cut: He would accept a call to office as President of the Republic (such a call is permissible under the Constitution) but he would do so under two conditions:

1. The dissolution of the present Parliament.

2. The adoption by the country in a referendum of a new constitution based on the U.S. model.

What then are his prospects?

Certainly, if disaster overtook the French in Algeria, his recall would become almost inevitable. But short of disaster let no one underestimate the capacity of French politicians to go on talking instead of acting.

Meanwhile it is once again useful to be a de Gaullist.

Friday, May 11, 1956

THE BARONET WHO HAD A LETTER FROM CRABB

He is upset by 'silly theories'

Sir Francis Rose, the 46-year-old baronet, who created a stir this week by claiming he had received a letter from the missing frogman, Commander Crabb, posted on the day of his disappearance, is one of the most colourful members of the British community in Paris.

Sir Francis came to see me this week in a state of considerable agitation.

He was upset for two reasons: first that reports concerning the Crabb letter which disappeared from his flat some time ago had

attributed to him theories which were palpably silly; and secondly, that his 20-year-old son, who is a Spanish subject, has been
held for the past six weeks in a French prison without the
detailed charges having yet been communicated to his defence
counsel.

Crabb, he says, was a very old friend of his (he calls him
'Crabby'), and the letter written on the notepaper of the Ports-
mouth hotel in which Crabb stayed before his disappearance
was a brief note saying he was now in funds 'because I have sold
my invention' and could now repay a small debt.

After Crabb's disappearance Sir Francis realised the possible
importance of the letter and filed it among his private papers.
Later when he decided to show it to the authorities, he found it
had disappeared.

He then went to see the British Ambassador, Sir Gladwyn
Jebb, and told him the full story. He does not for a moment
believe that his son's arrest is in any way linked with the matter.

Sir Francis, with his stocky figure, ruddy complexion, addic-
tion to snuff, and beautifully cut, slightly tweedy English clothes,
looks like an English country squire. He is, in fact, a painter of
considerable distinction.

He had until quite recently a large and beautiful flat overlooking Notre Dame, which he lost, and he now lives in what was
once his servant's bedroom in the same building.

This small room he has transformed with admirable taste and
ingenuity into a miracle of compactness. An effect of space is
created by differently coloured walls and as the need arises it
serves as kitchen, sitting-room or bedroom.

The walls are decorated with Henry Moore, Graham Sutherland and Christian Bérard originals.

Sir Francis was a great friend of Gertrude Stein, who was the
first to buy one of his paintings in 1930, and he has decorated the
cookery book written by Miss Stein's companion, Alice B.
Toklas.

Memoirs – 2

The second volume of General de Gaulle's war memoirs is now
out, and superb stuff it is, too. The publication was timed for the
anniversary of his famous June 18 appeal to France over the

BBC, and it covers the period from the spring of 1942 to the liberation of Paris.

These are the highlights:

* A closely reasoned, extremely moving and hitherto unpublished letter to the late President Roosevelt outlining de Gaulle's view of his own role in the war, disclaiming any ambition for personal power after the war, and pointing out the dangers inherent in treating with former Vichyites.

The President did not deign to reply to this letter.

* A verbatim report of a conversation with Eisenhower. At one point Eisenhower said to de Gaulle: 'I must confess that I have harboured some unjust suspicions of you.' De Gaulle responded in his painstaking English: 'You are a man.'

De Gaulle clears up the mystery of the roof-top firing which created panic in Paris the day after the liberation, when he and his followers walked in procession to Notre Dame.

The theory at the time was that the firing was provoked by Vichy and German elements still in the capital.

Not so, says de Gaulle: the Communists organised it, to create the impression that it was still necessary to retain under arms their resistance groups.

It is now clear that nothing since the war has enhanced de Gaulle's prestige more than the publication of these brilliantly written memoirs.

Friday, June 22, 1956

THE AGA KHAN GETS HIS
AFFAIRS IN ORDER

– and has the world wondering again . . . which son will succeed him?

The decision of the Aga Khan to establish, with his two sons Aly and Sadruddin, his and their legal residence in Switzerland – a country happily free from death duties – is the final step taken by the Aga to place his affairs in order.

It has naturally revived speculation as to which of his two sons he will name as his successor. To this there is an interesting pointer. It lies in the broken romance between Sadruddin and Miss Doone Plunkett of the Guinness family.

Because the young couple were very much in love, and because the marriage seemed entirely suitable, the sudden break up of the romance two years ago was a mystifying development. It is now being said by those who were closest to the young couple that Sadruddin, a dutiful son, had yielded to parental pressure in the matter.

According to this view the Aga is highly conscious of the rise of nationalism in the Middle East and feels that Sadruddin should marry a fellow Moslem.

Sadruddin is a complete opposite of Aly. He is a highly serious young man who has just completed his studies in political science at Harvard University.

On previous visits to France Sadruddin has led a somewhat remote existence, cultivating a circle of intellectual friends and interesting himself in the running of an American-edited literary review in Paris. He is now leading a more worldly life.

At the moment he is friendly with the former Nina Dyer, the now divorced wife of Baron Von Thyssen. As for Aly his marriage to the model Bettina is now considered certain, awaiting only the legalisation of his Reno divorce from Rita Hayworth in Switzerland.

As for the Aga his health at the moment is remarkably good, a fact which is largely attributable to the selfless devotion of that remarkable woman, the Begum.

Friday, August 24, 1956

PICASSO, 75, GETS A SURPRISE PRESENT

– A devotional book by a Dominican priest

I came here to see Pablo Picasso on his seventy-fifth birthday bearing a gift from a former mistress of his. She is Dora Maar, who lived with him during the 'thirties.

Mlle Maar is a Roman Catholic and the present she sent this gnarled old atheist was a devotional book by a Dominican priest.

I had a moment of apprehension on delivering it, fearing that Picasso might receive it with a touch of facetiousness – some joking reference to her efforts at converting him. Not a bit of it. His eyes positively gleamed with pleasure as he handled this paper-backed book.

The next moment there was uproar. Picasso seemed to be in half a dozen different rooms at once as he shouted for his present companion, Jacqueline Roque, 'Come at once, where are you? I have just had a present from Dora.'

I looked round the room during his absence. Chaos. A birthday chaos superimposed on the normal chaos. There were mounds of paper from unwrapped parcels everywhere, piles of telegrams and letters.

The room was uncarpeted, barely furnished. There were litters of newspapers, magazines, books, and canvases everywhere.

There was a similar chaos about the birthday preparations. No invitations had been sent out.

'I expect those of my friends who can make it to just drop in,' said Picasso. As a result about half a dozen people were already camped in the villa.

The house itself is a three-storeyed wedding-cake affair, built by a Victorian champagne millionaire.

Picasso bought it recently for £15,000, leaving the villa in the nearby pottery town of Vallauris, in which he had lived since the war, in the possession of a former mistress, Françoise Gilot, in whose name it had been bought.

The house remains in exactly the same state of neglect as when Picasso bought it, and this, combined with a neglected garden, gives the house an unlived-in look.

Picasso cares nothing for appearances, and simply does not see the ugliness of the house.

He likes to tease friends to comment on it by saying: 'Ah, good taste, what a dreadful thing. Taste is the enemy of creativeness.'

Apart from Mlle Roque and Picasso only two other people live in it, an elderly couple, the woman doing the cooking, and her husband the odd jobs and butlery.

Paul, Picasso's son by his only marriage, chauffeurs his father in a large American car which has replaced the now decrepit Hispano, which he used before the war.

Mlle Roque is a strikingly handsome woman, approaching middle-age, bosomy, short, with a beautifully cut profile, which is seen in a great deal of Picasso's latest work.

She is a native of Vallauris, and was formerly the wife of a minor French colonial official. She is a woman of superb poise, coupled with a very attractive directness of manner.

She dresses almost dowdily, in French provincial fashion, and her only affectation is a black handkerchief which she wears as a hat in something of the shape of a Spanish mantilla.

Picasso himself is an astonishingly dashing figure, with a peasant's rude health and vitality.

See him as I saw him yesterday dressed up to receive a civic welcome from the town council of Vallauris and he looks like an Andalusian rancher (he is, of course, an Andalusian) dressed in his swaggering Sunday best.

He was wearing a beautifully cut, almost skin-tight, pair of black trousers, a delicately knit black matador's jacket which shone like silk, and a string tie.

All that was missing were the high-heeled boots.

That was only one of the day's functions, for in the evening he was received by the pottery workers at Vallauris, where he blew out the seventy-five candles on his birthday cake in three lusty gusts.

He was still going strong late into the night, when everyone else was wilting in the over-crowded, over-heated room.

This boundless good health of Picasso's is no accident. He takes great care of himself. He eats sparingly and simply, drinks nothing apart from an occasional glass of champagne, or white wine.

He appears to smoke heavily – about thirty black tobacco cigarettes a day – but in fact he does not inhale. He sleeps late, rarely rising before twelve, and goes to bed well after midnight.

His eating habits remain Spanish – late afternoon lunches and near-midnight dinners. He is much shorter than his head-and-shoulder photographs suggest. He is, in fact, a small-boned little man with delicate hands, small feet and somewhat spindly legs.

Picasso is a strangely uncomplex character. He is superstitious and sentimental, hates old age and has a horror of death.

Part of the reason why his home is so cluttered up is that he loathes to part with anything, no matter how slight, which has a sentimental or symbolic value for him.

A friend summed up this aspect of his character to me:

'Picasso does not throw away things or people that have become part of him.'

His relations with the women who have played a part in his life is one of close friendship.

Similarly, both his art dealer, Daniel Kahnweiller, and his financial adviser are people he has known for nearly fifty years.

His loyalty to friends remains untouched, even by meanness or silliness on their part.

As to his membership of the Communist Party, that, too, is now encased in the hard shell of his loyalty.

There remains the question of his fortune which technically ought to be immense.

A Picasso sketch is worth about £700 and recently a small painting from his 'Blue' period was sold for £20,000.

His own tastes are simple, and all the women who have figured in his life have been similarly indifferent to money or developed extravagant tastes.

Only one man knows how Picasso's money is disposed of, and that is an old friend, a retired French banker, Max Pellequer.

Cannes, Friday, October 26, 1956

1957

WILL ONASSIS QUIT MONTE CARLO?

The fabulous casino has disillusioned him

Mr Aristotle Onassis, the Greek tanker owner, would now like to sell out his controlling interest in the Monte Carlo Casino. The entire venture on which he staked some remarkably naive hopes has turned sour and become a tiresome irritant.

Among the hopes which have been dashed was that of acquiring the Monégasque flag for his tankers, which, of course, the French would never permit, and of acquiring an influence over Prince Rainier, whose importance he, in any case, grotesquely overestimated.

But the whole climate in Monte Carlo seems inimical to the idea of using it as a business headquarters for his fleet.

Here his business and private life is a public spectacle played out against a background of endless banquets. It says a lot for his stamina and good humour that he survives it.

The other day while he was lunching at the Beach Club he became involved in a scene over a business deal with an irate American who towered over him and looked as though he was about to pick him up and throw him into the blue Mediterranean.

The American was Governor Averell Harriman's son-in-law, who announced himself as Stanley Grafton Mortimer Junior.

He had flown over to clinch a sale on fourteen Douglas DC 6's for Mr Onassis's Greek airlines.

Mr Onassis doubted whether Mortimer could deliver them by the promised date and added: 'The only difference between you and dozens of others who make the same offer is that you are Averell Harriman's son-in-law.'

Mr Mortimer, who looked as though he played American

football for his university, thereupon shouted that that was no way to speak to a member of the Harvard Club and the Racquet Club and that his father-in-law would see to it that the matter was taken up by the U.S. Ambassador to Athens with the King of Greece who, he added, 'won't even have you to tea'.

All this no doubt is of little importance but it is somewhat bewildering to find a man of Onassis's importance discussing even the most trivial affairs not only in the full glare of the Mediterranean sun but under the fascinated gaze of hundreds of bathers.

One feels a pang of sympathy for him especially as he has aged considerably in the past year and looks frayed, tired and worried.

Incidentally the other evening at a sporting club gala (£25 a head with champagne charged extra) the orchestra played over and over again a charming Greek song which is apparently a current favourite of Mr Onassis. It made one wonder whether they would not soon consider it appropriate to end an evening with the Greek National Anthem.

Gambling at the casino recently has been very heavy – and so has the tipping. Mr Niarchos won £20,000 in a burst at *chemin de fer* and passed over a £500 chip as a tip for the croupiers.

Mr Jack Warner is equally generous.

His bill for his party at the gala was £556, on which he paid a £100 tip.

Monte Carlo, Friday, August 9, 1957

PRINCE RAINIER AND ONASSIS QUARREL OVER MONEY

After years of enmity, Prince Rainier and the Greek tanker owner, Aristotle Onassis, are now engaged in their bitterest dispute to date. It is a dispute which may result in Mr Onassis having to move his business from the Principality.

The lease over the premises which he has in Monte Carlo and which is the headquarters for his fleet is owned by the company which controls the Casino and the leading hotels.

Mr Onassis is the biggest single shareholder in the company.

Prince Rainier, however, has veto powers over the company and is now threatening not to renew the lease for the premises which expires early next year.

The dispute has already led to the resignation of the president of the company. He is M. Pierre Ray, who is the Prince's nominee for this post and who is also the administrator of Rainier's personal fortune.

The dispute, as may be guessed, is over money.

Prince Rainier claims he is not getting enough money from the Casino. In an attempt to placate him, the directors of the company offered him a large cash sum in addition to the regular payments in receipts from them.

The sum is said to be £3,000.

This the Prince is believed to have refused on the grounds that it was insufficient.

Having to move his headquarters from Monte Carlo would present Onassis with considerable problems.

He is known to have been considering for some time a possible move to Tangier.

Otherwise he may be forced to go to Panama – his ships are registered there – but this would create great staff difficulties for him.

Prince Rainier's financial situation is better today than it has ever been before.

The reason for this is the vast increase in the flight of foreign capital to Monaco, especially capital brought over by rich French settlers from Morocco and Tunisia.

This has been accompanied by an increase in the number of companies registered in Monaco.

Permission for the formation of such companies has to come from the palace.

As a result, Prince Rainier can display a greater degree of independence as regards Mr Onassis than hitherto.

Friday, November 15, 1957

THE WINDSORS ARE MOSLEY'S LUNCH GUESTS

A ten-minute drive takes them to their neighbours' house
'Le Temple de la Gloire'

A close friendship has developed in the past two years between the Duke of Windsor and Sir Oswald Mosley.

The two men have of course known each other since pre-war days, but it is only in recent years especially since they have become near neighbours that they have become friends.

The Duke has his country home at Gif-Sur-Yvette on the outskirts of Paris, and Sir Oswald, the former British Fascist leader, lives at Orsay, only ten minutes' drive away.

They see each other almost every weekend, the Windsors being regular visitors to the Mosleys' Saturday lunch parties.

Sir Oswald and Lady Mosley live at the end of an underground railway line in a rather drab setting of allotments.

The house itself, however, is charming, a little architectural gem dating from 1830, and built by the man who designed the Madeleine Church.

It looks rather like a miniature Madeleine, but though small it is extremely luxurious.

The Mosleys have lived there since 1951.

Of all things, the house is named 'Le Temple de la Gloire' – the temple of glory.

The Mosleys entertain there frequently, and extremely well.

Their guest list includes such members of the international society as Mrs Daisy Fellowes and Mr Tony Pawson, Sir Charles Mendl and a variety of Troubetzkoys.

It also includes such brilliant intellectuals as the novelist André Malraux, a former Communist who became an ardent de Gaullist, and the political writer Bertrand de Jouvenel.

Then, too, there are some French wartime political figures like 65-year-old Gaston Bergery, a man of remarkable courage and political instability, a former left-winger.

He had the courage to return to France after the Liberation

and after spending five months in jail was acquitted of collaboration charges.

Another visitor is Jacques Benoist-Mechin, a former history professor who was first sentenced to death after the Liberation then had the sentence commuted to hard labour for life and was finally released from prison in 1954.

At these lunch and dinner parties at the Mosleys there is never a brick dropped. The Mosleys are excellent hosts, and there is never any tension or rancour in the conversation.

The Duke and Sir Oswald have a common interest in gardening.

CHRISTMAS NOTE: The Duchess of Windsor does her Christmas shopping for her staff at Cartiers. She spends between two and three thousand pounds on it every year.

Friday, December 20, 1957

1958

MEMO FOR 1958 – DON'T BE SORRY FOR THE FRENCH

It is now reasonably certain that the New Year will bring with it an end to France's four-year-old war in Algeria. The ceasefire will be brought about on French terms and will constitute a remarkable French victory.

Militarily speaking, the war is now all but over. The full scale of rebel desertions to the French have not yet been made public, but I understand that foreign military attachés who have been shown the evidence are extremely impressed by it. An electrified barrier along the Algerian–Tunisian border has now sealed off in Tunisia the only effective remnant of the rebel army.

One reason the French Government is withholding this news from the nation is that it wishes to get its framework law for Algeria through Parliament in a more-or-less unscathed state, so that the military victory can be quickly supplemented by a political settlement.

Right-wing MPs would begin dismantling the Bill if they realised the full scale of the military victory. This new optimism about the outcome of the Algerian struggle has given a marvellous buoyancy to the nation's mood at the opening of the New Year.

Nothing is more puzzling to me than the pitying condescension with which France is viewed abroad. There is nothing apart from Government instability to justify it.

On this point I shall venture a few prophecies for the New Year. The Gaillard Government will be maintained in power for just long enough to enable it to secure a new dollar loan. This loan of 400 million dollars is now virtually in the bag. I expect M.

Gaillard to fall in early spring, thereby producing another seemingly insoluble political crisis, to which, nevertheless, a solution will be found.

There will be no drama, no de Gaulle, no Right- or Left-Wing *coup d'état*. There will not even be any kind of constitutional reform, of a kind that the cunning of French MPs cannot circumvent. There is no revolutionary mood in the country, for the good reason that France has never been more prosperous and its people have never lived better.

This Christmas sales were sixteen per cent higher than last year, and 1,500,000 Parisians left the capital over the holidays for winter sports and Riviera resorts. Wages on the whole have kept up with prices – industrial workers have averaged a five per cent wage increase every year for the past four years.

Furthermore, productivity has increased over this period by seven to eight per cent annually – an achievement unequalled by any other country in the world.

For the first time in its history France finds itself a highly modern, highly industrialised nation. It is also being transformed by its bounding birth-rate from the oldest country in Europe to the youngest.

To sum up, my New Year message from Paris would be – don't be sorry for the French.

Friday, January 3, 1958

MR GETTY ('I'm worth 1,695 million dollars') GETS THE LEGION OF HONOUR

Paul Getty, 65-year-old American oil magnate, named by a recent financial survey as the richest American in the world, has been awarded the Legion of Honour.

The award was made by France's wartime Prime Minister, M. Paul Reynaud, who represents in Parliament some of the big North of France shipbuilding towns in which six of Mr Getty's super tankers (total tonnage of 350,000 tons) have been or are being built.

In speeches which followed the ceremony, M. Reynaud, with gallant delicacy, avoided any mention of the considerable material contribution Getty has made to the prosperity of the French ship-building industry.

Getty is well known and respected here, and he combines very good French with very good manners.

I have had many meetings with Getty and each one has revealed some unexpected aspect of the man. Take his linguistic abilities: he not only speaks very good French but also excellent German, good Spanish and Italian, and fluent Arabic.

This week Getty leaves his Paris hotel room, where he is staying under an assumed name, to visit his oil properties in Saudi Arabia.

He will probably fly there though he detests flying and this will be his first air journey since 1942. Getty does not keep his room in Paris – one of the most modest rooms in the hotel – when he is away on a trip.

Dozens of begging letters reach him every day and he goes through them as carefully as he does through the rest of his mail. At the moment he is packing for his trip which for him involves arranging himself innumerable packages, papers and documents which the hotel will store for him until his return. For his room is his only office and there is no typewriter, secretary or Dictaphone.

A great many of the facts and figures which he would need with him on his Middle East trip he simply commits to memory.

His own estimate of his fortune is one billion, six hundred and ninety-five million dollars (about £605 million). At the moment he is planning further expansion by building refineries in Germany and France.

The drop in freight charges which has hit people like Niarchos and Onassis hard has in fact proved 'very beneficial' to him as a producer of oil in the Middle East.

His decision to build refineries, like his decision to build tankers, arises from his deep-seated hatred of being 'at the mercy' of combines. He despises American big business with its managerial complex.

'Who pays for their fancy salaries and expense accounts? Why, it's the common shareholder and the producers who pay,' he says.

He has decided to stop adding to his collection of antiques and paintings. They are housed in his private museum in the United States which he has not visited for eight years.

'There is no more room to put anything,' he told me.

Friday, January 31, 1958

WILL A SLOGAN ('The Republic is in danger!') BE STRONGER THAN THE GENERALS?

Crossing the Champs Elysées early yesterday evening a French friend nudged me as he pointed at the long line of Black Marias stretching as far as the eye could see and said: 'There is a real Sixth of February nip in the air.'

He was referring, of course, to that historic date of twenty-two years ago when Fascist rioting in the Place de la Concorde over the Stavisky scandal so terrified the Left that it welded them into the triumphant Popular Front of Radicals, Socialists and Communists.

This was a coalition which has a strong survival value in French political mythology.

It even enjoyed the blessing of General de Gaulle himself for a brief period after the Liberation. That popular front is now in process of re-forming itself in answer to the military coup in Algiers.

This idiot coup is the French Communist's delight. Let no one underestimate the strength of Republican feeling in France. The cry of 'The Republic in danger' is the most evocative slogan in French national life. It overrides the largely superficial contempt for the Parliamentary game and is even stronger than the overwhelming popular support for the Algerian war. The French have bitter memories of generals as politicians.

Only two months ago General Massu, who with the de Gaullist MP, Jacques Soustelle, is clearly the ringleader of the revolt, underlined these memories in a private talk I had with him at his headquarters in Algiers.

I had asked him rather naively what he thought of Paris

suspicions that he might use his magnificent paratroopers as a Praetorian Guard for the overthrow of parliamentary government in France.

I recall the moment vividly. Massu is a heavy-nosed man with protruding lips. He spluttered with indignation.

'We'll never do it!' he replied: 'Never! never! never! The French army is like the Catholic Church; we have long memories and we learn our lessons. The church learned from the Dreyfus Case. The army will never forget the lesson of General Boulanger.'

Boulanger was a popinjay on whom anti-republican hopes were based at the turn of the century and whose melodramatic efforts to seize power from politicians was as seemingly hopeless as the present one and ended in a humiliating suicide.

Now that Massu's mask is off I see no reason to withhold further details of our talk. He spoke with bitter contempt of the reactionary elements among the French settlers 'who are asked to use us so that they can get back to the easy days as though nothing has happened and the clock has stood still'.

He added: 'Our next job will be to crack down on the Ultras.' He thought the major weakness of French policy in Algeria was the delay in applying overdue political reforms and the dishonesty with which even watered-down reforms were applied.

Both he and his wife, who was engaged in tireless social work, were a seemingly Mountbatten pair anxiously searching for Moslem Gandhis to embrace.

The ramifications and purpose of the conspiracy are intriguing. Clearly it was carefully prepared with the army giving the go-ahead signal to chosen leaders of French settlers' organisations to prepare the necessary rioting.

But what was expected to happen in Paris? A political infant could have seen that the Communists either by abstention, as was in fact the case, or if need be by outright vote would have rallied to Pflimlin.

Or could the Right have been so befuddled by wistful thinking that it believed its own tall stories of the Communists cunningly conniving at the return of General de Gaulle to serve some devious purpose of Russian foreign policy?

Or did they really think that they could force General de Gaulle's hand and make him emerge from retirement as a latter-day Pétain?

The ramifications of the plot are an even more interesting

subject for speculation. It was known that at least one Minister under the previous government played a direct role in countenancing the disastrous Sakiet bombing.

Was this so-called de Gaullist and ferociously ambitious politician in the plot?

It was fascinating the way tension was gradually built up over yesterday until it was clear by late afternoon that something very odd was afoot.

The Socialist resident Minister for Algeria in the outgoing Government, M. Robert Lacoste, refused to see M. Pflimlin, despite the latter's urgent appeals during the day.

Finally cornered in the Parliamentary lobbies and as a result of a direct appeal from the outgoing Premier M. Gaillard, he condescended to speak to the Premier Designate on the telephone.

He contented himself with saying that he had given all necessary instructions for the maintenance of order in Algiers and refused point blank to return to his post.

It became known too during the day through a leakage which shows that the Republic has its own means of keeping tabs on its generals, that General Salan, C.-in-C. in Algeria, had sent a highly secret note to his superior army chief in Paris indicating that an army revolt was imminent. As for Salan, all that need be said is that he is an insignificant political general with a long trail of military disasters to his discredit and that now he has been forced to bite the hand that promoted and sustained him.

Having said all this, it should be added that the agony of Algeria and the agony of the French army are two deeply moving tragedies.

The essence of the Algerian tragedy is that there is no alternative policy to the one at present being followed of pacification and free elections, other than the evacuation of Algeria by 1,200,000 Frenchmen who have been born there and whose forebears have lived there for generations.

Not even M. Lacoste's most bitter critics can formulate a valid policy that falls between these alternatives.

As for the army its tragedy is even more stark; it has suffered defeat after defeat ever since 1940, largely through no fault of its own. Now it is engaged at one and the same time in a stupendous humanitarian effort and a bloody guerrilla war.

It finds the thought of 'a diplomatic Dien-Bien-Phu' quite unbearable. But the fact is that the French Right and the French settlers in Algeria have now overplayed their hand.

They have assumed the role of makers and breakers of governments and they have forgotten the brutal arithmetic of the existing French Parliament. It is easy enough for the French Right to overthrow a government with the aid of the Communists as they did with the last Government.

But it is easier to make new governments with the support of the same Communists, and as for M. Pflimlin for once they have an opponent of great courage and character.

Wednesday, May 14, 1958

DE GAULLE:
I MUST BE OBEYED BY ALL

The French political crisis – easily the gravest since the war and one which brought the country to the very edge of civil war – is over.

General de Gaulle is assured of an overwhelming vote of confidence when Parliament votes on his investiture as Premier, probably tomorrow morning.

The Socialists, on whose vote everything depended, have gone over to him by a large, though as yet unspecified, majority.

In short, de Gaulle is in. This morning the general met at his Paris hotel twenty-six different leaders and representatives of all the non-Communist political parties.

The talks lasted seventy minutes. Afterwards the general asked them to see him again at five o'clock this evening to give him their assurances that he would get at least 400 votes to counter the 155 Communist votes against.

In the course of these talks de Gaulle gave a number of vital assurances. Among the most important was that in no circumstances would his former wartime right-hand man Jacques Soustelle, who largely organised the Algerian rebellion, be given a post in his Government.

De Gaulle was closely questioned by some of his last remaining implacable opponents, including the former Socialist Premier, M. Ramadier.

His reply to questions concerning the future of the Algerian Committee of Public Safety was simply to state: 'The powers of the Republic, once they have been entrusted to me, give me no other choice but to ensure that I am obeyed by all.'

He once again explained that he wanted a federal solution for Algeria with equal rights for Moslems and with Algeria being part of an alliance including Tunisia, Morocco and France.

General de Gaulle also gave details of the specialists he would include in his Cabinet.

These included at least three names anathema to the extreme Right.

He elaborated on the subject by making it clear that not only would he not ask Soustelle to serve on his cabinet but that everyone involved in the military uprising in Algiers would be ruled out of consideration for high office.

Saturday, May 31, 1958

THE POWDER KEG WAITING FOR DE GAULLE IN ALGIERS

*The big question: Can he please the army
and the settlers?*

There must be few circumstances in history as ironic as the contrast between General de Gaulle's arrival in Algiers today and that of his arrival fifteen years ago.

When he arrived here in 1943 he was the symbolic representative of all that was best in France – a kind of political giant breaking with the utmost ease the cobwebs of conspiracy between Washington and Vichy.

Roosevelt and Pétain – the oddest of combinations – wanted Giraud and Admiral Darlan to replace de Gaulle as the effective spearhead of the Liberation of Metropolitan France.

They were foiled by the obvious fact that only de Gaulle represented fighting France.

Now de Gaulle returns here in circumstances considerably different.

His spiritual companions of the war years have largely deserted him. He returns as the darling of the very people who in 1943 hated him the most.

A man like Alain de Serigny, the former Pétainist whose hand de Gaulle may not even wish to shake, is today the leading orchestrator of the 'de Gaulle to power' clamour.

This very city, which reeks of Vichyism, is preparing a triumphant welcome to de Gaulle – fifteen years too late.

There is no section of French public opinion which hates de Gaulle more than the traditional Right.

He is in their eyes the man responsible for all France's post-war evils.

It was he who permitted the semi-revolutionary terror against collaborators; he who brought back the Communist leader and army deserter Maurice Thorez from exile in Moscow, and he who re-created the pre-war popular front by having Communist Ministers in his government.

In short he is regarded as a traitor to his class and – final irony – a mutinous general who refused to obey Marshal Pétain.

Now this erstwhile mutineer returns to Algiers to re-establish State authority over an army in full rebellion.

Quite clearly the civilians here have used the de Gaulle slogan simply as a means of binding themselves to the army.

Now they are disappointed at the result and they are preparing to switch slogans.

A new one will be that a Cabinet post, preferably that of Minister for Algeria, be found for Jacques Soustelle, the leading intellectual light of the Algiers revolution.

The settlers here are clearly infuriated by the moderate charter of the men de Gaulle has surrounded himself with, and especially the inclusion of the hated M. Pflimlin whose close friendship with the Liberal mayor of Algiers, Jacques Chevallier, has long rendered him an object of great suspicion.

As M. de Serigny, with his customary delicacy, puts it: 'It was necessary for General de Gaulle to cheat a little in order to ensure his parliamentary majority and appease Washington.

'But now that he is in the cleaner air of Algiers we hope he can be relied on to do the right thing.'

It is difficult to see how de Gaulle can find a Cabinet post for Soustelle because he has given a solemn promise to the Socialists that on no account will he give such a post to anyone involved in the Algiers rebellion, and especially Soustelle.

Soustelle is a curious example of the sincere idealist exposing himself to exploitation by cynical mercenaries.

An intellectual former right hand of de Gaulle during the war, his ideas on the future of Algeria would, in any other circumstances, be considered exceptionally Liberal.

They are also however impractical, and it is because of their total impracticality that the Right-wing extremists have rallied to him.

Soustelle's idea of complete integration and equal rights between the Moslems and the Frenchmen would involve the French State in bankruptcy.

The settlers, however, prefer to rally to someone chasing political will o' the wisps rather than risk a solution which would deprive them of the presence of the French army.

In short, what the settlers want is a state of virtually permanent war in which their interests are protected by the army.

The situation regarding the army is a curious one. The army has no love for the settlers who, in fact, they detest for such simple reasons as profiteering and even charging troops for water.

All the army is concerned about is avoiding the humiliation of defeat. The sympathies of the junior officers are entirely on the side of equal rights for the Arabs and an end to the war which would combine a Liberal settlement with an army victory.

Here is another contradiction in the situation, one which involves an ultimate conflict of aims between the army and the settlers.

There is little doubt that the army will rally to de Gaulle – but only on condition that de Gaulle can give them a clear political aim.

Everything now depends on the frankness with which de Gaulle speaks when he comes here.

If he indulges in phrases which can mean all things to all men he will leave behind him an extremely explosive situation.

If he speaks out frankly and declares a policy, then the fury of the settlers may be bright. But the army and the Moslems, to say nothing of the opinion in France itself, will be behind him.

Algiers, Wednesday, June 4, 1958

1959

CAN DE GAULLE KEEP UP HIS BALANCING ACT?

Tomorrow General de Gaulle takes over the Presidency of the Republic from President Coty, and his faithful follower M. Michel Debré becomes France's first Prime Minister under the new Fifth Republic.

Thus ends the first stage of the revolution begun in Algiers last May and the second and more decisive stage opens.

Superficially General de Gaulle enters upon his seven-year Presidency in a France almost as thoroughly renovated as the salons of the Elysée Palace, which is now being spring-cleaned to receive the General, his wife and a huge secretariat.

It is as though all the windows have suddenly been opened in a house long shuttered against fresh air.

In the past two weeks while General de Gaulle's emergency powers have still been in force a cascade of some 200 fundamental reforms touching every phase of national life – the judiciary, education, national defence and even marketing – has descended upon a country dazed by the speed of it all.

Everyone in the past has agreed on the need of every one of these reforms; no government in France has ever dared tackle them for fear of offending some powerful lobby or losing a fraction of the support on which its life depended.

Symbolic of this sweeping away of much that is old and musty in France has been de Gaulle's last-minute attack on that almost feudal stronghold of entrenched privilege – Paris's central market Les Halles, the so-called 'Belly of Paris'.

For half a century the criminal absurdity of Les Halles's location has been denounced – and denounced in vain. Not only is it not near a railhead, not only does it cause fantastic traffic jams but it is the headquarters of hereditary middlemen whose activities are largely responsible for the low prices paid to the farmer and the high prices charged in the shops.

Now Les Halles is to be moved to a more suitable location and central markets near railway stations will be set up in all provincial capitals.

It is now almost thirteen years to the very day that de Gaulle resigned office and went into voluntary retirement. On that bleak January day in 1946 in a Paris largely unheated and hungry, de Gaulle first stunned and then delighted his Cabinet of bickering Socialists, Communists and Catholics by announcing: 'I have decided to resign; my decision is irrevocable.'

He then left the Cabinet Room while his ministers' faces gradually broke into broad smiles of relief like schoolboys witnessing the departure of a harsh headmaster.

They were relieved to see him go, not only because they were supremely confident of being able to rule France without benefit of de Gaulle, but also because they were impatient to revert to the profitable political intrigues and pastimes of pre-war France.

They never realised that twelve years later they would be pleading with de Gaulle to save them from the consequences of their own follies. A few days later de Gaulle made his first (and for several years only) public reference to his resignation. He said: 'The regime of the parties, unchecked by a strong executive responsible to Parliament but separated from it, will lead France into chaos and democracy to the abyss.'

De Gaulle now takes over a France far different from the one inherited after the war. It is now a country in plain renaissance in every field of activity and indeed it was the existence of this renaissance which made the revolutionary change in the outworn political system inevitable.

It has a bounding birthrate which has already changed and will continue to change even more drastically the old political allegiance.

The three dominating figures of the new Republic will be de Gaulle himself, his Prime Minister, M. Debré, and, in the wings for the time being, M. Jacques Soustelle.

Forty-seven-year-old M. Debré is a man of strong opinions but whatever his views he will carry out the General's wishes in all fields of policy.

He dislikes the new Budget, but he will apply it; he loathes the Common Market, but he will swallow it; he detests the

Germans, but he will be nice to them. An extreme Nationalist, his nationalism takes the form of complete identification with de Gaulle.

Debré's intense nationalism probably springs from the fact that he is Alsatian. His grandparents left Alsace in 1870 because they did not want to become Germans. His grandfather was a rabbi. He is an intellectual and the author of the New Constitution. Unlike other de Gaullists, he consistently refused to hold office under the old Republic. He was a thorn in the side of successive governments and averaged at least ten extremely embarrassing parliamentary questions a week.

Soustelle's future is a mystery – a mystery bound up with a so far indiscernible outcome of the de Gaulle experiment itself. So far de Gaulle is refusing him any of the key posts in the Government – Interior, Foreign Affairs or Defence – and it may well be that Soustelle will stay out of the Government altogether and devote himself entirely to the leadership of his new party, the UNR, the largest in the present Parliament.

Two aspects of de Gaulle's policy as they may affect Soustelle to say nothing of France itself have now become clear.

1. France will stay in Algeria hoping that military pressure and economic betterment will produce the conditions for a settlement on terms far short of the present rebel demand. Soustelle will oppose negotiations with them on any terms.

2. De Gaulle has chosen a financial policy so classically Conservative that one has to go back to the 'twenties in Britain to find a parallel.

This is completely opposed to the policy advocated by Soustelle and his party, which is one of continuing with the present inflationary boom. Soustelle at the moment intends to lie low, consolidate his party, and emerge as an effective Left-wing Opposition leader should de Gaulle's policy fail. This is completely in character with the man who started as a revolutionary and remains one.

Not only is he himself essentially a man of the Left, but his electoral support is very largely Left of centre. It is no accident that his party picked up over a million former Communist votes in the last election.

He has heavy support, too, among the junior ranks in the army, and the French army of today is not the traditionally Conservative force it used to be. It is heavily impregnated with the mystique of a kind of French National Socialism.

I doubt if Soustelle's success in the elections was due to his party's seeming identification with de Gaulle. If de Gaulle had given his public blessing, say, to the Socialists, I doubt very much if that would have gained them one extra seat or cost Soustelle's party any important loss of votes.

The fact is the old parties, with the possible exception of the Communists, are finished – their numbers are not only insignificant in the present Parliament but their doctrines and slogans are meaningless in the ears of the new generation.

M. Mollet has, of course, resigned from de Gaulle's government and refuses to serve in the new one. Instead, he has told the General that he and the Socialists will go into 'Constructive Opposition'.

The Socialists could not really swallow the new budget, and fear that they would be outflanked by the Communists in industrial opposition to the budget was sufficient to ensure a Socialist withdrawal from the government.

But who in ten years' time will vote for M. Mollet's Dickensian Socialists, or the Radicals? In the new Parliament the great debate will be between the two bulk parties – M. Pinay's Conservatives on the Right and M. Soustelle's revolutionary Nationalists on the Left.

Between them, if the new economic programme falters in the next six months, de Gaulle will hold an uneasy balance.

Wednesday, January 7, 1959

NO NEED FOR ME TO WHISPER – THAT'S HOW THE PLACE HAS CHANGED

This is where it all started – in this dazzling city on the bay of Algiers with terraced skyscrapers rising from it like some mammoth monument to French achievements.

Here it was that a band of youngsters, whose rioting had for years reduced the Paris Government to palsied indecision, stormed the building from which Algiers is administered, and later, joined by the army, overthrew the Fourth Republic and paved the way for General de Gaulle's return to power.

Now, one year later, the crucial question is whether de Gaulle has tamed the tiger of civil and military revolt on which he rode to power.

The answer is that he has pulled some of its sharpest teeth and pared some of its most menacing claws.

The problem for de Gaulle is how to impose a liberal and humane solution to the five-year-old Algerian war on a European population 1,200,000 strong, which sees in any weakening of the tie with France a menace to its own existence; and on an army which bristles at a mere suggestion of negotiations with the enemy.

De Gaulle's immediate purpose, which he has pursued with consummate cunning, is:

1. To avert any possibility of another explosive fusion between army and civilian feeling which produced last May's revolution. Without the army the settlers are powerless; with the army they can plunge into civil war.

2. To split the settlers themselves and especially to isolate their Fascist-minded leaders.

3. By pursuing the war to convince the Moslems, and especially their educated élite, that this time France's promise of revolutionary reform, under which political power will pass to the Moslem majority, will be kept.

The solemnity of the promise is underlined by the magic of de Gaulle's name, and this magic still works with the Moslem population.

How successful has de Gaulle been in these three directions?

He has met with considerable success, and in any case has completely dissipated the great fear which hung over France last May that he would become the prisoner of the forces which brought him back to power.

The change in the atmosphere is noticeable from the moment we arrived at Algiers Airport. As usual, on arrival, I carefully left behind on the airplane any Left-wing newspapers or periodicals, only to find them on open sale at the airport book-stall.

Even in the Hotel Aletti bar, the stronghold of rich settlers and army officers, which usually teems with police spies, people were openly reading so-called 'treasonable' newspapers barred here under the Fourth Republic.

A year ago, in this very spot, one dropped one's voice in conversation and was careful whom one met.

Now little trace of that police state atmosphere remains.

A Moslem who would not have come into the bar a year ago eagerly suggested that we meet there. Patrols are less numerous and less menacing.

The curfew has been advanced from midnight till 1 a.m. and the whole city has the air of an American Middle West boom town set on a Mediterranean shore.

New skyscraper flats are shooting up everywhere, every hotel bar is full of American oil men fresh from oil surveys in the Sahara, and the swaggering paratroopers have the air of characters out of Western films.

The Moslems are moving in greater and greater numbers into what were hitherto considered exclusively European quarters.

One sees more unveiled Moslem women than ever before, and even many of the veiled ones walk on arrogant high heels.

On the political plane the change is even more striking. The former all-powerful Committee of Public Safety, which came into being during the May revolution, is now a rump from which all the army officers, all the de Gaullists and the Moslems have resigned.

What is left of it is boycotting the May 13 anniversary and proclaiming it as a day of mourning to mark de Gaulle's 'betrayal' of their initial aims.

The army officers who played such a prominent part in the revolution have almost all been dispersed. Only General Massu is still here, because he is considered an especially docile de Gaullist.

General Salan, who took over the leadership of the May 13 movement, must still be painfully wincing from the mighty kick upstairs he received when he was made military governor of Paris.

Civilian control has been completely re-established and a remarkable new Governor-General, M. Delouvrier, the brilliant economist, has moved in here with his own staff, thereby putting himself in the position of being able to by-pass the so-called administration.

Unlike previous governors, Delouvrier has succeeded in making it clear that he is Paris's representative in Algiers.

On the military side the situation has greatly improved, largely owing to more mobile tactics introduced by General Challe.

The military successes, however, are counter-balanced by a revival of terrorism in the big towns.

This is the pall of fear that hangs over Algiers on the eve of tomorrow's anniversary. If a bomb is thrown on that day it may rouse the highly-inflammable European population into widespread rioting.

Even on the briefest visit one inevitably receives some personal and poignant impression of this tragic, and now largely senseless, war.

On Sunday I drove with some friends to a nearby beach. The road ahead, as far as the eye could see, glistened with cars in the brilliant sunshine. The sandy beach was crowded with bathers and the whole scene might have been taking place on the Riviera.

My host's 14-year-old son broke the spell by asking his father why the terrorists did not plant bombs. The company suddenly froze.

Why not indeed? Or rather when will they think that one up?

We drove back just as dusk was settling. With the dusk everyone grew noticeably edgy. The unending line of cars passed village after village, each one emptying of Europeans while lolling, expressionless Moslems looked on.

One had an eerie feeling during moments in that drive of being a member of an evacuating convoy.

Algiers, Tuesday, May 12, 1959

NEVER HAS DE GAULLE RIDDEN SO HIGH . . .

The fog of melodrama which has descended on French politics recently should not be allowed to obscure the principal features of the situation here, some reassuring, some menacing.

The most reassuring is that General de Gaulle is now more popular in France and enjoys more esteem and affection – popular affection never before felt for him – than at any time since he came to power eighteen months ago.

This is of major importance because it gives him greater authority in dealing with malcontents on the Right, especially the army, and the doings on the Left, especially the trade unions, who might be tempted to exploit this winter's renewed upward trend of crisis.

The rise in de Gaulle's popularity dates from one event – his broadcast to the nation offering self-determination to Algeria.

This speech was so noble in its terms, so courageous in its decisiveness, so moving in its sincerity, that it has had all the impact of a Churchill wartime broadcast.

Before that the delphic obscurity of his speeches on these key subjects had caused general exasperation, and in consequence a sharp dip in his popularity.

Now he has still further strengthened his grip on public opinion by pulling off last week's diplomatic stroke – getting Krushchev to Paris and securing a postponement of the summit conference.

This double triumph fits in with the general mood here that France's allies have taken France for granted for far too long.

De Gaulle's renewed authority is a major factor making for stability.

The major factor making for instability is simply the reverse of this particular coin.

By exercising such sweeping authority de Gaulle has magnified the worst features of his Constitution and allowed to fall into disuse all the checks and balances on presidential power which had been so carefully devised.

What we have in France today is one-man rule with all the advantages and perils that such rule involves.

The government matters little, parliament even less.

Only one minister in the present government speaks up for his views and that is the Finance Minister, M. Pinay.

The French Foreign Office might be operating on another planet for all it knows of de Gaulle's intentions.

Often on key policy questions not even the cabinet is fully taken into de Gaulle's confidence. And if it is it is usually in the form of a last-minute briefing.

What of the army? If the long-term consequence of personal rule even by a man of such innate decency as de Gaulle may be considered frightening, the consequences (not so long term) of the political role the army is playing are positively hair-raising.

A feature of de Gaulle's character which has emerged most strikingly in the past few months is his supreme self-confidence.

Not only does he not believe that there was any serious plot against the regime last week but he refuses to believe even in the possibility of one.

A plot against de Gaulle, especially by the army, is to him as inconceivable as parricide is to a normal parent.

His minister in Algeria, M. Delouvrier, may live in genuine fear that one of these days he will find himself under arrest by a military junta in his summer palace in Algiers.

His C.-in-C. in Algeria, General Challe, may warn him, as he has done twice in recent months, that there is growing anti-de Gaulle feeling among senior army officers.

De Gaulle simply refuses to heed these warnings. Some action has clearly been taken recently – as it was after the May 13 revolt – against suspect officers.

But this has been on an insufficient scale and not of a kind to break their long-range influence over Algerian events.

It is safe to say that the writ of Paris stops more surely on the other side of the Mediterranean now than it did before the May 13 uprising.

The army having tasted the elixir of one successful revolution has been flexing its new-found political muscles ever since.

The heart of the situation is that there is a fatal misunderstanding between de Gaulle and the higher echelons of the army.

The army is prepared to go along with de Gaulle's self-determination policy for Algeria on the assumption that it is humbug designed for foreign opinion and especially the United Nations.

They therefore consider that they will be left free to carry on with the war and organise a referendum in the distant future in their own way.

That is why the flashpoint of danger will come if and when – and it is hard to see how it can be avoided – the rebel leaders come to Paris to discuss cease-fire terms.

Such terms will have to include giving the rebels the freedom to campaign for Algerian independence.

It is tempting to share de Gaulle's optimism regarding the future.

After all an army revolt against him at a time when he can be certain of the support of ninety per cent of the nation seems doomed to failure.

Frenchmen who watched with apathy the death agonies of the discredited Fourth Republic will rise to de Gaulle's defence.

Nevertheless the warnings are open and insistent.

Almost every senior officer in France from Marshal Juin down has expressed his opposition to the honest application of de Gaulle's Algerian policy.

Wednesday, October 28, 1959

THE GENERAL'S MEMOIRS OUTSELL FRANÇOISE SAGAN

– and look like making him more than half-a-million

To the book-embattled Field Marshals of Britain, I bring news of a mere Brigadier-General who is out-selling the lot of them.

I refer, of course, to General Charles de Gaulle, whose final volume of memoirs is selling here at a rate which puts him well ahead of Françoise Sagan as the biggest money-spinner in French publishing history.

This latest volume, published last week at 30s. – twice the price of a Sagan – is selling at the rate of 5,000 copies a day.

The first volume of General de Gaulle's memoirs sold 115,000 and the second 70,000, in France alone, and both are still selling briskly in cheaper editions.

Because of the increased interest in de Gaulle since he returned to power, the first print order for the present volume was 143,000, and the sale will almost certainly touch the 200,000 mark.

How much money then can Operation Memoir be expected to net the General?

From the figures available it is almost certain that de Gaulle will make from sales and syndication rights well over half-a-million pounds.

It has been commonly assumed in the past that all the profits from his books go to a private charity supported by the General and Madame de Gaulle.

This is not so.

Profits from the book sales go to de Gaulle's private account at the Rothschild Bank in Paris.

It is only the profits from syndication, on which incidentally de Gaulle has struck a very hard bargain of taking eighty-five per cent of the profits, which go to this particular charity.

The foundation is dedicated to the care of retarded children.

De Gaulle's keen sense of the dignity of his present office has led him to make an interesting change in the syndication policy for France.

No single newspaper or periodical has been sold the exclusive rights for the publication of extracts from the present volume, as was the case with its predecessors.

Instead all are free to publish it – on payment of a stiff fee.

De Gaulle's publishers, the House of Plon, merit a close look.

It is one of the oldest in Paris and was once the official publishing house of Napoleon III.

Today control is shared between the great newspaper distributing firm of Hachette and various Rothschild interests.

De Gaulle's financial affairs are controlled by Georges Pompidou, the director of the Rothschild Bank, who served on de Gaulle's personal staff after his return to power.

Footnote – While I was talking to a director of Plon, a telephone call came through from M. Pompidou.

He wanted to know when the last cheque had been despatched to the General.

He was told that the cheque for £10,000 had been sent two days before.

Friday, November 6, 1959

1960

REVOLT GROWS

The Algiers rebels are still holding out

General strike in three cities

The Algerian uprising is spreading in Algiers itself and has also spread to the other two principal cities – Oran and Constantine.

There is a general strike in all three cities and in Algiers the population is reinforcing two rebel strongholds which have held on throughout the night.

One is commanded by a former parachutist and now an MP, M. Lagallarde, who played a leading role in the May 13 revolt. His headquarters is in part of Algiers University.

The other stronghold is commanded by M. Joseph Ortiz, an Algiers café proprietor, who has taken over the leadership of the revolt.

His stronghold is in a skyscraper building facing the central post office. Both Oran and Constantine were relatively calm yesterday. But today unofficial reports reaching Paris said that in Oran there are 25,000 demonstrators in the streets.

M. Ortiz issued a declaration today calling on President de Gaulle to reverse his policy of self-determination for Algeria before there could be any question of the rebels laying down their arms.

Following the state of siege declared last night in Algiers after rioting in which nineteen were killed and 141 wounded, Algiers today is cut off from all but official communication with Paris.

All civilian telephone calls and cables are forbidden even inside Algeria and the official French news agency announced that it was unable to establish contact with its Algiers office.

According to the last messages to reach Paris, there is no public transport in Algiers and the only vehicles on the streets are military ones.

Despite the heavy censorship and official efforts to calm the public, both here and in Algeria, there is great apprehension in official circles.

It is felt that unless the revolt is mastered in the next two or three days the situation may get out of hand.

Great disquiet is felt here that the authorities in Algiers are apparently not prepared to use paratroops formerly commanded by General Massu to help restore order.

In their place paratroopers of the Foreign Legion and those commanded by the famous Colonel Bigeard have been moved in from other parts of Algeria.

Disquiet is also felt over the fact that two senior officers – one from the headquarters of the Commander-in-Chief, General Challe, and the other formerly on the staff of General Massu – appeared on the balcony with one of the principal ringleaders of the rebellion, M. Joseph Ortiz, while he harangued the crowd yesterday afternoon.

A helicopter today flew low over Algiers scattering copies of President de Gaulle's broadcast to the rebels 'to rejoin the nation'.

These leaflets were seized by the crowds and immediately burned. The civilian Governor of Algeria, M. Delouvrier, today moved his headquarters from the imposing Summer Palace in the centre of Algiers to a locality which is being kept secret.

All streets leading to the Palace are barred with barbed wire and the Palace itself has been transformed into an army headquarters.

In Paris the Prime Minister, M. Debré, who talked to President de Gaulle at 3.30 a.m., saw the Minister of Defence, M. Guillaumat, and later saw the President again.

An official communiqué on the situation in Algeria is to be published later in the day. Meanwhile all demonstrations and all gatherings of more than three people are forbidden throughout France.

A Cabinet meeting, presided over by President de Gaulle, has been called. Paris itself is outwardly calm, but police and Republican Guards are guarding key points, Ministries and the Parliament buildings.

Observers in Paris are puzzled that troops who were stationed yesterday on the main roads leading into Algiers to prevent demonstrators reaching the centre of the city apparently let most of them through with the result that the crowd in the heart of Algiers, much of which consisted of armed territorials, was allowed to swell to more than 20,000.

It is ironic that the most reliable military force in Algiers today should be the Foreign Legion paratroopers, a very heavy percentage of which are Germans.

M. Bidault, former Prime Minister and Foreign Minister, who is violently opposed to General de Gaulle's self-determination policy for Algeria, was believed today to have escaped from police surveillance.

However, he returned to his home today after a weekend in the country.

General Massu is also in Paris, living in an apartment set aside for him at the Ministry of War.

The early-morning broadcast by General de Gaulle appealing to the settlers to 'rejoin the nation' underlined the gravity of the situation.

He asked them to give up their attempt at insurrection and called yesterday's uprising 'a foul blow against France and Algeria, against France and the world, and against France and the heart of France itself'.

He added: 'Nothing is lost to Frenchmen when they rejoin Mother France.'

He concluded: 'I shall do my duty – *vive la France*.'

Government officials said that whatever happened President de Gaulle would go ahead with his scheduled visit to Algeria on February 5.

He also indicated that if the attempt at insurrection were abandoned no charges would be made against ringleaders but if it were persisted with then they would lay themselves open to the charge of high treason.

The uprising was Algiers' answer to President de Gaulle's dismissal of General Massu on Friday for insubordination. Clearly the rising was an organised and prepared affair. If it had been a spontaneous outburst of popular anger at Massu's dismissal then it would have broken out on Saturday instead of two days after the event.

This is the most frightening feature of the rising.

Clearly it was part of a conspiracy and the problem is to know both its instigators and its scope.

It has been well known for months past that Right-wing organisations in Algeria were waiting a signal for an uprising, the timing of which would be dictated both by assurances of at least some army support and parallel action in Metropolitan France.

Did the signal come from France?

Who gave it?

Who gave the assurances, if any, of at least a degree of army support?

These are the questions which are worrying the French Government at the moment and which the events of the next few days will disclose.

Monday, January 25, 1960

SO *THESE* WERE THE MEN WHO MADE FRANCE TREMBLE!

Coming to Algiers from Paris is like walking through a mirror. On the Paris side the figure of de Gaulle looms to a size almost too big for it; on the Algiers side it shrinks to almost that of a postage stamp.

In Paris one sees only the triumphant assertion of presidential authority.

Here one realises with sickening despair that de Gaulle's will counts for little with the only force that matters – the army.

Let no one be deceived by the humiliating collapse of the so-called insurrection this week. What it proved was that the Algiers mob, before which successive French Governments had trembled, was venal, vain-glorious and cowardly.

The rising came as the result of prior assurances of Army benevolence and lasted only as long as the army was prepared to protect.

It could have been ended easier much earlier by a two-day blockade.

To give one an idea of the quality of the men behind the

barricade it is only necessary to recount the sequel.

Only a week earlier they had been screaming at the riot squad police before opening a murderous fire at them: 'Why don't you go and fight the FLN?' That is to say the Moslem guerrilla army which launched the war against the French five years ago.

When the surrender came they insisted as part of the terms that they should be given a chance of joining the army to fight for French Algeria. What happened?

Of the 600 armed and mostly able-bodied young men who surrendered, 140 jumped from the army trucks which were taking them to barracks immediately they were out of the centre of the city.

Of the remainder only 120 took out short-term enlistments of from one to six months. The rest went back to mum.

This was the force which made the majority of the French cabinet quail as though it was facing a 1940 onslaught of 120 panzer divisions.

This was the force which reduced the Governor-General M. Delouvrier to hysterical supplication.

This was the force which army officers assured Paris would make a new Budapest of Algiers if it were attacked.

Poor Budapest. Not even Moscow radio has insulted it so woundingly.

To return to more serious matters: what is eating the army? Simply this: the army is not prepared to accept any settlement which will involve its departure from Algeria now or in the foreseeable future.

The army will mutiny against two of the three choices de Gaulle has left open to Algeria in a future free referendum. It opposes any form of loose association with France which the army believes can only lead to independence.

The army considers that only the complete integration of Algeria with France will justify its bitter five-year-old war and provide a sufficiently clear political objective for the war itself.

The army believes that de Gaulle's policy has produced wavering and uncertainty among the Moslems whose support is essential in a guerrilla war such as this.

They sum up their predicament with a query that has become a slogan: 'How can you rally the Moslems to a question mark?'

It is because virtually the entire officer corps has been won over to the view that uncertainty regarding Algeria's future is hampering them in their operations that a thorough purge of the army seems an impossible undertaking.

What is the use of sacking some generals and colonels if their successors will think exactly as they did in six months' time, if they do not do so already?

Furthermore, de Gaulle's belief that after a negotiated cease-fire free elections can be held with former rebels as candidates or actively participating in the campaign is totally unacceptable to the army.

Indeed, the moment cease-fire talks are open with the rebels the balloon will go up here.

The present situation is that the army has temporarily rallied to de Gaulle but only in order to enforce its terms later. Its great fear is a possible split in the army. It is now planning to avert any possibility of a split.

War or no war Algiers is an extraordinarily pleasant city, especially when as is happening now the sun beats down with a ferocity Londoners only know in a particularly lucky August.

It may look with a number of troops in it like Southampton on the eve of D-Day but it is a Southampton on the southern shores of the Mediterranean with splendid French and North African cooking and local wines so heady that they would make a plotter out of the most timid citizen.

Plotting is almost a full-time occupation here and any self-respecting plotter makes himself available for interview with attendant police spies at least twice a day either at the Aletti Hotel Bar or the St George Hotel.

The Aletti is rather sleazy and thuggish; you get a higher-class type of plotter and police spy at the St George – a rambling country house type of hotel on a hill overlooking the city.

At either you can find the young man who was behind the barricades yesterday serving behind the bar today. A short walk will bring you to the somewhat fly-blown café of M. Joseph Ortiz, one of the leaders of the uprising, whose wife would be happy to give you the latest news concerning his health.

A beefy leader of the revolt who was promising to die on the barricades last week is proudly standing drinks to friends today.

The very best restaurant called in Arabic 'The Old Camel Saddle' is as quiet as ever with the Algiers rich. They have little to worry about as their money is being repatriated to France just as quickly as France is pouring money into Algeria.

There is only one note of complaint: an American engineer

here for a few days from the Sahara complains bitterly that the local golf course was closed during the insurrection. 'I worked all over South America and no Latin American revolution ever succeeded in closing the golf course,' he said.

Algiers, Friday, February 5, 1960

1961

HOW DID DE GAULLE DO IT?

What went wrong with the generals' plans? They must have expected de Gaulle's outright defiance. It is thought here that the major factors were:

The restlessness that was beginning to show itself in the ranks of the conscripts who formed the great majority of the army in Algeria;

The cast-iron loyalty of the navy which was preparing to carry out orders to make landings at Algerian ports;

The failure by generals in Metropolitan France to deliver on the promissory notes to join the mutiny which they had given to Challe before the insurrection broke out.

Whatever the technical reasons for the collapse, the defeat of the rebellion represents a triumph of character – de Gaulle's character.

It was his firmness and leadership which prevented a rout. Had any other Government been in power in Paris the military would already have been in control. The first major consequence of the rebellion is an end to the Fascist threat that has hung over France for three years and an end to the Algeria-is-French legend.

Ironically enough it is the mutinous generals themselves fighting to keep Algeria for France who have finally disposed of any possibility of doing so.

The negotiations with the Moslem Nationalist rebels will now begin with only the shortest possible delay with de Gaulle tragically weakened in bargaining power as a result of the mutiny.

It also seals the death warrant about to be pronounced on the Foreign Legion. This mercenary force composed of eighty per cent of Germans is certain to be disbanded.

So too are the élite Paratroop Regiments who have acted as the Praetorian Guard of French military Fascism.

This shameful episode will also have important international consequences. Relations between France and Franco Spain will become sub-zero in temperature, for General de Gaulle will never forgive Franco for the role his regime played in helping the plotters and allowing General Salan to 'escape' from Spain.

Also, de Gaulle, deeply conscious of his nation's humiliation, will become even more touchy on matters concerning French prestige than ever before.

One would like to be able to say that his countrymen feel an individual sense of shame at the events of the last four days. This unfortunately would not be true.

On all sides in Paris these last few days one heard prominent people say that the best solution to the crisis would be if de Gaulle resigned.

There was a readiness in many circles to collaborate with the prospective invaders. There were all sorts of politicians ready to jump on the military band wagon if it had rolled on to Paris.

Many on the Left worked with might and main to frustrate any liberal settlement rather than that de Gaulle should have the honour of settling the war. The other side of the coin presented by the Algiers mutiny is the notorious appeal launched by Sartre and other Left-wing intellectuals recently to French troops to desert.

The silences of some people throughout the insurrection is also noteworthy. There was not a word throughout from such a respected figure as the conservative leader M. Antoine Pinay condemning the uprising.

Nor did France's most distinguished soldier utter a word. One might have expected that Marshal Juin, though in disagreement with de Gaulle's Algerian policy, would have condemned the mutiny. Not a bit of it.

All the generals involved in the mutiny are products of the putrified parliamentary system of the Fourth Republic.

Under the Fourth Republic, as under the pre-war Third, generals were appointed for political reasons or because of their friendships with different political cliques.

General Salan, for example, is a typical Fourth Republic product. He was promoted under it for political reasons and he was notorious as an entirely political general.

The same goes for Marshal Juin. Juin was made a Marshal by a Socialist government solely because they wanted to give prestige to another general to counter-balance that of de Gaulle.

Small wonder the generals despise the politicians and the politicians live in fear of them as one lives in fear of blackmailers.

An enormous amount still remains to be revealed regarding the accomplices of the mutineers in high places – especially in the security services – in Paris.

Summary arrests are likely to continue for some time. A defeat for the military Fascists, the collapse of the revolt is also a devastating defeat for the classic French Right. Those politicians who have toyed with conspiracy or shown sympathy to the conspirators are doomed men at least politically speaking.

Some of them are now in flight, including Jacques Soustelle, who left the country secretly last night.

At the same time de Gaulle's position will, in the long run, be weakened. With a threat of a military *coup d'état* finally removed, a peace in Algeria in sight, the French Left and Centre will begin showing increasing impatience with the de Gaulle regime and a growing nostalgia for the bad old days when every MP could expect to be a Cabinet Minister from one weekend to another.

In short they will wish to return to the very kind of political life which is basically responsible for the present tragedy.

Wednesday, April 26, 1961

FRANÇOISE SAGAN:
ANOTHER £100,000 COMING UP . . .

The Françoise Sagan phenomenon continues unabated like some stratospheric object well out of range of critical fire.

This weekend a new Sagan will make publishing history as Sagans have been doing regularly every two years since 1954.

This one is a slimmer volume – slimmer by seven pages than her standard 192 – entitled *Marvellous Clouds*.

Unlike her two previous novels dedicated to her ex-husband Guy Schoeller, this one is dedicated to 'My friend Phillipe'.

The dedication evokes a tragedy. Phillipe is Phillipe Charpentier, a talented 25-year-old photographer – Mlle Sagan herself it should be noted is now all of 26 – with whom she fell in love and who committed suicide earlier this year.

Thus tragedy continues to stalk her but leaves her curiously unmarked like someone still young enough for emotional wounds to heal fast.

This new book has made her a small fortune even before its publication. A newly launched weekly bought the serial rights, which because of the novel's brevity ran to no more than six instalments, for £40,000.

A condition for the pre-publication sale was that the plot of the book should be kept a close secret. It was an unnecessary precaution because by now a Sagan plot is as standardised as the Michelin Guide.

It concerns middle-aged men falling for younger girls, younger girls falling for middle-aged men and, to add a certain complexity to matters, everyone is everyone else's best friend.

It is all as charmingly unsophisticated as the babblings of a precocious schoolgirl who had access to a forbidden part of her father's library. And it is all accompanied of course by a cacophony of creaking bed springs.

In addition to the £40,000 serial rights, the book has a pre-publication order of 130,000 copies. At a modest estimate this alone will net her a further £60,000.

A noted French critic examining the Sagan phenomenon points out that it had its beginnings when her first novel, *Bonjour Tristesse*, was hailed by that doyen of French novelists François Mauriac as 'the work of a new Stendhal'.

M. Mauriac has since refrained from passing an opinion on her subsequent work. The critic then adds a penetrating note. He points out the unintended eroticism of her work, is an eroticism wholly in the reader's imagination.

He says: 'If she writes "The maid entered the room and announced that dinner was served" one immediately conjures up a picture of a couple caught in disarray.'

Apart from being seven pages shorter, the latest novel has other innovations. For the first time working-class characters appear, one of whom, a fisherman, actually has a love affair with one of her gilded characters.

This broadened outlook even extends to motorcars. Instead of everyone driving round in the latest sports cars, one of the leading characters owns only a beaten Chevrolet and another the cheapest of French family cars.

Friday, June 23, 1961

DE GAULLE ESCAPES BOMB
DEATH-TRAP

'This is just a little joke in very bad taste,' he says

A bomb-in-the-road attempt to assassinate President de Gaulle was made last night as he drove along a lonely road from Paris to his country home at Colombey-les-deux-Eglises, it was revealed today.

An official statement issued by the President's office said: 'An inflammable mixture with an explosive charge attached was placed between Nogent and Romilly on the route which the Head of State had to take to Colombey-les-deux-Eglises.

'The inflammable mixture caught fire, without causing an explosion, towards 10 p.m. while the Presidential cars were passing.'

President de Gaulle ordered the cars to halt. He climbed out on to the road and scoffed: 'This is a little joke in very bad taste.'

Then the 70-year-old President got back into his car and drove on. He arrived at Colombey on time.

Police later found an 8 lb charge of plastic explosive in the road. The inflammable material was apparently intended as the fuse.

The plastic explosive is a powerful, putty-like substance which has frequently been used in bomb attacks by Right-wing European extremists who oppose de Gaulle's Algerian policies.

A cordon was thrown around the area and police arrested an unidentified man but there was no immediate indication whether he had anything to do with the assassination attempt.

This was the first officially-confirmed attempt against de Gaulle's life since he returned to power in 1958. There were vague reports of another attempt in April during the revolt in Algeria.

The attempt has heightened the tension in Paris and Algiers.

An enormous police operation is at present going on throughout France and Algeria against members of a secret army organisation. Details of arrests are largely secret, but it was learned that a senior army officer was arrested in Paris early today.

Others arrested include a prominent Paris businessman who is alleged to be the treasurer of the secret army and a middle-aged woman whom police say acted as courier for ex-General Salan in Algeria.

Salan has been in hiding since the collapse of last April's *putsch*. But officials in Algeria have reported that his car, flying the flag of a five-star general and escorted by motor-cyclists, has been openly driving along roads near Algiers in the last two days.

Saturday, September 9, 1961

EVERY DAY, KILLINGS, BOMBS
BY THE SCORE

Viewed from Paris, events in Algeria take on an almost lunar unreality.

Here on the spot the problem takes on flesh and blood – especially blood.

The Algiers newspapers have now taken to running two adjoining columns of local news under the succinct headings of 'Assassinations' and 'Explosions'. The average in the past week in Algiers alone has been twenty assassinations daily and twenty-three explosions.

Most killings – a grenade tossed into a café, a bullet fired into the nape of someone's neck – are the work of the Moslem Nationalist Underground, the FLN. The plastic bomb explosions are the work of the European Underground, the Secret Army Organisation (OAS) led by ex-General Salan, in hiding since the failure of last April's *putsch* somewhere in, or near, Algiers.

What officials here call 'the infernal cycle' continues – killings followed by funerals, followed by riots, followed by further funerals.

Last week seven Arabs were hideously lynched following the funeral of a young European murdered by the FLN. That meant seven more funerals, this time of Moslems, giving the Moslems seven separate occasions for revenge.

Mainly in order to fend off a possible Arab descent into the European quarters, the city has been in a virtual state of siege throughout this week as funeral followed funeral.

I went to the Bab-el-Oued to see a café proprietor friend. Bab-el-Oued, perched high over Algiers, is the working-class suburb – dockers, railwaymen, bus drivers, clerks and minor officials – with a minority Moslem population.

Before the Moslem rebellion broke out seven years ago it was solidly Communist. Today it is solidly OAS.

My friend, of Spanish origin, had never been to France, but his café evokes Paris. The neon lights flash out its name: 'The St Germain-des-Près of Bal-el-Oued.' Then underneath 'Atmosphere, gaiety, joy'. It was deserted.

'What do you expect?' said the proprietor. 'People are afraid.'

It was getting dark and there was the steady rumble of half-tracks as troops and riot police moved in to occupy Bab-el-Oued for the night.

Behind them they had created an enormous traffic jam and motorists were klaxoning their impatience to the tune of slogan 'Al-gé-rie Fran-çaise'.

When conversation became possible my friend gave vent to his bitterness: 'We fight. You say it's hopeless and maybe you're right. Nevertheless we fight rather than go to a France we don't know and which doesn't want us, or hand over the county we've made to the FLN.'

He was shamefaced about the lynchings: 'What do you expect? It was blind fury. The boy was well known in the district.'

Outside, gangs of shirt-sleeved youths from the surrounding tenements lounged at every street corner in the steamy heat. There was not a Moslem to be seen.

The following night I dined in a different setting as the guest of a wealthy Frenchman at the Algiers Yacht Club. He took me there because, he said, it provided the best view of the nightly plastic bomb explosions.

A perfect sickle moon hung low over the city and the explosions started shortly after 9 p.m. Usually, my host pointed out, each explosion is greeted with applause by the elegant Yacht Club patrons but they were silent that night.

We counted twelve explosions in an hour and a half. Across the harbour came the wail of an ambulance siren.

'It may be nothing, of course,' said my host, 'even in Algiers people get appendicitis.'

Of all the forms of terrorism plastic bombing is surely the most cretinous and cowardly. It requires about the same amount of courage to wedge a piece of Plasticine containing an explosive charge into a crevice of a wall at night, as that needed by a schoolboy to scratch the first letter of a four-letter word on a wall.

Furthermore the plastic explosions never continue after the midnight curfew.

Who are the chief targets for the plastic bombs? Mainly Europeans selling out and planning to leave Algeria, and Government officials loyal to Paris.

These latter forming a small group at the top of the administration, and all recruited from the Civil Service and Metropolitan France, are caught in the cross-fire of hatreds.

And, to add to their frustrations, they operate an administrative machine largely permeated by the OAS.

In these circumstances their efforts to help catch Salan and the other fugitive officers becomes a will o' the wisp chase in which every move is transmitted to the fugitives themselves beforehand.

Civilian complicity with the OAS is paralleled by army complicity. No army unit, for example, is ever expected to betray Salan to the authorities.

Nevertheless, the army is more mute than mutinous, sullen at the continuing treason trials in Paris, rising from last April's *putsch*.

It will not betray Salan but neither does it share any longer his crackpot dreams of French Algeria. It realises that even if de Gaulle is overthrown his Algerian policy cannot be reversed and in these circumstances the most imminent dangers are those of a purely futile uprising or an inter-racial blood-bath in the major cities of Algiers, Oran and Constantine.

Now, for the third time, peace talks between the French and FLN are about to resume and this time they are likely to succeed.

Two major policy decisions are necessary on both the French and the FLN side to avert the danger of catastrophe.

In the first place, de Gaulle must swallow his pride and talk directly to the poor whites of Algeria as though their fate was in principle, as well as in fact, his major preoccupation. Secondly, the FLN must call off its gunmen in the cities.

The apple of independence is about to fall into their laps. If they shake the tree too hard at this moment, the apple will be rotten when it drops.

Algiers, Friday, September 22, 1961

WHEN A WOMAN CHOOSES TO LIVE
WITH A LEGEND . . .

Two women out of Picasso's past, who are both painters in their own right, are worth noting this week as the master's 80th birthday is being celebrated on the Riviera.

Mlle Dora Maar, now in her fifties, still bears traces of the beauty she was when she lived with Picasso in the 30s.

She has become a deeply religious woman and prays regularly for the unlikely miracle of Picasso's return to the Catholic faith.

The other is 39-year-old Françoise Gilot, who lived with Picasso from 1943 to 1953 and is the mother of two of his children, Claude, fourteen, and Paloma, twelve.

Mlle Gilot is more earthbound in her attitude to Picasso.

She speaks of him with amused affection and without a trace of idolatry.

She denied a remark widely attributed to her at the time of her separation from Picasso that life with him was 'like living with an ancient monument'.

'It was someone else who made that remark,' she said. 'And in any case it's absurdly untrue.'

What then is life like with Picasso?

'A little tiring,' she said. 'But fun.'

She went on: 'The most striking thing about Picasso is his sense of complete freedom. It is a freedom which communicates itself to anyone who is with him and who feels freer in his presence as a result.

'That man has too much of everything. He is more than a painter, he is extremely clever. He can open people like a box. He loves laying traps for them. He adores the game of life.

'He finds, for example, the Philistine Russian attacks on him very funny.

'He enjoys the paradox that he a Communist should be derided in Russia while he is sold for enormous sums in the U.S.'

We talked of his attitude to money.

Mlle Gilot said: 'He knows the price of a packet of cigarettes and after that he thinks in millions. Anything in between he finds very expensive.'

Mlle Gilot owns two Picassos – one, *The Girl Flower*, painted in 1946, and the other a portrait of her, which to me looks like a brilliant parody of the *Mona Lisa*, painted in 1949.

The two children spend their holidays with their father, but they are taking a week off from school this week to be with him on his birthday.

Both are average pupils, but the boy is showing signs of precocity.

He, shrewd fellow, has decided that he wants to be an art dealer.

Friday, October 27, 1961

THE LONELY LIFE OF THE DANCER WHO RAN AWAY . . .

Rudolph Nureyev, who deserted from the famous Leningrad Kirov Ballet Company last June, just after it had completed a Paris season and was about to depart for London, is a far from happy man.

Ever since his defection Nureyev has made plain his keen disappointment at the professional future the West holds out for him.

He doesn't consider the de Cuevas Ballet Company is of sufficient standing to provide an adequate background for his talents.

This has made him a difficult colleague – silent and moody.

Nureyev seems to have good reasons for discontent.

He had hoped for a contract with the Paris Opera but this has been judged 'diplomatically premature'.

This young man of twenty-three is now beginning to feel a heavy loneliness closing in on him.

Meanwhile the pressures on him to return to Russia are beginning to become equally oppressive. He receives daily phone calls from Moscow.

Usually they are either from his mother or his dancing teacher. Both assure him that if he returns all will be forgiven.

There was, in fact, no political motive for his defection. It was a piece of artistic wilfulness.

Not cricket

Relations at the moment are strained between Yugoslav Royalist circles in Paris and the U.S. Embassy here.

What has happened is that the U.S. Embassy has refused a visa to an eminent Yugoslav refugee. He is M. Arsene Gazivoda, a former courtier and diplomat who served in London and Paris.

M. Gazivoda was invited to spend Christmas in Chicago by a Palmolive-Colgate heiress, Mrs Pearce Sherman.

His visa application was refused under the clauses in the United States Immigration Laws barring political undesirables.

M. Gazivoda, who has the Legion of Honour and who is treated with special courtesy by the French Foreign Office, rated a one and a quarter hour interview on the subject of his visa with the United States Ambassador, General Gavin.

Speaking excellent English he told General Gavin, 'Look here, this is just not playing cricket.'

General Gavin may not realise it but a foreigner who can use an expression like that is clearly above suspicion.

Friday, December 1, 1961

1962

DE GAULLE MOVES THIRTY-TWO TANKS INTO STREETS OF PARIS

Tough security measures taken in Paris during the past twenty-four hours have led to speculation on whether the Government has information indicating an imminent coup by the extreme Right-wing Secret Army Organisation (OAS).

This the Government vehemently denies. It claims that the increased security measures are aimed at warding off any spectacular act of sabotage or terrorism the OAS may intend.

Government sources speak with contempt of OAS strength in Metropolitan France. They consider that at the very most there are only 3,000 active OAS agents in the whole of France.

They also note that the OAS in Metropolitan France has to recruit desperadoes from Algeria to carry out the greater part of its plastic bomb and sabotage terrorism.

The security measures, however, are on a spectacular scale. Thirty-two light tanks suitable for street fighting and manned by the para-military gendarmerie moved into Paris during the night.

They have taken up strategic positions in and around the city.

This force will be brought up to 100 tanks during the weekend.

The gendarmerie also has at its disposal a force of some 150 light armoured cars.

Total number of police in the Paris area stands now at 30,000 and the force can be mobilised within two hours.

The precautions are partly connected with the broadcast de Gaulle is to make on Monday.

Documents captured by the police following the arrest on Wednesday of the leading OAS terrorist figure in France, Phillipe Castille, show that the OAS planned to blow up radio and television transmitters on top of the Eiffel Tower before de Gaulle's broadcast. As a result the Eiffel Tower is the most densely guarded strategic point in the city.

Castille himself has been under continual round-the-clock grilling since his arrest. As a result ten of his accomplices have been arrested and further arrests are expected.

In Algeria the OAS last night carried out one of its most spectacular acts of sabotage so far when it blew up the Algiers police radio transmitter.

This has isolated the Algiers police from police in the rest of Algeria and from Paris.

The show of force in Paris is unaccompanied by the slightest show of nervousness on the part of the population. The general public shares the Government's contemptuous assessment of OAS strength in France.

Friday, February 2, 1962

HOW DE GAULLE WON THROUGH

Three months ago it was possible for a Liberal newspaper in Paris to write: 'Only de Gaulle's obstinacy prevents a settlement in Algeria.' At the time this was published the precise opposite was the truth: Only de Gaulle's obstinacy was keeping the tiny flame of negotiations alive.

During the past three years two basic misconceptions regarding de Gaulle's policy have flourished. To the Left de Gaulle was a reactionary and it was inconceivable that he should follow a liberal colonial policy; to the Right, which had perceived the true course of events much earlier, he had broken a pledge to keep Algeria French.

Both sides accuse him of Machiavellianism in not revealing his true intention earlier. The answer to both is that if after six months of de Gaulle rule they still had any illusions as to where he was going, then these illusions were entirely self-induced.

Why then did he proceed so warily as though walking through a minefield? The answer is that he *was* walking through a minefield and if he often stopped to dismantle a mine instead of treading on it who can blame him?

It may of course be argued that the minefield is now more dangerous than ever; this is simply not true: the Algerian problem was acutely dangerous only while France itself was hopelessly split on the issue.

Just how split it was is proved by the fact that before de Gaulle's return to power not even such figures on the Left as M. Mendès-France dared advocate immediate negotiations with the Moslem rebels.

It is de Gaulle's achievement to have united French opinion on this issue.

But the French Left was not only deaf to de Gaulle's words, it was also blind to his acts.

For example: how was it possible to mistake his intentions when within less than a year of coming to power he freed fourteen French colonies at a stroke?

And how was it possible to depict as a bleak reactionary a man who set in motion a programme which now makes France the biggest contributor of aid to underdeveloped countries in the world?

Now as to the Right-wing charges of duplicity. Oddly enough M. Jacques Soustelle, who makes the freest use of this charge, provides the best evidence to the contrary.

M. Alain de Serigny, one of the chief organisers of the May 1958 revolt which brought de Gaulle back into power, records in his memoirs that M. Soustelle reported to him that not only was it impossible to persuade de Gaulle to commit himself beforehand to a 'French Algeria' policy but that the General expressed his total disbelief in its feasibility.

M. de Serigny adds that Soustelle's view at the time was that de Gaulle could be forced to accept this policy after he was brought to power.

Really M. Soustelle should have known his de Gaulle a little better. In truth only by wrenching a few phrases from de Gaulle's speeches out of context can the charge of duplicity be sustained.

As for the actual history of the negotiations it is distortion of history to blame the earlier failures on the French. Sovereignty of the Sahara, held to be the reason for the failure of last summer's talks, was in fact privately conceded to the rebels then and publicly conceded by de Gaulle last September.

What was so baffling and frustrating was the apparent unwillingness of the rebel delegation to get down to basic problems.

The reason became clear only a few weeks later when, in a shake-up inside the rebel leadership, out went Ferrat Abbas, the so-called pro-Western moderate, to be replaced as the rebel chief by the tough revolutionary, Ben Khedda.

While the Left wailed that peace was now further off than ever, de Gaulle privately welcomed the change. The reason for his apparent complacency has now become fully apparent: Only a revolutionary and not a 'liberal' front man could impose on a revolutionary movement the kind of compromise essential to an agreement.

The details of the agreement are comparatively unimportant: What is important is that the new state will be built with French aid.

This means that it will be the kind of state envisaged by de Gaulle from the start – independent, but closely associated with France.

Doctrinaires may call it neo-colonialism but clearly the Algerians prefer it to near starvation. This is the ultimate triumph for de Gaulle – to have won his gamble that enlightened self interest would ultimately triumph over sterile fanaticism.

The Algerian war, in the divisions it has created among Frenchmen, has often been compared to the Dreyfus Case. The comparison goes deeper than that. The victory of the Dreyfusards snapped yet another link with a 19th-century past.

The Algerian peace marks a final break with that past.

The birth-pangs of the new France may be agonising but the future should be glorious.

Monday, March 19, 1962

NO DOUBT WHOSE YEAR THIS HAS BEEN!

This, even more than any other year, has, as far as France is concerned, been General de Gaulle's year.

Writing in this column exactly a year ago I prophesied 'with the utmost confidence' that 1962 'will be a year of peace and dazzling prosperity for France'.

It is a measure of the transformation that has taken place in the course of the year that this prophecy at the time could have been reasonably regarded as hazardous if not downright reckless.

Recall the circumstances: The Algerian war as yet unfinished and its end seemed further off than ever; the OAS had succeeded in solidly implanting itself both in Algeria and France and was on the rampage in both countries; Paris within a few weeks of the New Year was the scene of murderous clashes between police and demonstrators.

Now the Algerian war is ended, the OAS is reduced to a handful of forgotten conspirators, and the power and prosperity of France stands at a level it has not enjoyed since the turn of the century.

There are miracles within this miracle. Take one shining example: The absorption by France of nearly 1½ million refugees from Algeria. Among them are so many Moslems that the extraordinary situation has now been reached in which there are twice as many Algerian Moslems in France as there are Europeans left in Algeria.

This vast population of varied social, racial and religious backgrounds which it was feared would provide the OAS with a solid basis in France have been rehoused and rejobbed with little more disturbance to the nation's life than that involved in an outbreak of gangsterism in Marseilles.

What is so notable, too, is the patience and goodwill the French continue to show to the new Algeria, despite Castro-style verbal and physical provocations.

Aid continues to pour into the country. Algerian labourers continue to be received in France at the rate of 1,000 a week. The French army in Algeria, once noted for its indiscipline, now shows an exemplary self-control, and schoolteachers continue at their posts, often in isolated and dangerous circumstances.

The result is that patience is beginning to triumph over demagogy and Algeria's future despite all set-backs is being forged in association with France.

How near did France come to Fascism in 1962? Very near indeed, for it is now quite established that an electoral victory over de Gaulle would have produced a general amnesty for the OAS.

The OAS had already reached agreement with several important French political leaders that it would play its part by declaring itself dissolved once de Gaulle was overthrown.

Such a dissolution followed by such an amnesty could have had only one result: an eventual OAS take-over in France.

Friday, December 28, 1962

1963

DID SOMERSET MAUGHAM BREAK A PROMISE MADE TO HIS DAUGHTER?

No novel Somerset Maugham ever wrote has so many ingredients for his talents as a story-spinner than those contained in his present dispute with Lady John Hope.

That in his eighty-ninth year he should renounce his daughter seems both bizarre and brutal.

That at the same time he should adopt his 53-year-old secretary-companion as his son gives the story just that element of farce essential to all real tragedy.

It is at this point that outsiders should be warned against hasty or too obvious conclusions.

That very big money indeed is involved in the dispute is in a sense almost irrelevant. If that were the only issue involved it would have been to everyone's interest to have come to a satisfactory compromise.

To Maugham now his major moral and financial obligation is not to Lady John Hope or her children but to Alan Searle who has served him unstintingly for the past thirty years.

In the last few years as age marked Maugham more and more, Searle's relationship to him has become one of almost utter servitude.

Searle is an immensely likeable, gregarious man who has in a sense voluntarily committed himself to a monastic order.

As for Lady John Hope, financial considerations apart, clearly she could not accept Maugham's public renunciation of herself as his daughter.

It seems to me that Maugham's hatred of Lady John Hope's mother has festered with the years and the final breaking point came when to general surprise Maugham published his memoirs.

After that it was difficult for both to regard each other as father and daughter.

I discussed this with Lady John Hope and she claimed that Maugham had given her repeated assurances over the years that he would specify in his will that his memoirs were not to be published, not merely in his own lifetime, but not until thirty years after her own death.

The reason was to spare pain to her children.

She admits it was difficult for her to bring herself to see him for several months after the publication of the memoirs.

How comparatively recent the bitterness between them is can best be shown by the fact that when Maugham turned his South of France villa into a public company in 1950 he made 500 of the 12,000 shares over to her and later transferred to her another 11,000.

Lady John Hope made a final fitting comment:

'It's a pretty miserable situation.'

Nice, Friday, June 14, 1963

SNAP! NOW ONASSIS HAS *HIS* ISLAND, TOO

Aristotle Onassis has at long last succeeded in matching his ex-brother in law, rival shipowner Stavros Niarchos, with that rarest of all status symbol possessions – a private Greek island.

It is five years now since Niarchos bought the island of Spetziapoula in the Aegean, transforming it in the process into a cross between Eden Roc and a Scottish grouse moor, and I forecast then that Onassis would seek to match him in this acquisition.

Now at long last he has succeeded. He has bought for £35,000 the Island of Scorpion in the Ionian Sea near Corfu.

It is a better and cheaper buy, I consider, than Niarchos's island which cost much, much more.

It is likely that Sir Winston Churchill, at present cruising with Onassis, will be taken to see Scorpion.

The island, which is 400 acres in size, is almost self-sufficient. As in Niarchos's case it was bought from an impoverished Greek aristocratic family.

Unlike Niarchos's purchase, however, Onassis's is not the result of a mere whim. Behind the purchase lies a shrewd business intention.

Scorpion lies off the island of Lefkas and Onassis is at present negotiating with the Greek tourist office to develop Lefkas as a holiday resort complete with casino. If the deal comes off Onassis will be strategically placed to keep an eye on Lefkas.

Lefkas, like Scorpion, is thickly wooded, provides excellent fishing and superb swimming in its deep blue waters. Now rivalry between the two Greeks is at an intense pitch.

Both are playing a role in Greek politics with Niarchos a king's man, and Onassis a supporter of the opposition.

Onassis is seeking legal permission to start a shipbuilding yard in competition with the one operated by Niarchos.

The guide

I commend a book about to be published here, *The Gaullistes*, by the political correspondent of *Le Monde*, Pierre Viansson-Ponte.

It is amusingly presented in the style of a Michelin guide to hotels and restaurants. Like a Michelin it is prefaced by a list of symbols this time indicating the political history and the degrees of intimacy and fidelity shown by the 100 or more of de Gaulle's followers and henchmen whose potted biographies are given in this book.

It is a fascinating volume which begins with Aron, Raymond, the great French pundit, and ends with a little-known member of the constitutional council, Waline, Marcel.

What the book shows clearly is that no one who ever met de Gaulle was left unmarked by the experience.

As a result there is an astonishing range of characters from men of such sublime talent as the novelist Malraux to someone as comparatively brutish as the paratroop general Massu ('Still an ass?' the General asked Massu. 'Still a Gaullist,' Massu replied).

De Gaulle evoked such strong emotions among his followers that there was never any compromise between total fidelity and total revolt. As a result many of the men mentioned in this book are either in exile or in prison.

The book makes clear, too, an interesting phase in France's post-war history. It is that the one Government of all the multitude which ruled France before de Gaulle's return to power, which ruled almost by direct proxy from the General, was that of Mendès-France.

Mendès-France never took a step in national or international affairs or even made an important appointment without consulting de Gaulle.

So much so that the entire Mendès-France administration was permeated with Gaullists, and Gaullists, headed by de Gaulle's first Prime Minister, Michel Debré, flooded the Mendès-France weekly *L'Express*, with their contributions. The most fateful appointment of Mendès-France was made to send Jacques Soustelle, then a Liberal in colonial affairs, as Governor-General to Algeria.

This was made in direct consultation with de Gaulle. Here the book produces a remarkable piece of evidence showing that de Gaulle's trust in Soustelle was always something less than total. It is that de Gaulle always refused to Soustelle an honour which he granted to all his other wartime associates, that of membership of the Order of Liberation.

Friday, June 28, 1963

1964

THE SAD DECLINE OF MELBOURNE, STILL THE CITY OF SNOBS

This is where the treasure is buried. Sydney may have its harbour and its bridge but it's in this prim flat city of Melbourne where the money is.

Melbourne has always remained essentially a rich provincial 19th-century city but now it must rank as one of the richest communities in the world.

Of Australia's forty-odd ranking millionaires I should say at least half of them live here. It is now a major world banking centre and it is also the centre of Australia's pastoral wealth and retail trade.

Australia's snowballing mineral wealth is represented here too by the fabulous Broken Hill Proprietory Limited. Wealth has always made Melbourne a smug and, by Australian standards, an outrageously snobbish city, with such impregnable social citadels as the Melbourne Club, which is the oldest in Australia, and such a suburb as Toorak, which, as an address, is almost an essential passport into the higher reaches of Melbourne society.

This is a city where trams still run through main streets and which remains a stronghold of Australian 'wowserism', as local militant Puritanism is called.

Here pubs still shut at six and the only change in the licensing laws is that now you can drink with your meals till ten instead of, as previously, having bottles whipped off tables punctually at eight.

This Puritanism, combined with a sprawling suburbia which now stretches almost to the foothills of Dandenong Ranges twenty miles away, is destroying Melbourne as a city, draining it of almost all life at dusk.

This is a pity as the city was originally planned with a certain style and even grandeur. Now all that remains of the old Melbourne are isolated patches of elegance in Collins Street and in Eastern Melbourne and in the city's magnificent parks.

The trouble is that Melbourne is now repeating on an even larger scale the tragic mistakes it made fifty or sixty years ago.

The passion of early migrants to escape cramped European conditions led to haphazard growth of hideous suburbs and this is now being repeated by present-day migrants. There seems nothing can be done about it in view of the passionate desire of European migrants to achieve something they could not achieve in Europe – their own home and garden.

Being located in flat country there are no natural barriers to its growth and there are no focal points for its population like the harbour in Sydney, apart from a muddy creek called the Yarra River.

There is no one more typical of the new Australian tycoonery than 55-year-old Reginald – 'Reg' to all Australia – Ansett. He started by operating a small bus service in the bush and now bosses the largest transport empire in the Southern hemisphere.

It is he who operates the Australian-wide private airline company which competes with the Government-owned network. It did so originally but now it is truer to say that the Government airlines compete with his.

He has just pulled out from New Zealand, which is his first setback in his career, as a result of the unco-operative attitude of the New Zealand Government but his relations with Australia's Liberal Government are excellent.

Ansett boasts that his is the only airline in the world which must operate at a profit and claims that a two-airline policy provides the essential stimulus of competition.

The Liberal Government which is wedded to a concept of private enterprise naturally agrees with him and this produces the curious phenomena of Liberal members of Parliament preferring to travel Ansett while Labour members patronise the Government airline.

No real element of competition seems to exist, however, and Ansett's decision on the types of airplane chosen are meekly followed by the Government airline.

It was Ansett, for example, who blocked the purchase of Caravelles for Australia, choosing Lockheed Electras instead. He is now negotiating the purchase of Boeing 727s. Says Ansett:

'It's I who set the pattern. It would suit me better if the Opposition didn't always play safe.'

Lean-jawed, beak-nosed, and with an accent like a rasping saw, Ansett looks and talks like a typical Digger. He commutes to work by helicopter from his country home and his morning arrivals in the city produce a city-wide craning of necks.

Melbourne, Friday, August 21, 1964

1965

HOW THE TATE GOT A NEW PICASSO . . .

The Tate Gallery, I am able to reveal, has purchased a superb Picasso, the market value of which is in the region of £60,000.

The acquisition of this picture, with which Picasso had long refused to part, is the result of secret negotiations conducted by Picasso's old friend and disciple, Mr Roland Penrose, who organised the famous Picasso exhibition at the Tate seven years ago.

The Tate Gallery described the picture today as one of Picasso's 'great canvases'. Originally known as *Les Trois Danseuses* of 1925, it will in future be known as *The Three Dancers*.

The picture, 7ft 1in. high by 4ft 8in., will be regarded as an outstanding acquisition by the Tate. The gallery ranks the Picasso with Cézanne's *Grandes Baigneuses* (recently purchased by the National Gallery) as 'a supreme example of a particular (though of course different) phase of modern art which has had far reaching influence'.

The Three Dancers forms part of Picasso's private collection. It was painted at a particularly interesting period in his development, marking his transition from Cubism to Symbolism.

The noted art historian, Mr Douglas Cooper, states that it belongs to the painter's 'metamorphic' phase.

He described it thus: 'In this phonetic composition Picasso has transposed a favourite subject into a period jazz idiom. It treats the three dancers in a simplified synthetic, cubist manner, detaching them from the background with a bold schematic use of black shadows.'

The Tate Gallery add 'Here it is evident that the post-war hopes of a new golden age shared by so many had vanished and yielded to a desperate ecstatic violence, expressive of frustration and foreboding.

'The painting is the first to show violent distortions which have no link with the classical serenity of the preceding years. It heralds a new freedom of expression.'

Mr Penrose has striven for some time to persuade Picasso to part with it. He finally succeeded only ten days ago.

Picasso's principal dealer, Kahnweiller, had nothing to do with the transaction. He told me that it was negotiated directly between Penrose and Picasso.

Although the Tate Gallery does not disclose what it pays for works of art, a hint at the price of *The Three Dancers* is contained in the trustee's statement: 'A purchase of this magnitude could scarcely have been contemplated if it had not been for the existence of the Tate's special purchasing grant for early-20th-century paintings announced by the Treasury in 1963, and valid for five successive years at the rate of £50,000 a year.'

'Owing to the working of the gallery's financial year this particular purchase was, even so, only made possible through handsome contributions from the Friends of the Tate and the Contemporary Art Society.'

The picture is now on its way to London.

The acquisition of this picture through the agency of Mr Penrose for the Tate is a tremendous achievement on which both are to be greatly congratulated.

I personally would like to see Mr Penrose's efforts in this matter receive the only possible fitting reward – a knighthood.

Friday, February 12, 1965

HOW DE GAULLE SEES VIETNAM: JOHNSON PLAYING CHINA'S GAME

United States policy in Vietnam is viewed with dismay in Paris. Even that is a considerable understatement. It would be truer to say that General de Gaulle regards the United States as China's best ally at the moment.

To get at the essence of the argument it is necessary to clear a

considerable amount of jungle foliage. Washington, for example, is convinced that de Gaulle's attack on the United States
over Vietnam is part and parcel of his general anti-American
position on a par, say, with his attack on U.S. gold reserves in
Fort Knox.

This theory strikes an immediate snag, for experience seems
to suggest that de Gaulle can be as staunchly pro-American as he
is apparently anti-American at the moment.

Thus, for example, over Cuba he refused to play to the
neutralists – and especially Latin America – gallery and instead
came down unhesitatingly on Washington's side. Why, then, is
he taking an opposite line on Vietnam? The answer, as I have it
from leading Government figures in Paris, is twofold.

ONE: The United States is mistaken in the view that the
outcome in Vietnam can threaten its security.

TWO: In reacting as it has, it has walked into a Chinese trap.

Take the last point first. The French argue that it is in China's
interest to increase the U.S. military commitment to South
Vietnam. Let the Americans increase their Air Force installations in South Vietnam, let them increase the number of Marines
guarding the Air Force installations, and finally let them send
troops to guard the Marines who guard the Air Force installations.

This is a development which, the French argue, the Chinese
welcome. The bigger the commitment, the bigger the trap, and it
is a trap which the Chinese are in no hurry to close.

Why should they be? The French are convinced that there will
be no military reaction in the near future from the Chinese.

Meanwhile, the American commitment, now on a scale which
makes it clear that it is Washington's war and has nothing to do
with Saigon, bedevils U.S.–Soviet relations, and forces the
Soviet Union, for reasons of its own sagging prestige in South
East Asia, to bolster up the Hanoi regime and provides Peking
with precisely the posture it wishes to assume – that of protector
of the yellow races everywhere.

The fact that the Chinese will not be providing any effective
military aid need not embarrass them in view of the fact that,
unlike the Russians, they are not yet in a position to possess a
nuclear arsenal.

It is a situation ideally suited both for guerrilla warfare on the
local level and for Chinese political exploitation throughout
South East Asia. Only one thing can change this picture and that

is an American decision to escalate the war to the point of bombing Chinese atomic installations, but by that time – if that stage is ever reached – the world will be engulfed in such large disasters as to obliterate even the memory of how the whole thing started.

In the circumstances, the French Government feels that the only policy it can follow is one of which might be described as 'ostentatious dissociation' from Washington. This, it feels, is what the British Government would like to do but cannot because, among other things, of its dependence on U.S. support in Malaysia.

The French are freer in the matter and feel that this is an occasion on which they should exercise this freedom. One reason they feel this freedom to dissociate themselves from U.S. policy in Vietnam may be valuable in the future is that when, short of total disaster, the possibility of a negotiated settlement arises its freedom from commitment to the United States will enable her to play a fruitful role.

They point in this connection to the sterility of the discussions between Mr Gromyko and British Foreign Secretary Mr Stewart in London last week, and attribute this to the fact that the British Government is committed to supporting the U.S. policy.

The French then make this further claim: That they have never suggested to Washington a policy of scuttle. On the contrary, they claim that they have agreed with the Americans on the need to step up the war as a pre-condition to negotiations, but they have always insisted that this should be accompanied by an outline of conditions for an overall settlement.

Their policy, they claim, has been 'bomb by all means – but propose at the same time'. They have met in this matter precisely the same refusal from Washington to outline its political aims as they claim the British have so far met in this regard.

A great deal of the difference between Paris and Washington points of view on Vietnam stems from totally different assessments of the nature of the war itself. The Americans, to the exasperation of the French, tend to see the war in Vietnam through the colonialist spectacles of former French governors and military chieftains in that country.

According to the latter, as with the former, everything would be peaceful if it were not for 'interference' across the border.

The French, who have planted their culture in that country,

and who maintain a formidable but non-professional intelligence network inside it, claim to know better.

They claim that the civil war in South Vietnam is largely nationalist in character and only superficially Communist. In any case, de Gaulle is not the man to quail at the Communist character of a regime, if only because he has long ago ceased to believe in the international character of Communism.

According to him the Vietnam revolution, if allowed to take its natural course, is bound to produce a kind of Far Eastern Titoism. What is delaying this natural process, in his view, is foreign interference in the war, which forces a choice for the Vietnamese between the Communist and the American blocs.

The French can point, with a certain amount of despair, to advice which they have given to Washington over the years and which has been ignored. For example, long before de Gaulle the French advised against the choice of Diem as Chief of State for South Vietnam.

Since Diem's fall the situation has deteriorated to the point where only phantom governments can come into being in the South.

At the moment, to sum up, the French are deeply pessimistic about the outcome in Vietnam. They are convinced that as recently as three months ago, the Chinese could have been brought to conference on a settlement, but that now it is too late.

China's interest now, they consider, is to see that the war goes on.

Tuesday, March 23, 1965

SAD, LONELY FAREWELL TO A
TOAST OF THE '20s

There were more pall-bearers than mourners at the funeral of Nancy Cunard in the British Embassy Church in Paris this week.

Of the latter there were five, of whom I recognised Miss Flanner, the Paris correspondent of the *New Yorker*; Mr Desmond Ryan, an old Irish friend; Laurence Vail, an American poet; and the man she named as the executor of her will, the art historian Mr Douglas Cooper.

There were no members of her family present but they had sent a wreath – a huge garish affair almost big enough to decorate the bow of a Cunard liner and bearing a gold-printed inscription: 'With love from your cousins.'

It was hard to realise that this was the funeral of one of the great stormy spirits of the '20s and '30s, a woman who numbered friends by the thousand in Paris and London. She was the most intelligent of the three reigning beauties of her generation, the other two being Iris Tree and Lady Diana Cooper.

She took her radicalism seriously and her enticing physical beauty and elegance as a matter of course. She fought tyranny everywhere with an almost self-destructive passion and when she had money she used it to help its victims with reckless generosity.

At one point she so scandalised her family that she was disinherited, but her mother, Lady Cunard, left her some American holdings and it was on the diminishing proceeds from these that she lived in the latter part of her life.

For the last eight years of her life she lived in a cottage in Central France in failing health and great physical pain. Her very last days form a tragic epilogue. She had been staying with a friend in the South of France when she abruptly left and caught the Blue Train to Paris.

On the train she claimed to have lost her ticket and on arrival in Paris she was handed over to the police. Mercifully they took her straight to hospital where she died. Her will, which she carefully made out, reached Mr Cooper only after her death.

It begins: 'I have little indeed to dispose of.' Oddly enough, although she herself did not realise it, this is not strictly true. The Cunard family ironically enough should benefit fairly handsomely from her estate.

For example, she left a valuable Manet. This Mr Cooper has now traced. It is in the hands of a German art dealer living in Paris. Miss Cunard entrusted it to him because she could not afford to pay the insurance on it.

Mr Cooper is in no doubt that legally the picture can be claimed as her property. Finally, in her last days, she had something of a windfall. A visiting U.S. professor equipped with the large funds available to U.S. universities bought her witty and lively history of the publishing house she founded in Paris in the Twenties.

The sum paid for it, I understand, is quite substantial.

Friday, March 26, 1965

A JUKE BOX AND SEX HIT THE RUSSIANS

This city even smells like no other. The acrid, sour smell of Soviet petrol fumes hits one immediately on arrival at Moscow airport and stays with you like some kind of smog throughout.

But the sights, as distinct from the smells, are on the whole pleasing, as though there is a kind of political springtime in the air. In Eastern Europe, new aspirations, or old ones long suppressed, struggle to break out after the great post-war freeze-up. This is clearly evident in Moscow, too.

The place, one realises with a pleasant shock, is not as drab and cheerless as one had feared it might be.

One notices the high heels, the daintily designed frocks, the gleaming hair-dos of the women. The young men one sees are almost invariably neatly dressed in reasonably cut Italian-style suits.

In fact the entire Soviet clothing industry is undergoing a major crisis because people with plenty of roubles in their pockets are refusing to buy the vast quantities of shoddy clothing piled up in warehouses and are waiting for something better to turn up.

Much the same is true of furniture, with the more prosperous citizens prepared to pay much more for Polish or Czech importations rather than buy the hideosities which only the Soviet furniture industry can produce.

There has even been a break-through on the architectural front with a superbly designed Palace of Congresses and a much more modest but still creditable Youth Hotel. These are small mercies, however, from the architectural horrors of the Stalin era, constructed in a style which can only be described as Coney Island Gothic and which gives the city a nightmarish appearance.

It was sad to note in this context that a 26-storey hotel is being constructed just behind St Basil's Cathedral, which will effectively ruin one of the best conceived and most beautiful architectural clusters in the world.

The big subject of conversation at the moment in Moscow, however, is the introduction of the city's first ever juke box and the publication for the first time since 1917 of a manual on sex. The juke box, installed in a youth club, is the subject of passionate interest as it blares out jazzed-up versions of Russian folk songs.

The manual on sex, published by the State publishing house, was sold out in a matter of hours when it made its unannounced appearance on street bookstalls. It is a product of a vigorous debate that has been going on here for many months on the need for providing Soviet youth with some knowledge of the subject.

It begins promisingly: 'There are fundamental differences between man and woman.'

Another event is the arrival in Moscow of a consignment of bananas which have produced long queues.

What's on in Moscow? There are four Brecht plays on at the moment, two Chekhov plays, *My Fair Lady*, *Lady Windermere's Fan*, a play by a new Soviet playwright, Padjinski, entitled *104 Pages of Love*, and a strikingly modern stage version of John Reed's *Ten Days That Shook the World*, in which even the theatre ushers are actors.

The literary event of the week is the publication of the latest instalment of Ilya Ehrenburg's autobiography in which the famous writer savagely denounced Stalin, an attitude which is believed to be not altogether fashionable at the moment in official circles.

The dramas of daily Soviet life are confounding. I called in at the Intourist office in my hotel to ask them to ring for me an old friend who works for *Pravda*, the leading Soviet newspaper.

Drama.

Did I have the telephone number of *Pravda* by any chance?

No, I didn't – and then I realised the difficulty – there are no telephone directories in Moscow. After a half-hour of telephoning round we finally found the number.

There are some thirty restaurants in Moscow, a city of eight million, and most of the principal ones are located in hotels and serve the national dishes of the Eastern capitals they are named after.

For what I hope were non-ideological reasons I have been put in the Hotel Peking where Chinese food is served of a kind which almost constitutes anti-Chinese propaganda.

The best and liveliest are those founded by the Armenian and Georgian feeding authorities, the Ararat and the Aragvi.

The Aragvi has private dining-rooms and it was in one of those that Vassall was ensnared by the Russians.

Both restaurants are patronised chiefly by what might be described as the Soviet expense account crowd consisting of officials on business in the capital.

The service, especially in the hotel restaurants, can be agonisingly slow, but there is a complaint book which can be called for as a kind of final ultimatum and which when filled in with details can cost the waitress a fine.

However, as it takes longer to get the complaint book than the food it is better not to insist.

It is an intriguing sight in a Socialist society to see people pulling rank as a means of jumping the restaurant queue.

One of the minor mysteries of Moscow life is where the higher echelon of Soviet society go to have their fun. The answer is clubs. Moscow surely is the most club-ridden city after London. The Central Committee has its own club and so have architects, writers, journalists and so on.

It is almost impossible for a foreigner to penetrate one of them, but they are reported to be highly luxurious, enjoying special privileges in the matter of food, drink and service.

Moscow, Friday, May 21, 1965

MAUGHAM AND CHURCHILL:
A MYSTERY

I can now throw light on the nature of some literary works which it is known Somerset Maugham destroyed towards the end of his life. They consisted of fourteen short stories which were read possibly by three and certainly by one other person.

Two who possibly read them were Maugham's secretary and

companion, Alan Searle, and Lord Beaverbrook. The one who certainly read them was Sir Winston Churchill.

The reason why it is certain that Sir Winston had been shown the stories is that it was at his request that they were destroyed. The subjects dealt with in the stories are covered by the Official Secrets Act. They cannot be revealed. They show that during the Second World War Maugham carried out some secret mission or missions, probably directly for Sir Winston.

Maugham was a compulsive writer who could not resist committing any experience, especially his own, into fictionalised form. The fourteen stories were clearly an extension of the fictionalised version he gave in the Ashenden series of his experiences as a secret agent in the First World War.

The request to destroy the stories came to Maugham five years ago in a cable, stating simply: 'Have destroyed my papers, hope you will destroy yours.' Maugham was in bed when he received the cable. He rose from his bed, collected the manuscripts and put a match to them.

The whole matter of these destroyed short stories is immensely intriguing. What could they have contained which was so explosive and dangerous that they could not be published as fiction, not merely posthumously, but literally never? Could they have concerned France or the United States where Maugham spent the greater part of the war?

My own guess is that they most likely concerned the desperate days of 1940 when Maugham was still in France.

There was a singular appropriateness about Maugham's desire to be cremated in Marseilles before his ashes were flown to England. Marseilles was his favourite port and it was from there that he set out on his great travels.

Now the Villa La Mauresque in St Jean Cap Ferrat stands vacant ready to receive its new owner, Maugham's daughter whom he tried to disinherit.

Searle is about to leave for Rome. The house is a husk – the pictures long since sold and the library given away to King's College, Canterbury.

After Christmas the servants will be given one month's notice. There are twelve of them, of whom the cook and chauffeur have been with Maugham for forty and thirty-eight years respectively. The youngest of the rest of the staff had been with him for seventeen years.

In recent years the villa became enormously expensive to run despite the fact that Maugham and Searle lived there alone and did little entertaining. The average running costs came to about £2,000 a month.

For Searle himself – he is now touching, if not over, his 60s – there is a life ended and a life to remake. He is financially secure because Maugham's Swiss fortune goes to him. He will keep Maugham's valet and would like to keep the cook too. An East Londoner himself, he is toying with the idea of going back to live in London or settling in Yorkshire.

One of Searle's oddest gifts from Maugham is a life interest in Maugham's Soviet royalties. Maugham has become a best-seller in the Soviet Union in recent years and the royalties which were carefully banked for him in Moscow made him a rouble millionaire.

Maugham himself often thought of going back to Russia but hesitated because of his anti-Bolshevik activities during the First World War. Searle will now probably go to Moscow if only for the pleasure of spending some of the accumulated royalties. The Soviet Union does not respect international copyright covenants but despite all the careful arrangements it had made for banking Maugham's royalties in Moscow there was a recent miscalculation and Maugham suddenly found himself enriched by £500 worth of roubles.

Searle himself looks a good twenty years younger than his age. Like Maugham he was a client of the famous Swiss rejuvenating expert Dr Niehans. Churchill himself inquired about the treatment but when told that it involved giving up smoking and drinking for three months, lost interest in it.

Thursday, December 23, 1965

1966

MY, HOW THE OLD PLACE HAS
CHANGED – AND SO HAVE I

With this column I complete twenty years with the *Evening Standard* in Paris.

Françoise Sagan was still a schoolgirl, Brigitte Bardot was an 11-year-old and General de Gaulle had retired into the shadows of history when I arrived here.

The ensuing changes have been such as to make me feel that the only stable feature of the Parisian scene is my almost structural relationship with the Crillon Bar.

There were still the almost audible gasps of relief at de Gaulle's resignation in January 1946 and there was even a certain grudging generosity towards him on the part of the politicians.

It was generally agreed that he had resigned with dignity – and within weeks of his departure the country was engulfed in scandals and government crises.

What was significant about 1946, however, was the way France drifted into prolonged war in Indo-China.

This was the first of the post-war colonial blood-lettings which finally left the Fourth Republic drained of all life.

The Paris of 1946, just emerging from the moral and physical subjugation of the Occupation, was undergoing a kind of faded revival of the night-club glories of pre-war Paris.

The principal promoters of this revival were Latin American millionaires and its chief actors were the so-called Lost Generation of the war years. Most of these are now established actors, musical performers and authors.

The great change that has come over the city is that it is now the most bourgeois of the three great capitals. What is happening in fact is that the Parisians are enjoying a delayed arrival into the affluent society.

117

It is this revolutionary aspect of French life – the French being dragged into the contemporary age – which I think is the most striking feature of the past twenty years.

The rage and frustration of this transformation from a 19th-century France into a 20th-century one still echoes. The fact remains that all the great divisive issues which have plagued France since the French Revolution have now been largely resolved but one should never despair of the ingenuity of the French in finding fresh ones.

The heroes of the immediate post-war years were the great larger-than-life figures who lived in the shadow of post-war shortages. All found a refuge in Paris.

They were George Dawson, scrap-iron millionaire, 'Black Max' Intrator, who profited from British currency restrictions and of course Sydney Stanley, the 'spider' of the Lynskey Tribunal.

Here is a report from 1950 of an interview I had with Stanley in Paris which catches the flavour of the period.

He had telephoned me to give me 'the story that all the world has waited for'. He went on: 'This is the story – the Russians haven't got the atom bomb – yet.'

When I met him he told me: 'They've got everything but just this little bit.'

As he said it he shoved a grubby forefinger in front of my eyes, enveloped it firmly in his right hand, obscuring all but the nicotine stained fingernail.

'Just a little bit, that's all they need. But until they get that little bit – and take it from Sydney Stanley – they haven't got the atom bomb yet.

'What the Russians want now is just that little bit – and they've come to me – Sydney Stanley – to help them get it because it's true as I'm sitting here – the Russians haven't got the atom bomb yet. They have offered me millions of dollars, enough to paper a house, to work for them. I told the Yard all about it and the Yard and me have worked together ever since.

'You can come up to my room and see messages and messages from the Yard and from "M fifteen" telling me what a good job I'm doing for England.

'Last week a man speaking English as good as you or me telephoned and asked me to meet him at a certain café.

'He said, "Stanley, I'm glad to meet you. You are the only man in England that can help us." I said, "What's your business?'' and then, as true as I am sitting here, if we had one brandy we had thirty-six. It turned out he wanted me to put him in touch with certain people in the Ministry of Supply. He said, "You know everyone in England and I may as well be frank with you. I am working for the Russians and – we haven't got the atom bomb yet. We've got that much – but we haven't got the whole thing.''

'Anyway, to cut a long story shorter, he wanted me to go to Vienna to meet the Russian boss of "M fifteen''.'

That was the last I saw of Stanley.

Friday, January 7, 1966

WHAT DE GAULLE'S SIX DAYS DID TO RUSSIA: AND WHAT THEY DID TO ME . . .

Gallivanting round the Soviet Union with General de Gaulle is an experience which might be described as specially designed as a human survival test.

In the past six days we have criss-crossed the length and breadth of this country in so frenzied a manner and to the accompaniment of bewildering time changes that twenty-four hours after returning to Moscow none of us was still quite sure that we were firmly earthbound.

From the ensuing haze of impressions it is inevitable that the dominant one is the sheer continent-like size of the Soviet Union.

And yet as the numbness wears off there is another dominant impression – that of the enormous friendliness of the people and the growing well-being of the country. In that sense this frantic travelling was good for us for it broke the spell of cynicism and scepticism which Moscow engenders.

Here in Moscow even the welcome de Gaulle received was doubtful in its spontaneity. No such doubts were possible in the provinces.

The welcome we received – and I say 'we' advisedly for the cheering and waving and clapping lasted until the last car in the Presidential convoy disappeared – was of a kind that recalled to me the welcomes Allied troops received in the liberated cities of Western Europe during the Second World War.

In Novosibirsk, in Leningrad, in Kiev and in Volgograd, the sheer delight of the populace at our arrival was infectious even to the most blasé and weary members of our party.

As for the growing well-being of the population, this was manifest in the appearance of their clothes and the total absence of the kind of provincial shoddiness one might have expected. The housing looked adequate and in some cases even attractive, the sparklingly clean tree-lined boulevards and numerous well-cared-for public parks in every city indicated civic pride and a care for the amenities and life on the whole seemed easier and more abundant than in Moscow.

But what was especially impressive was the scale and thoroughness in a city like Volgograd which was completely razed at the battle of Stalingrad. Wandering through this city it is only by an effort of will that one recalls that it was the scene of the decisive battle of the Second World War. Everywhere, too, to complete the general impression, we found excellent modern hotels and glittering well-designed airport buildings.

Speaking of the war, however, one of the most striking impressions one forms travelling through the country is the ever-present sharp recall of its horrors in the Russian mind. For us the war ended twenty years ago; for the Russians it might have ended last year. Wherever one goes the horrors of the past surge back into memory: in Kiev it is the ravine in Babi-yar which still awaits a monument to the 40,000 Jews who were slaughtered and buried there; in Leningrad it is the vast cemetery for nearly 1,000,000 civilians who died from hunger and cold during the siege of the city; in Volgograd, as in Stalingrad, there is no need for a monument – there is a scarifying one on the heights overlooking the Volga and everywhere, too, there are the living maimed of these various hells.

The Soviet Union is appallingly backward in the production of artificial limbs, and the therapy that goes with their use. The result is that crutches still serve as the only means of movement for the legless, and the armless have nothing but their stumps.

One is filled with horror at the number of maimed one sees. Is there no hope or is it already too late for our international effort to help the Soviet Union cope with this problem?

Of all the cities we visited it was Novosibirsk which intrigued me the most. As a city it is only a little more than twenty years old and only came into existence some sixty years ago as a staging post on the trans-Siberian railway. It is engulfed by boundless steppes and immense forest and the River Ob on which it is located matches the Dnieper and the Volga in immensity.

The large colony of scientists and engineers who live in the so-called 'science city' near by are obviously as excited as schoolboys at the vast terrain of research and discovery Siberia offers them. The picture they give of Siberian life is in total contrast with what one imagines it to be.

The winter is long, there are heavy snowfalls, but after that the popular image of the place is shattered. One skis across the country in dazzling sunshine wearing only a shirt, but the cold is so dry it does not pierce. And the hunting is fabulous.

Novosibirsk itself is so sophisticated that it dealt me a shattering humiliation. I was trying to make a call to Paris from my hotel room and the French-speaking young woman telephonist who was trying to cope with my French finally gave up in despair saying: 'I don't know what kind of language you are speaking, *monsieur*, but it is certainly not French.'

Other memories return with a dream-like quality. Those two white nights in Leningrad. As though the city were not already magical enough, it had at this time a special quality that a brief dusk and a 2 a.m. sunrise gave. This is the ideal time to go sight-seeing, for everything is suddenly seen in relief as though on a stage set.

The gardens of the Winter Palace and the banks of the Neva echoed to the revolutionary hymns of our times. It was guitar-strumming Leningrad youngsters trying to catch the beat of the Beatles. The Soviet soldiery also never ceased to fascinate me. They come in all sizes and a dozen races, yet they all look of incredibly tough peasant stock.

And I always lingered behind at airports to watch the military displays in de Gaulle's honour. At Leningrad the officer commanding the guard of honour was about 6ft 4in. tall, as slim as a polo player and might have been the reincarnation of the Captain Vronsky who ran off with Anna Karenina.

On most of the aeroplane journeys across Russia de Gaulle was accompanied by Soviet Premier Kosygin and the two men spent considerable time in abstract political discussion. One of de Gaulle's themes was that France, too, had had a revolution to which Kosygin replied: 'We still have ours.'

De Gaulle's response was: 'After revolution follows evolution.' Whatever the trip achieved it re-established France in the centre of the Russian imagination.

The Marseillaise was a revolutionary song in Russia up to and even after the Bolshevik cease fire. De Gaulle himself kept repeating to Kosygin his favourite theme that France was still waiting for the world at large to respond to the French revolutionary slogan of Liberty, Equality and Fraternity.

All this would be slightly absurd if it did not carry with it a total conviction in de Gaulle's mind of what he has called 'a certain idea of France'. France has always had an enormous appeal for the Russians for it expresses their deepest longings to be European. In this connection one of the most touching sights I saw on the entire trip was in Volgograd where I glimpsed a young woman in a crowd carrying a placard with the one word on it: *'Liberté.'*

Whatever political diplomatic consequences this trip may have, it constitutes above all a triumph for France and for 'a certain idea of France'. That it should have been achieved through this old man with fallen arches and failing eye-sight is yet another, and not the least of the services he has rendered his country.

Moscow, Friday, July 1, 1966

IN THE CITY OF COMMUTERS WHO DRIVE WITH LOCKED DOORS

A t the moment of writing, the White House shimmers in a heat haze and the American Legion is in town for its annual convention.

There are some 50,000 members of this powerful ex-servicemen's organisation and although banners over hotels, restaurants and bars announce 'Welcome to the Legion' all the hatches are firmly battened down and Washington resembles a fragile frigate which is about to enter a notoriously stormy sea.

The lobbies of famous hotels like the Mayflower and the Blackstone are full of the wilting widows of late middle-aged commandos. The legionnaires themselves, bellies bulging over

low-slung trousers and wearing fancy forage caps, are storming
the city's bars as though they were barricades.

I was an innocent victim of this invasion the other evening
when I entered a dimly lit bar and, after having finally attracted
the barman's attention, was told by him in gentle fashion:
'Listen, bud, don't you think you've had enough already?'

In the ensuing vehement debate it appeared that my husky
lean-jawed all-American appearance had led the barman to the
assumption that I was a member of the Legion convention. In
subsequent apologies over the misunderstanding, which was
only finally dispelled by the production of a British passport, I
was offered a drink on the house.

All this is taking place against a background of Washington
dignity, of an August somnolence, of Southern gentility and an
architecture which ranges from Cheyne Walk to Hampstead
Garden Suburb.

The Deep South impregnates Washington, with Virginia and
Maryland as its neighbouring States, and it is easy to forget in the
silky charm of manner of Negro taxi-drivers, waiters and maids
that this is no longer the Washington of old but the first city in the
United States to have a Negro majority in its population – but
with integration has come other and more serious problems. As
Negroes move in on hitherto white areas, white families cross the
Potomac into Virginia.

Violence simmers on the outskirts and motorists commuting
between their Virginia homes to their Washington offices drive
with car doors firmly locked all the way. It is easy to find all this
incredible, especially while here in the magnolia-scented suburb
of Georgetown.

Europe seems very far away here. The problems are War,
Peace and Bobby Kennedy. Soon – very soon – there will be half
a million American soldiers in South Vietnam. Two gigantic air
and naval bases are being constructed near China's borders. It is
difficult to escape the impression that whatever will to moderation undoubtedly exists here, the logic of being a Super Power
makes its own implacable demands.

This place purrs with power until it is almost like a constant
drone in the ears. Meanwhile, the U.S. Press is flooded with
stories of Goyaesque horrors of war. Illegitimacy, prostitution,
the total disruption of Vietnamese life and culture, a mounting
suicide rate among the Vietnamese – one is forced to ask
whether victory bought at such a price can ever be meaningful.

Yet even as the horrors mount, blueprint after blueprint flows from Washington government departments taking care of the future welfare of the Vietnamese.

By comparison, the French war in Algeria was a minute little skirmish but on the French side as on the American it had this in common – the combination of horror and well-intentioned Boy Scoutism. Nobody here seriously believes that American public opinion, conscious of its country's power, will tolerate a long drawn-out struggle.

The best hope, in the words of one important diplomat whose country is supporting America with troops as well as with words, is that North Vietnam may weary of the struggle before the United States and that 'one day, sooner than we expect, we will discover that the North is no longer reinforcing its troops in the South.'

Meanwhile the U.S. will continue its military withdrawal from Europe and, despite the denials, there is no intention of replacing 20,000 already withdrawn and earmarked for Vietnam.

Air Force units withdrawn from France and allegedly being moved elsewhere in Europe, are in fact being moved to Vietnam. As one authority put it to me, 'Mr de Gaulle has done us a favour without knowing it. He has given us the moral excuse for doing what we would have done anyway.'

The same authority took the view that the resulting vacuum in Europe will be filled by West Germany with U.S. support.

And now a word about the third subject of U.S. preoccupation – the future of the last President's brother, Bobby. Will he make a bid for the Presidency in 1968 or hold his horses until 1972, when he will be all of fifty?

Bobby, it should be noted, is much more old Joe Kennedy's son than was the late President. John Kennedy was able to take a detached view of his father which Bobby remains unable to do. Furthermore, despite his boyishness and ploughboy grin, he has to a greater extent than his brother his father's qualities of single-mindedness and ruthlessness. His campaign methods have nettled and irritated Johnson to a point where the President reacts to the mention of his name as though it were a bad smell. His campaign has struck me, I must say, as being short on scruple.

He has needled the President on Vietnam by implying but not stating another policy. He has courted in the most blatant fashion the Negro vote by his recent visit to South Africa and, characteristically, has been more outspoken on the issue there than he has been here. He has also played up his image-making potentiality as the candidate of the under-forties by even saying some kind words about the drug LSD.

To produce all this elaborate equivocation a permanent brains trust and batteries of speech-writers are fully employed. In short, what is happening is that with the aid of the Kennedy millions a kind of shadow government exists within the President's own party. This in itself is exasperating enough but as though to rub salt in the wounds there is a constant campaign of hints that all of the present misfortunes would have been avoided if President Kennedy had remained at the helm.

My own present reading of the situation is that Bobby hasn't a chance of snatching the Democratic Party's nomination from the actual presidential incumbent and it would be fatally humiliating for the one as for the other to consent to Bobby running as Johnson's vice-presidential running mate.

I therefore conclude that the Kennedy ambition is in for a six-year postponement. . . .

Washington, Wednesday, August 31, 1966

LADY DIANA GIVES A HINT ABOUT MOVING OUT . . .

It may be – and I cross my fingers on the subject – that the longest British occupation of French soil since we gave up our claim to Calais is drawing peacefully to a close.

I refer, of course, to the château in Chantilly Lady Diana Cooper has lived in ever since the war and which was originally placed at her husband's disposal by the French Institute for use as a weekend home when, as Sir Alfred Duff Cooper, he was British Ambassador in Paris.

Lady Diana's tenancy of the château has been plagued by a melancholy misunderstanding.

Lady Diana was under the firm impression that the château for which until three years ago she paid only a nominal rent, and which now costs her £7 a week, was leased to her and her late husband for their individual lifetimes.

The Institute takes a different view. It claims that the château was leased to the Duff Coopers only for the period during which they were at the embassy here and that since then it has wished to lease the château to other ambassadors and was prevented from doing so by the fact that Lady Diana remained in occupation.

Three years ago Lady Diana received a curt notice asking her to leave. The notice was later withdrawn and a new lease was signed fixing a rent for the property and containing a no-sub-letting clause.

Now Lady Diana has been telling friends that she intends to leave France and settle permanently in England.

News of this reached the Institute who promptly asked Lady Diana to confirm these dismal tidings.

Lady Diana informed the Institute that she would not leave the château before the end of the year and only if she found suitable accommodation in England.

Lady Diana intends to give the furniture of the house, which was previously the property of Otto Abetz, the Nazi Ambassador in France during the war, and which she bought after the Liberation at a knockdown price, to her son John Julius.

This includes Abetz's remarkable library, which the Duff Coopers always kept under lock and key.

The reason is that many of the books carry tender inscriptions to Abetz from very prominent Frenchmen.

Friday, September 30, 1966

1967

AN EYEFUL OF LONDON – AND WHY IT GAVE ME A CRICK IN THE NECK!

The first ailment to hit me in London was a crick in the neck. It was one, I reflected, which must afflict most tourists of this city. Clearly long residence in Paris had atrophied my neck muscles for lack of exercise.

I can, for example, walk down the length of the Champs Elysées without once glancing back, whereas here just to cross Sloane Street is a risk to neck and life.

I am talking about the London women of course.

Bird watching, however, was not the main reason for my coming to London. I last lived here during the War and occasional weekend visits over the years have only whetted my curiosity about a city which was becoming to me the most foreign in Europe.

I have been to a few parties, visited the House of Commons, talked to a few of the all-important young, and the impression of a revolution having taken place is almost numbing.

It is in the social world of London where the revolution is most clearly marked and the contrast with Paris is most striking. Whereas Paris society is the most compartmentalised and uncurious in the world, London's crackles with ideas and curiosity like a bonfire. It is indeed a bonfire in which the old barriers and barricades are being put to the flames.

What is emerging, it seems to me, is a kind of meritocracy, a society of achievement which despite its follies and nonsenses gives to London today the true stamp of a civilised city.

There are shocks and unpleasant surprises, however. Drugs is one, politics is another. I had no idea that drugs and marijuana smoking, which barely exist in Paris as a social problem, had taken such roots in London. I was astonished to find it pointed out to me at a cocktail party how many of the young were not touching alcohol, and having it explained that this was an easy way of recognising those who took drugs in one form or another.

Since then I have been offered explanations of how drugs were a civilised substitute for alcohol and that the police drive against marijuana was based on prejudice and ignorance.

I have misgivings also about the political scene, especially Mr Wilson's position in relation to his own party. I knew about the disenchantment among sections of the Labour Party with their Prime Minister. What I did not realise was that it was so general and expressed with such embittered cynicism.

I felt in the lobbies of the House almost as though I were once again back in the corridors of the French Assembly in the bad old days of the Fourth Republic. Here again were the same charges against the Prime Minister of having no principles other than survival, of living from day to day by gimmickry and of betrayal of what one once imagined were deeply held beliefs.

That these charges should be made by the Opposition is understandable, but that they should be made by wide sections of his own supporters is disturbing.

Shortly after these lines are published Mr Harold Wilson will be sleeping in a four-poster bed (period Louis-Philippe) in the restored Trianon Palace in Versailles as the guest of General de Gaulle.

As I pointed out last week, considerable honour has been done him and Mrs Wilson in being the first overnight guests at the Trianon which will henceforth be reserved strictly for Heads of State.

The suite allotted to the Prime Minister and his wife is so vast that, if Mrs Wilson chooses a separate bedroom, a sixty-yard corridor walk will separate the two.

Although the main bed is Louis-Philippe, the general décor is Louis XV.

Mr Wilson might also be interested in the almost sacrilegious kitchen arrangements for banquets. The adjoining chapel serves also as a shaft for dishes coming up from the kitchen and the food is served to waiters from the altar.

On the political side it seems clear that Mr Wilson will be offered a special relationship with the Common Market rather than negotiations for immediate membership. A chance that sounds much better in French – *Les Relations Speciales* between consenting adults, as it were.

Sonia Orwell, widow of George Orwell, who is now in the process of editing a volume of Orwell's immense and brilliant journalism, has cleared up a considerable minor mystery.

It concerns the identity of the great Paris hotel in which Orwell worked as a dishwasher in 1929 and whose kitchens he described with so much off-putting stomach-turning detail in his volume *Down and Out in Paris*.

For many years suspicion hung over the Paris Ritz. It is now clear, however, that the hotel concerned was the Crillon. I can testify that the Crillon's kitchen conditions have been transformed since 1929.

There are even old clients who complain that today's highly hygienic aspirations have had a detrimental effect on the quality of the Crillon's food. Orwell himself, of course, was never deceived by appearances and always preferred being down and out in Paris to a 'tea, bread and margarine' alternative in the Britain of that period.

What shines through this forthcoming collection of articles is his robust English socialism which, had he lived, would have made him such a scourge of present-day society.

It was only with the publication of *Animal Farm* late towards the end of his life that he earned any real money, and for the greater part of his writing life his income was on the £3 a week level.

Now both *Animal Farm* and *1984* remain steady best-sellers, providing his widow with an income far, far in excess of anything Orwell himself aspired to earn.

London, Friday, June 16, 1967

POLES APART – THE ASTONISHING STRUGGLE STILL GOING ON

Here in Warsaw you can see probably better than anywhere else in Eastern Europe the melting away of the last ice floes of the European cold war. It is a refreshing sight and one which would have been almost unimaginable only ten years ago.

What it shows is the hollowness of ideologies and the durability of nations. Technically of course Poland remains a Socialist state and politically it is a dictatorship of the Polish Communist Party.

But the erosions in both economic and political life have been such that eighty per cent of agriculture is in private hands and what could have been an intolerable tyranny has been mellowed by reluctant and somewhat cynical national acceptance into a tolerable way of life.

In the arts, literature, lively political discussion, the easiness of personal contact, Poland is setting the pace for the whole of Eastern Europe. Indeed, to a dour Moscow party functionary a visit to Warsaw must be almost as unsettling as a visit to, say, Paris.

Part of this is due to the famed quixotic perversity of the Polish character and part – the acceptance of a Communist regime – is due to a deep sense of national interest. History has dealt the Poles a terrible lesson. Their absurd pre-War feudal ruling class dreamed dreams up to the last moment of playing a role in Hitler's anti-Bolshevik crusade.

In the end 6,000,000 Poles – a fifth of the nation – were slaughtered by the Germans along with such despised minorities as Jews, Ukrainians and others. The dreams of conquest to the east dissolved in tragedy and instead Polish nationalism has now hardened into anti-Germanism.

Yet something of the past now finds expression in the current titanic struggle between the Communist leader, Gomulka, and the Primate of Poland, Cardinal Wyszynski. It is literally a struggle for the soul of the nation. A direct confrontation between the two would be a disaster, yet both are too stubborn and stiff-necked to reach a compromise.

It would be easy to write of the Cardinal as something of a martyr but that would be nonsense. The church is flourishing and there are now more priests in Poland than there were before the war.

The Cardinal's views are theocratic – Poland belongs to the Church – and they would be unacceptable to any lay State. Both men are patriots, both are scarred by imprisonment by the first post-War Communist regime. Gomulka is respected, the Cardinal revered. The unchallengeable position the Church holds in

130

Poland and its identification with Polish nationalism gives the Cardinal a potentially explosive strength.

It is astonishing that such a battle on such issues should be waged anywhere in the second half of the 20th century but that it should be waged in a Communist-ruled country is wholly fantastic.

The Cardinal, in his late 50s, is a comparatively young man. He can continue to wage the struggle for years. Rome, with all its diplomatic skills, seems unable to intervene effectively.

Certainly de Gaulle will try to influence the struggle in the course of his present State visit but as I understand it he has lost patience with the Cardinal.

One of the interesting aspects of the Warsaw scene is the evidence of the reluctance of members of former Polish aristocracy to become emigrés. Many of the most famous names are still around doing humble jobs.

For example, the head of the Radziwill family, Prince Radziwill, still lives in Warsaw. Shorn of his estates and his castles, he lives in a modest flat in the city. His son, Edmund, brother of Stanislaus, who is married to Jackie Kennedy's sister, works in a brewery. His wife works in a publishing house.

She has recently been awarded a high Socialist decoration. She herself is a Bourbon-Parma. Prince Radziwill often travels abroad and the authorities keep hoping that each time he goes abroad he will decide to stay there. But no – each time he returns to resume his ordinary life in Warsaw.

At the moment of writing, the entire vast French Press corps accompanying General de Gaulle to Warsaw is engaged in a search for the General's alleged mistress with whom he is supposed to have had a fling when he was here as a staff officer in 1920.

Having preceded them here by two days I could have told them, but didn't, that the woman is dead. She was the Princess Thérèse Czetwertinska and she died in Warsaw just after the War. She was the wife of a Polish colonel at the time and it is doubtful if the so-called *affaire* was anything more than a warm friendship.

In any case a year after his return to France the General married his present wife.

The General also developed a strong taste for Polish pastry

while he was here. He lived above the premises of a renowned pastry cook on Warsaw's main street, Nowy Swiat, called Blikle. It's a third generation business and the present owner not only writes elegant verse both in French and Polish but also sends a regular consignment of pastry to the Elysée Palace.

Referring to the matter of de Gaulle's alleged love affair in Warsaw, I discussed it with a former Polish Ambassador to Paris. He became a close friend of de Gaulle while he was in France and he assured me that the General never made any inquiries about the Princess.

On the other hand he told me that on one occasion he was taken aside by Mme de Gaulle who said to him: 'Your Excellency, is it true that my husband became attached to a Polish lady before he married me?'

The Ambassador unhesitatingly replied: 'Madame, I have never heard of such a thing.'

Modestly enough, he regards this as his major diplomatic triumph in a long career.

Warsaw, Friday, September 8, 1967

THE LAST TIME I SAW PARIS
(AT DAWN, I MEAN)

How to cope with the nightclub problem in Paris? This is a matter which is now exercising some of the finest and most subtle minds in this city, including mine.

Time was, and this until fairly recently, when Paris boasted a night life of remarkable charm and sophistication and of a social and topographical diversity which kept one happily afloat till dawn.

And speaking of dawn, I can make no more telling commentary on the present situation than by confessing that I have now almost forgotten what a Paris dawn looks like. All this is, of course, in marked contrast to the situation in London, New York and Madrid, all of which cities Paris used to serve as a beacon and an example.

In case anyone is tempted to dismiss these as the jaundiced

views of an ageing roué, I can only reply that I am supported by a wide range of visitors to the city who are on the average twenty years my junior.

What has happened, whatever the profound, sociological reasons may be, is that Paris night life is now leaden and provincial. The recorded music blares and blares away to a maze of the same familiar faces.

There is no one to insult and almost no one one would wish to befriend. I tried to insult Gunther Sachs at the New Jimmy's recently, but it was no use. He couldn't hear me.

All this is a far cry from the old Jimmy's, now unhappily closed, when table hopping, bickering and frenzied flirtation could all be conducted to the accompaniment of the excellent music of a Latin American band and superlative service.

Now a man called François Patrice, or the Marquis de St Hilaire to give him his full title, has decided to do something about it.

I'm not sure that I altogether approve. His nightclub, which is on the site of the once-famous Éléphant Blanc in Montparnasse, is on three levels with a dance floor which can be seen from anywhere floating in the middle. There are no tables but instead metal trees on which you can hang your bottle and glass.

There are no ash trays, either; butts are swallowed up by shafts. The disc jockey operates from the small tavern, going up and down like a lift.

All this sounds very fine, but when will someone revert to the old-fashioned idea of a night club as a place where one had a pretty girl as a captive audience?

When the history of our times is written two names will be inexorably linked in the chapter devoted to France: General de Gaulle and Brigitte Bardot.

Both are now regular New Year's Eve TV performers – de Gaulle with his New Year greetings and Bardot with her annual cabaret romp. As a feast it's like ripe pheasant and the youngest Beaujolais.

Having seen Bardot's performance privately screened, there is no danger of French TV viewers sharing the British disappointment with the Beatles.

This is the best of the four or five New Year's Eve shows she has so far given. This time she has chosen as partner the singer

Serge Gainsbourg, whose sad and unconventional looks act as a perfect foil to her own sexy, kittenish image.

She is naked or half naked a good deal of the time, first as a kind of modern motor-bike-riding Lady Godiva, then she is transformed into a fur-clad panther of a woman. Then again she is Salome, dressed in diamonds and then a kind of Superwoman with long straight brown hair, pink tights and a heavy chain around her hips.

Then we find her on a lonely beach, singing of the lost summer and then in her St Tropez home, an interior of great charm and simplicity.

The scene then switches to the front of Buckingham Palace, where she parades in a Hussars uniform. This time she sings in English, ignoring the aitches in the best Maurice Chevalier manner.

One of her best songs is titled 'I Feel Strange Desires Creeping up the Back of My Kidneys'. It is done with enormous charm and talent. In fact one recognises Brigitte's talent as an actress much more vividly in these sketches than one does in any of her films. It makes one regret that she has never had a film role worthy of really testing her.

Friday, December 29, 1967

1968

GISCARD – THE MAN WITH THE KENNEDY TOUCH . . .

This man Giscard d'Estaing is becoming more and more the Bobby Kennedy of France with probably a better chance of becoming President of his country than Bobby has of becoming President of the U.S.A. He has just initiated a move which has the true Kennedy stamp to it, being both far-sighted and self-assured to the point of arrogance.

What he has done is to form a company designed to come to the rescue of any newspaper or periodical which finds itself in financial difficulties.

The company will not only bring financial aid but will also 'advise on technical, administrative and editorial changes'.

The offer is nicely timed. It comes just when large sections of the Paris press find themselves in difficulties and when the press as a whole is apprehensive about the forthcoming introduction of advertising on the state-owned television which threatens to milk it of much of its advertising revenue.

For the ambitious Giscard the advantages are obvious. It offers him the opportunity of creating a nation-wide press devoted to him and his policies well before the Presidential elections in five years' time.

He has already made a start by taking over the influential financial fortnightly, *L'Economie*.

By 1973 Giscard will be well placed to make a bid for the Presidency. He will be only 46 while his principal rival, the present Prime Minister, M. Pompidou, will by then have had ten years of gruelling office.

But there is another advantage which Giscard will have over Pompidou. He is the golden boy of French big business and finance. They're not waiting till 1973 to 'go with Giscard'. They're with him now to a man.

Big money in France has long ago become disillusioned with de Gaulle. It is scared stiff of his foreign policies and apprehensive of his domestic ones.

It backed the luckless Jean Lecanuet in the last Presidential elections but has now dumped him for the much more impressive and much better placed Giscard.

When Giscard, therefore, makes a promise of financial aid to newspapers, he is not talking lightly. The money is there, and lots of it.

The main danger for Giscard is that he can be too clever by half. A former de Gaulle Finance Minister, he is technically a member of the Gaullist majority in Parliament. He is also leader of an independent party whose forty-one MPs give the Government its majority.

If he withdraws, then the government falls and new elections are held. He has been pressed to withdraw in the recent past, but he insists that the time is not now and probably never will be while de Gaulle is alive.

De Gaulle, however, is no mean tactician, either, and it is just possible that he may slit Giscard's political throat before Giscard even realises what has happened.

Friday, January 26, 1968

IS MR SOAMES A PRESENT FOR THE GENERAL?

Christopher Soames's appointment as Ambassador to France has delighted Paris socially and politically. Socially, of course, his wife Mary should prove a dazzling hostess and politically the appointment of Sir Winston Churchill's son-in-law is considered as something of a feather in General de Gaulle's diplomatic hat.

There are no two ways about it – in Paris the appointment is considered to be deliberately calculated to please the General. It now remains to be seen what impact Soames has on de Gaulle and this will, of course, greatly depend on his brief from the Government.

The most important conclusion here is that the British Government has now decided to drop its 'all-or-nothing' policy in relation to the Common Market. In other words, it is assumed here that Mr Wilson will now accept some kind of 'association' with the Common Market rather than continue with the policy of trying to force his way in.

This means, according to Paris, that Britain will drop all attempts to line up the Five against de Gaulle and particularly that it will no longer seek to win Bonn away from Paris. If this turns out to be in effect the new British policy then it will undoubtedly improve the climate of Anglo-French relations.

One cannot help but feel considerable sympathy for the outgoing British Ambassador to Paris, Sir Patrick Reilly. He is the second victim of Britain's two failures to break de Gaulle's veto on the British Common Market application, the first one being his predecessor, Sir Pierson Dixon.

In a very real sense Sir Patrick is the scapegoat for the second British failure. In addition there is no doubt that the Foreign Secretary has a penchant for drama in ambassadors as a way of overcoming serious political problems and he always hankered for an ambassador in Paris who could 'shine'.

The idea that de Gaulle can be charmed or flattered into doing something to which he is opposed is, of course, a kind of kindergarten fiction which no adult should ever be deceived by.

More storms in Monaco

Is Princess Grace in danger of losing Prince Rainier his throne? I ask this question because recent events in Monaco and the so far muted but distinctly foreboding reaction to them in Paris indicate that a new showdown between France and the Principality is in the offing.

Two weeks ago in an interview the Princess bitterly attacked the French State-controlled television for its allegedly anti-American bias in reporting the war in Vietnam. This has been duly noted here and filed away – it follows an incident last year when Prince Rainier criticised de Gaulle's 'Free Quebec' speech and was forced to retract.

Meanwhile the steady Americanisation of the Principality proceeds apace. The hotel side of Pan American Airways is taking over Monte Carlo's chief hotels, including the Hotel de Paris, and an American has been named as director of the Société des Bains de Mer, the company which runs the casino and the hotels. He is Mr Wilfred Groote and rightly or wrongly he is considered in the Principality to be Princess Grace's direct choice.

The famous general manager of the Hotel de Paris, M. Jean Broc, is resigning shortly and though he refuses to give any reasons – yet – for his departure it is clear that he is a victim of the changes that are taking place. The new director will be a Pan Am man, M. Max Blouet. At present, after the fiscal agreements forced on Monaco by the French in 1963 – which largely destroyed the Principality as a tax evasion haven – companies registered there enjoy only a ten per cent tax advantage over France.

When the agreement comes up for revision the French, no doubt, will even sweep that away.

Meanwhile the Prince has had no lack of warnings. His own officials in Paris are in despair. Whatever efforts they make to sweeten the French in Paris something either deliberate or fortuitous happens in Monaco to wreck their efforts.

For example, there was the almost farcical incident which they tried to explain away to the French as an accident – and it was indeed an accident – when the U.S. warship *Constitution* happened to sail into Monte Carlo's harbour in the course of celebrations of Monaco's National Day.

The Prince may, of course, be banking on General de Gaulle's reputed love for royal trapping and even minor royalty. He should know, however, that he has a resolute enemy in the Protestant French Foreign Minister, M. Couve de Murville.

M. de Murville was a French Ministry of Finance official before he became a diplomat and he knows his Monaco dossier backwards.

Friday, March 8, 1968

THE AMBASSADOR WHO WAS SACKED AND MR BROWN

Or what really happened at the French Embassy

The sacking of Sir Patrick Reilly – for that is what it is – as British Ambassador to Paris, has inevitably led to speculation as to whether his personal relations with George Brown were as bad as those which forced the resignation of Sir Con O'Neill from the Foreign Office.

They were not as bad simply because Sir Patrick did not have such steady personal contact with the Foreign Secretary as did Sir Con, but they were pretty dicey all the same.

Sir Patrick has much the same background as Sir Con, including a Fellowship of All Souls, and those characteristics of donnishness which seem to bring out the bully in Mr Brown. The two men, of course, got off to an appallingly bad start even before Mr Brown became Foreign Secretary.

The occasion was a dinner at the French Embassy in London attended by the French Prime Minister and Foreign Minister, and an accurate account of Mr Brown's behaviour that evening has never before been given. The French have always maintained an admirable discretion over the incident – which shocked them greatly – but with the passage of time it is possible to tell the full story.

Mr Wilson and the then Foreign Secretary, Mr Michael Stewart, were to have been guests of honour at the dinner but at the last moment they cancelled the engagement, claiming urgent House of Commons business – an explanation which the French could not wholly credit. Mr Brown was then wheeled in as the Government's representative.

Meanwhile, on hearing that the Prime Minister would not be coming, the French changed their plans for the dinner, making it an informal one with batches of guests distributed at small tables.

Mr Brown was placed at Mme Pompidou's table and found himself seated between Lady Reilly and Mme Simone Servais, the beautiful and brainy French Prime Minister's Press Attaché.

Mr Brown asked Lady Reilly who the French woman next to him was, and was given her name and function. He lapsed into silence, and then a few minutes later repeated the question and got the same answer. Then for some mysterious reason, possibly either doubting the accuracy of the information or considering himself badly placed, he exploded.

Waving an arm at Lady Reilly, he shouted: 'You are not fit to be an Ambassador's wife.' There was a stunned silence. People at other tables turned round and then everyone fell to trying to make desperate conversation.

But Mr Brown continued: 'You are not fit to be an Ambassador's wife.' By this time Lady Reilly's eyes were dimming over and she was on the edge of tears.

I am not suggesting that this incident played even a minor part in the sacking of Sir Patrick. There were other differences, especially Mr Brown's belief that he could storm into the Common Market and Sir Patrick's chilly appraisal of the prospects.

Sir Patrick until very recently was looking forward to another eighteen months in Paris and when Mr Soames's name was first mentioned in connection with the Paris Embassy a year ago Soames wrote to him telling him he knew nothing of such a move.

As for Sir Patrick's professional abilities, I can only repeat what I have written before – that in my modest view he was the most effective of any of the five British Ambassadors I have seen come and go in Paris.

Friday, March 15, 1968

A MOST UNLIKELY SPY:
DE GAULLE'S DEVOTED AIDE

I am now at liberty to disclose the identity of the so-called French Philby who, it is alleged, has been master-minding General de Gaulle's anti-American moves.

He is 55-year-old Jacques Foccart, whose official position and title is Secretary-General for African Affairs at the Elysée Palace.

The title, it has often been alleged in France, is a cover for his real job, which is that of co-ordinator and supervisor of the French secret services. In that role, real or imagined, M. Foccart is thoroughly inured to slander.

No scandal now occurs in France without the opposition press laying the responsibility for it at his doorstep.

He is a tubby, balding man, married with two children. By profession he is a businessman dealing with the import and export of rum and sugar from the Martinique.

He is a Jew and politically a man of the Left. He is a man of almost corrosive intelligence and of the utmost discretion. He was never in London with General de Gaulle and he only joined him after the war. Ever since then he has been one of his most trusted and closest followers.

His devotion to the General and to France is total, and unlike others in the General's entourage he has never sought to carve out a career for himself.

When the General leaves power Foccart will revert to his modest import-export business.

He continues to run his import-export business from an office in the Boulevard des Capuciles, only five minutes' walk from the Elysée. The background of this whole story is, as in all good spy stories, slightly sordid. It begins with the defection to the Americans of a French Secret Service man, Col. Thiraud de Vosjoly, way back in 1962. Up to that time he had been stationed in Washington as a French liaison man with the CIA.

Then he moved to Mexico where the sources of his livelihood remained something of a mystery. Some three years ago he made contact with the American writer, Leon Uris, and gave him the background for his fictionalised Spy in the Elysée story, recently published with the title *Topaz* – the alleged code name of the Elysée spy operation.

This book, which is a best-seller in the U.S. – it will shortly be published in Paris – provides de Vosjoly with fifty per cent of the author's royalties.

Is de Vosjoly being used as part of some anti-French CIA campaign? It is a more likely theory than the possibility that M. Foccart is a Soviet agent.

De Vosjoly's collaboration with the CIA was very close. In any case it was in 1963 that de Gaulle decided to break up the cosy relationship that existed between the CIA and the French intelligence services on the grounds that it was a one-way set up, with the French informing the Americans and the Americans not informing the French.

It was around that period that President Kennedy did, in fact, write a personal letter to General de Gaulle warning him that the interrogation of a Soviet defector indicated the presence of a highly-placed Russian spy in Paris.

It was around this time, too, as I reported, that the French asked that part of a considerable army of CIA agents in Paris should not be accredited to the French Foreign Office as diplomats but to the Ministry of the Interior as CIA men.

Nothing is more deliciously tempting than to imagine that General de Gaulle has been 'influenced' in his policies by a highly placed Soviet agent. Unfortunately, however, so many people have had cause to realise over the years that General de Gaulle is not a man who is easily influenced.

Friday, April 19, 1968

WHY THE STUDENTS (UNDERSTANDABLY) ARE KICKING UP SUCH A FUSS

This week's great student revolt in Paris should serve as a catalyst for a long overdue overhaul of the entire antiquated French education system.

If it does this, it will, paradoxically enough, still further enrage many of those who are today in the forefront of the student protest movement.

The explanation is not far to seek: like much of the peasantry in France, like small shopkeepers, like many small family-owned firms, like the creakingly antiquated legal profession and legal apparatus, the French higher educational system is one of the fortresses of the old France, doomed to erosion and final disappearance.

It is, in many ways, an agonising process; but it is an inevitable one, if France is to enter fully into the second half of the 20th century.

The French educational system is essentially a Mandarin one, heavily slanted in favour of the arts and humanities; and producing a race of erudite scholastics, most of whom are doomed to go through life as frustrated dons. Such a system might work reasonably well if the university population were smaller. Today, however, France has three times as many university students as there are in Britain, and there are almost as many in Paris alone as there are in the whole of the United Kingdom.

Part of this large number is due to the commendable efforts of the Government to increase the number of students from working-class families: and these now number ten per cent of a total university student population of 660,000.

What France needs clearly is more students trained in business colleges and fewer with high-sounding literary degrees; more engineers and scientists and fewer lawyers. Yet the whole French university establishment, backed by many parents and students, remains rigidly facing in the opposite direction.

As a result, any effort at large-scale reforms will be met with fierce opposition, not only from the professors themselves, but from many students who are wedded to an existing way of life; one which, while they are students, confers on them considerable privileges.

In many branches of university studies, except the ones concerned with the sciences, students study for years, accumulating degrees, only to find, when they emerge in the harsh light of the outer world, that there are no jobs for them. It is significant that the trouble at the Sorbonne started among students engaged in arts courses, who are most affected by the prospect of not finding a job when they leave university.

The problem is further accentuated by the fact that there is virtually no 'selection' among those seeking an entry to a university – any student who has successfully completed his secondary studies can enter a university. The result is that there are about fifty per cent of failures after the first year at a university but remarkably few drop-outs. This means that the great majority of those who fail in the first-year examination repeat their course for a second, and sometimes a third, year.

Only between thirty to fifty per cent complete their university studies successfully. One result of this overcrowding is, of course, to reduce to an almost negligible extent direct contact between students and professors. The situation is particularly grim in the red-brick universities, where there is virtually no university life outside the lecture halls.

Friday, May 10, 1968

SOMEHOW I'VE GOT THE FEELING I'VE BEEN THROUGH ALL THIS BEFORE!

One almost wishes, even if it were only for the sake of allowing some originality of comment, that French history did not follow so stage-managed and repetitive a pattern.

Watching the events of the past three weeks was rather like watching a new cast playing out a well-worn melodrama. Here were all the ingredients of 1789, 1848, 1870, 1936, 1940 and of course 1958, to mention only a few dates.

The very fact that all this should be happening day for day on the tenth anniversary of de Gaulle's return to power is in itself a supreme irony and an indication that though God may not be a Frenchman he jolly well ought to be.

Of course the obvious parallel is with the events which led to the fall of Louis-Philippe in 1848.

He was a monarch-president from the Orleans branch of the French Royal Family which made him not too legitimate a monarch to offend Republicans and yet not too distant from genuine royalty to offend a bourgeoisie anxious for some kind of royal restoration.

He was genuinely popular and ruled the country for 18 peaceful and prosperous years.

Yet suddenly out of a clear blue sky the lightning struck, he was literally spat upon by people who had fawned on him only a few weeks earlier, and he was bundled out of the country to take refuge with Queen Victoria.

Revolutionary reaction with intervening periods of order – this seems to be the pattern of modern French history.

Since 1800 the country has seen two emperors, two monarchies, five republics and the wartime Pétain regime.

In the last thirty years it has had four different regimes – the

144

Third Republic, the Pétain 'new order', the Fourth Republic and the present Fifth Republic.

There are still coins in circulation which bear the Pétainist inscription Honour and Country.

It is of events in 1940, however, that the present situation most reminds me.

Let me be frank about this – I do not regard the present upheaval as a justified popular popular uprising against an intolerable tyranny. The Gaullist regime, whatever its faults, has on the whole been liberal and progressive and this government and president remain the elected representatives of the nation.

The present upheaval is profoundly anti-democratic in character aimed at unseating an elected government and president by insurrection. If it succeeds it will mean a Left-wing dictatorship dominated by the Communists to be followed no doubt by a Fascist one.

It is fascinating to see today so many people on the extreme right come out for M. Mendès-France. They are shrewd enough to realise what is meat for the Left-wing goose today is sauce for the Right-wing gander tomorrow.

It has been a shattering experience this week to hear men whom one has always regarded as democrats talking openly in *coup-d'état* terms. Thus M. Mitterrand and much more shockingly M. Mendès-France have given countenance to the idea that governments should fall not because they are defeated in Parliament but because they face strikes and riots.

Without so much as blinking an eyelid each of them has proposed themselves to lead a so-called provisional government composed only of the parties of the Left without a thought to the fact that the legal government is in office or that the entire nation is not composed of people on strike.

What the exteme Right – which fortunately de Gaulle has emasculated – could do with such a doctrine in the years to come is of course a chilling idea.

Nor is it any use saying that this behaviour can be excused by the claim that de Gaulle came to power as a result of an army *putsch* in Algiers.

De Gaulle was voted into power by an overwhelming majority of deputies including an overwhelming majority of Socialist ones.

It is true that Mendès-France voted against him but he did not

Sam White's Paris

do so on constitutional grounds. His own words at the time were: 'If I believed that de Gaulle could end the Algerian war, restore discipline in the army and maintain democratic liberties I would vote for him.'

One of the very undemocratic liberties which Mendès-France now enjoys is that of sedition and subversion.

It is this which brings me to the comparison with 1940. The events of the past few weeks have involved France in a moral collapse almost on the scale to that which followed defeat and occupation in 1940.

Six weeks ago the French Institute of Public Opinion poll showed that sixty-two per cent of the population was glad that de Gaulle came to power in 1958, and sixty per cent expressed themselves as satisfied with the government.

Suddenly, as though by a miracle, there seemed to be no Gaullists at all – until last night, when de Gaulle spoke and made a show of force.

In fashionable and rich circles the hatred of him became frenetic.

'Rather the Communists than that old dope,' an elderly dowager spluttered at me.

There was a marked tendency everywhere to come to terms with the potential new masters.

The rich began shipping out their money and in many cases their persons. Then there was the most sinister and frightening aspect of all – public opinion as expressed in the Press evaporated.

Where was the thunder and lightning, the cut and thrust of some of France's most famous editorialists?

Apart from an occasional squeak they were all silenced and silenced in the most humiliating fashion.

The weeklies could not come out and the dailies allowed an on-the-spot censorship by the printers.

In the case of one newspaper the censorship was applied by a shop steward who in 1940 had helped to produce the German Occupation newspaper in Paris.

Petrol was strictly rationed to priority groups yet there were mammoth traffic jams all over Paris.

I recalled the fact that only four months before D-Day Marshal Pétain had received a wildly enthusiastic welcome in Paris, only to face, a year later, a grotesque mockery of a trial almost without a single voice raised in his favour.

146

But, really, it is the famous French historian Tocqueville, writing more than a hundred years ago, who, writing of the French, summed up the matter perfectly.

He wrote: 'Non-docile by temperament, at the same time it always accommodates itself better to arbitrary rule, even violent rule, than to that of regular government full of liberal principles. Today it is the declared enemy of all obedience: tomorrow seized by some passion that even nations best-fitted for servitude cannot attain, it is led by some kind of thread that no one can resist, to submission.

'Ungovernable, once some example of resistance is given, it always deceives its rulers who either fear it too much, or too little.'

I will end this gloomy tale with two cracks current in Paris. One describes Paris as the Saigon of the West; and the other sums up General de Gaulle's policy with the words: 'Let them eat chaos.'

Friday, May 31, 1968

WHY DE GAULLE MADE TWO MYSTERY FLIGHTS TO SEE HIS GENERALS

Wednesday a week ago General de Gaulle was a man almost as alone as he was in June, 1940, in London. Here is the inside story of what happened on that historic May 29, 1968, when the General cancelled a Cabinet meeting and announced that he was going to reflect on his future at his country home in the village of Colombey-les-deux-Eglises.

Preceding his departure he had received advice from members of his Cabinet and from Gaullist deputies that he should resign. He was also involved in a dispute with his Prime Minister, M. Pompidou.

It has since been said by the political correspondent of *Le Monde*, who on that day reported that de Gaulle would resign, that the Prime Minister had pressed him to do so.

In fact, M. Pompidou's conduct was impeccable. The General wanted a referendum and M. Pompidou pressed him to dissolve the Assembly and hold General Elections. De Gaulle was reluctant to do so, seeing in the dissolution of the Assembly, while the Government enjoyed a majority, a capitulation to the general strike and the street demonstrations. In the end – twice – M. Pompidou warned him that if he did not follow this course then it would be best if *he* resigned.

It was at the height of this disagreement that the General announced to everyone's astonishment that he would leave that Wednesday morning for Colombey. The Presidential party took off in three separate helicopters from the military airport of Brétigny. In the first helicopter were General de Gaulle, Mme de Gaulle and his naval ADC.

The second helicopter carried M. Jean Ducret, the chief of security at the Elysée Palace, and members of General de Gaulle's personal bodyguard. The third helicopter had on board twelve men from the Gendarmerie Nationale, who formed part of the Elysée Palace guard.

Shortly after take-off M. Ducret noted they were not following the well-known route to Colombey. He questioned the pilot, who told him that his instructions were simply to follow the Presidential helicopter. M. Ducret then tried to communicate with de Gaulle's pilot, who refused all conversation. The two helicopters finally landed at the airport of St Dizier, about 150 miles east of Paris, where the President's Caravelle awaited them. General de Gaulle took the Caravelle to Baden Baden, headquarters of the French Forces in Germany.

There, the General assured himself of the loyalty of military commanders with the French Forces, including the famous parachute general, General Massu. De Gaulle then took off for Mulhouse and Metz for similar meetings with army chiefs. Meanwhile, the helicopter carrying the twelve palace guards landed near Colombey with no sign of de Gaulle.

The news of his non-arrival at Colombey was greeted with genuine amazement both in the Elysée Palace and in the Prime Minister's residence at the Hotel Matignon. In fact, only two members of the Elysée staff knew that de Gaulle would not be going direct to Colombey.

When he finally reached Colombey at 6.30 in the evening, de Gaulle's first action was to telephone M. Pompidou. He told him only two things:
1. That he would be back the following day, and
2. That he was not resigning.

As a price for conceding to Pompidou in the matter of General Elections, General de Gaulle insisted on naming most of the members of the new Cabinet himself and without reference to the Prime Minister. As a result, the former Foreign Minister, M. Couve de Murville, emerges as the strongest figure in the new Government, and has been given full powers to deal with the impending economic crisis.

The most striking example, however, of an appointment made directly by de Gaulle, which was bound to displease M. Pompidou, is that of the Left-wing Gaullist M. René Capitant, named as Minister of Justice. He and Pompidou cordially detest each other.

Asked what he thought about serving under Pompidou, M. Capitant replied: 'For General de Gaulle I can swallow even that particular snake.'

Capitant, a 67-year-old law professor and Deputy for the Latin Quarter, is the nearest thing French politics have to a kind of Michael Foot. A man of passionate integrity, he resigned his seat rather than be forced to vote by conscience against the Government in the recent confidence debate.

An Old Guard Gaullist from 1940, he has fortnightly sessions with de Gaulle, and is one of the few of the General's intimates who permits himself the luxury of lecturing the General rather than being lectured by him. His political credo is summed up in the phrase: 'Gaullism has no future if it identifies itself with the Right.'

He will be the conscience of the Gaullist Left inside the new Government.

Another veteran Gaullist who has received promotion is 55-year-old Yvon Morandat, who was parachuted into France in 1941 as one of de Gaulle's direct representatives with the Resistance. He knew so little of politics that when, just before the liberation of Paris, he was ordered to take the Hotel Matignon, which is in the Rue de Varenna, he and his wife cycled fruitlessly up and down the Avenue Matignon looking for a hotel of that name.

De Gaulle is not, as his foreign policy has shown and his domestic policies in different periods have indicated, a man given to unconditional anti-Communism. Why, then, is he basing virtually his whole election campaign on the Communist issue?

After the War he brought Communists into his first provisional Government, although – to their fury – he barred them from the key posts of Interior, Defence and Foreign Affairs. Electorally, of course, after the events of recent weeks the anti-Communist appeal will pay off: but he is too far-sighted not to see the danger of polarising French politics in this way.

Nevertheless, it seems to me that some commentators like Raymond Aron have gone a little too far in the opposite direction in claiming that in the recent crisis the Communists have been a factor for stability and virtual allies of the Government in bringing the crisis to an end.

In fact, the Communists have deliberately prolonged the strikes in the metallurgic and motor industries, largely to show that it was they who could end a strike and not the Government.

It is absurd to pretend that the Communist Party is a party like any other; and only commentators in Britain who enjoy the luxury of a minuscule Communist Party can permit themselves this type of light comment.

The French Communist Party is totalitarian in structure and totalitarian in aim. It now knows that it has the Gaullist regime by the throat; and, whatever the results of the Elections, its grip will tighten.

Friday, June 7, 1968

IN THIS ONCE-IMPERIAL CITY, I WATCH THE AGONY OF THE NEW REFUGEES

A utumn has come a little early to Central and Eastern Europe this year. As though to match the chill in men's hearts produced by the Russian invasion of Czechoslovakia a cold wind from the eastern plains is blowing across Vienna and withered leaves like withered illusions are falling fast.

Here, like some medieval merchant venturing into little known parts, the traveller bent on going eastwards pauses to sift the latest gossip and rumours and to provision himself for the rest of the journey. Which tribes are hostile or well disposed? Which visas can be collected in the course of the next few days?

How stand's one's stock of soap and toilet paper, pens and

150

cheap cigarette lighters? From all these points of view Vienna is the ideal starting point for a journey through Eastern Europe. Once the imperial capital of what is now the outer ring of the Soviet Empire its own basically Germanic people is deeply impregnated with Magyar, Serb, Croat and Bohemian blood.

Its proximity to the lands it once ruled comes home to one when one sees road signs in the centre of the city indicating the routes to Prague and Budapest. The frontiers of Czechoslovakia and Hungary are less than an hour's drive away and at one frontier post you can see the former Imperial Palace of Bratislava so clearly that you feel yourself almost physically in the city.

There is another good reason for using Vienna as a starting point for a journey such as this – it stirs even the most sluggish memory. A short drive to the outskirts of the city brings you for example to Karl Marx Hof, that once model working-class housing estate which was the pride and crowning achievement of Viennese Socialism. Red-painted and squat it now looks pathetically inadequate, almost like a rather attractive barracks, but in the twenties and thirties it was a showpiece of enlightened Socialist civic planning and administration. It was here of course that the Viennese working class made its last stand against a relatively mildly reactionary Dolfuss regime before both were overwhelmed by Hitler.

Finally, there is the ever-present reminder here of refugees. Some 14,000 Czechs are in Austria at the moment, and the overwhelming majority are holidaymakers who profited from the first-ever general issue of exit permits for Czechs to travel abroad.

They have gone in family groups in their own cars – many with camping equipment – little knowing when they set out just how useful this might turn out to be. They have been flooding into Austria all the week from Italy, France and the Dalmatian coast.

Now in camps all over Austria, with their money gone and dependent on Austrian charity, they are engaged in the agonising debate on whether to return or not. The great majority are opting to go back. Most of them are professional people, doctors, engineers, lawyers – totally different in character from the wave of Hungarian refugees who passed through Austria after the 1956 Hungarian uprising.

They are solid citizens, with a stake in their own country. I talked to one engineer from Bratislava, here with his wife and two daughters after an Italian holiday, who had opted to abandon everything and start a new life in the West.

The family had only their summer holiday clothes, and their decision not to return was made at a family conference literally at the frontier post and within sight of their home town.

Like many others, they were going on to Switzerland – where asylum, and financial support, was most readily available – and then the hope of a job in West Germany.

There is, inevitably, interesting speculation here in Western embassies as to the motives of the Russian intervention in Czechoslovakia. For many shrewd analysts here the main reason boils down to a Russian fear of the unknown. This was a novel and thoroughly perplexing situation for the Russians to face, in which a kind of quiet revolution was taking place not against the ruling Communist Party, as it happened elsewhere, but on the Party's own initiative – and with the support of the nation at large.

Where such an experiment could lead, and the daunting example of other Eastern countries to adopt the same techniques of moving towards greater freedom – these were the aspects of the Czech situation which worried and puzzled the Russians. It was all the more puzzling for them that the Czechs are not a people with a revolutionary temper given to overthrowing regimes – and Czechoslovakia is a member of the Eastern bloc, which had freely voted for a Communist regime.

In the opinion of observers here the Russian occupation of Czechoslovakia will now become permanent, but unobtrusive – as is, for example, the case with the twenty-two Russian divisions stationed in East Germany, the two in Poland and the four in Hungary.

This is a kind of 'real estate' occupation, without any overt interference in the day-to-day running of the country occupied.

There is every reason to believe the Russian decision to move in was a hasty one, made at the last moment, with carefully-prepared contingency plans but without any of the political preparations which usually accompany such a military move.

Meanwhile, life in Vienna continues along its placid course.

The opera is going full blast, with a performance of *Don Giovanni* and *The Magic Flute*. Culturally replete, a crowd enters the Three Hussars restaurant after the show. Leonard Bernstein is in town, and so is Ray Charles. There is also a World

Philosophical Congress in session – which adds a fairly comic backdrop to the Czech tragedy.

There are some 3,000 delegates, including forty-seven Russians and, for some reason, forty-two are Bulgarians. The Russians are falling over themselves to avoid all doctrinal and political disputation and are more than usually friendly to their Western colleagues.

One hard-line Marxist philosopher introduced a paper on the theme of the necessity of using violence in order to defend liberty, but it was made clear that this paper had been prepared long before the Czech events.

John Huston is also here making films in the Vienna woods. My stay here has been lightened by contact with three younger members of his cast – his 17-year-old daughter, Anjelica, who will star in the film; Assaf Dayan, the 19-year-old actor son of the Israeli general; and Anthony Corlan, 21-year-old actor from Birmingham Repertory.

The three of them, dressed in the latest Carnaby Street gear in staid Vienna, have been desperately trying to make the city swing. They have failed and confess their failure with amused resignation.

Vienna, Friday, September 6, 1968

Memo to the Russians:

IF YOU INVADE, COME IN FIGHTING!

If the Russians invaded Rumania they would have a fight on their hands. It would, of course, be little more than token resistance, but there would be resistance and there would be bloodshed.

Of this all experienced observers are convinced despite the total absence of any signs of Rumanian military preparedness on its frontiers with the Soviet Union.

Rumanian Communist leaders make no secret of their hope that this is understood in Moscow and that the consequences to world Communism of a bloody, as against a bloodless, invasion of a fellow Socialist country act as a major deterrent to a Soviet military move against this country.

In this connection the Rumanians do not hide their disappointment that 'for history's sake' the Czech army did not put up a token fight.

Among the disastrous consequences for world Communism of a Russian invasion they do not even rule out the possibility of the Chinese, with whom they have good relations, making a military move against Manchuria.

The dominant mood of the Rumanian Government and Asia, I think, can best be summed up by saying that they are nervous, certainly, but afraid, no.

The leaders have, of course, now curbed their tongues and their Press in the matter of attacks on the Soviet Union, but they have made no concessions on any points of policy and principle.

On the contrary, it was they who insisted that Mr Stewart's visit to Rumania this week proceed as scheduled despite repeated British offers of postponement. Basically what worries them is what worries the rest of the world, and that is the element of irrationality introduced into Soviet policy by the invasion of Czechoslovakia.

Before August 21 they considered a repetition of Hungary in 1956 unthinkable; now they think that anything is possible.

One of their hopes, of course, is that rational men will regain control in Moscow and that sometime soon, in six months or a year, there will be a palace revolution in the Kremlin. Geographically Rumania is at an advantage because it has no common frontier with the West and therefore, unlike Czechoslovakia, it cannot be made to appear to the military mind as a crumbling bastion.

Ideologically, too, it is difficult to see the Rumanian Communists – who are rigid Marxists and have not fooled around with any liberalising tendencies – as a menace. Here of course comes the rub, for the Rumanians have caught what in super-power eyes is the most dangerous disease of all – nationalism.

Their brand of national Communism is now the most eroding factor in the Russian empire. Stalin realised the danger early and he spent the last years of his life purging Communist party after Communist party to remove anyone with the remotest pretensions to national leadership.

He did this work particularly bloodily in Rumania. The present Rumanian leaders are the survivors of these purges. Their minds are full of memories not only of brutal Russian intervention in Rumanian affairs, but of the way the Russians pillaged their country. The result is a depth of anti-Russian feeling of astonishing ferocity.

Nationalism has made the Rumanian Government strong and acceptable. Without it, it would be a fragile thing indeed.

The leader of the Rumanian Communist party, Nicolae Ceauçescu, is something of a rough-neck, crude in manner and, to Western eyes, uncouth.

He is only fifty and his official biography is remarkably meagre. He was a cobbler by trade and joined the Rumanian Communist party at the age of sixteen. Like so many of the more independent Communists in Eastern Europe, he spent the war not in Moscow, but in prison in his native country. He is clearly a man of considerable courage and character.

His favourite phrase in conversation and in speeches typifies the man. It is: 'I want to be boss in my own country.'

He is flanked by a prime minister whose background and sophistication is the very opposite to himself. He is Ion Maurer, a man in his middle sixties, an intellectual and a lawyer by profession.

A former Socialist, he made a speciality of defending members of the illegal Rumanian Communist Party before the war, a task which he performed so well that he finally finished up in jail along with one of his clients. He is a man who greatly impresses foreign visitors as a statesman of international calibre.

One of the ironies of present-day Rumania is that this country, which, before the war, was the most virulently anti-Semitic in Eastern Europe, should now be the only Communist state to have diplomatic relations with Israel.

These relations, it might be added, are excellent, and were reinforced when, in May 1967, Rumania – seeing in Israel a small country like itself – refused to condemn it as an aggressor at the United Nations.

There are now only a little over 100,000 Jews left out of a pre-war population of one million, and, unlike in the Soviet Union, they suffer from no administrative anti-Semitism.

Such endemic anti-Semitism as exists is strenuously fought by the government. There are eighteen synagogues in Bucharest and – an astonishing paradox in a normally atheist country – the

Jewish minority is represented in parliament by the chief rabbi.

This is not to the liking of many younger Jews who have drifted away from their faith.

Rumanian nationalism, of course, has a solid economic basis as the Rumanian leaders, good Marxists themselves, are the first to admit.

It is a country which has been deeply humiliated throughout its history, always caught in a kind of historical cross-fire. It was trapped between the Roman Empire and the Barbarians, between the Austro-Hungarian, early Ottoman empires, between Germany and the West in two world wars, and it has always been a story of pillage, humiliation and semi-colonial status.

Now the realisation has sunk in that this is potentially a very rich country and not simply destined to be a subsidiary granary for the Soviet Union.

This produced the first clash with Moscow, which had precisely such plans for it, in its own Moscow-dominated Eastern equivalent of the Common Market.

Unique among the erstwhile satellite countries, Rumania is rich in oil and natural gas and in an abundance of raw materials which it can sell to the West, and especially West Germany, pouring back the profits to equip the country with machinery and plant from the West.

Rumania is, in fact, the eastern counterpart of the famous West German economic miracle. Here, central planning and Communism really work; here, too, Western capitalism – which in the inter-war years plundered Rumania – fulfils at high rate of profit the useful function of modernising and industrialising the country.

Before the war, Bucharest was the Paris of the Balkans and its ruling classes were without any doubt the most corrupt, indolent, lecherous and decadent in the world. This was the Rumania, of course, of Lupescu and King Carol, of orgies at the Hotel Athene, of great banquets and great poverty.

There is, I regret to say, very little left of what one might describe as the more decadent aspect of Bucharest life. Superficially, the city has a striking resemblance to Paris, with everything on a miniature scale.

The pleasant-looking villas which line the boulevards are now occupied by the new ruling class known as the Apparatniks. They are the members of the ruling bodies and they flit between their offices and their villas in curtained black Mercedes cars.

Nobody looks poor, except professional gipsy beggars. There are three or four good restaurants in town, one of which is now managed by its former owner.

He might be still a head waiter out of Maxim's, and his impeccable French and the solicitude he displays for a clientele which is composed largely of tourists from East Germany and oil technicians on a weekend spree in Bucharest from Transylvania is a touching indication of how a member of the old regime can maintain his morale simply by continuing to practise his profession.

If you want to see the new ruling class play, then Saturday night at the Lido Hotel is an eye-opener of festive guzzling to the accompaniment of the noise of an artificial wave-making machine coming from a swimming-pool.

For those in need of rejuvenation, there is a famous rejuvenation clinic here, and while I was getting my prescription for a special hair tonic and wrinkle-remover cream, I was delighted to see that my old friend, appropriately enough the French Ambassador, had arrived at the clinic for his daily jab.

Bucharest, Friday, September 13, 1968

WHAT THEY THINK ABOUT
CZECHOSLOVAKIA HERE IN HUNGARY
(INVADED IN 1956)

Order reigns in Budapest. Order has of course reigned here since the 1956 uprising was crushed by the Red Army.

Since then the Hungarians have travelled a long way towards establishing the kind of peaceful co-existence with their rulers and through them with the Soviet Union.

In effect they have gone further than that and the regime now enjoys a fair measure of acceptance. Life has been steadily getting better since 1956 and fear of arbitrary arrest and torture has lifted from the land. Indeed, in many ways the liberalising process, especially in the arts, has been carried further here than in any other Communist country except for a brief period in pre-invasion Czechoslovakia.

Sam White's Paris

All this has been accompanied by an ingenious policy of economic reform introduced recently – aimed at decentralisation, more power for factory managers and in general an economy more motivated by consumer needs and profit for reinvestment. Though it is feared by Communists and non-Communists alike that all this may have to be slowed down, if not abandoned, in the light of the Czechoslovakian experience.

The invasion of Czechoslovakia has had a traumatic effect on the Hungarians who inevitably see in it a parallel to what happened in Budapest in 1956.

It is therefore not too much to say that the fact that Hungarian troops took part in the invasion has evoked feelings of deep shame and indignation. Privately, Communist leaders explain that the Czechs tried to go too far, too fast and that once invasion measures were decided upon Hungarian participation was unavoidable.

Dubček himself received a rapturous welcome in Budapest shortly before the invasion and relations between himself and the Hungarian Communist leader Janos Kadar were extremely close. In fact Kadar tried to play the honest broker between Prague and Moscow, urging Dubček to put the brake on, and trying to inform Moscow of the realities of the Czech situation.

Since the invasion Kadar, a likable and humane man, has not appeared in public and has not made any statement on the affair. His attitude is mirrored by the Hungarian Press which, unlike the Polish one for example, has maintained a notable restraint on the subject.

What infuriates Hungarians is that they, who have maintained a steady liberalising policy for the past decade, should appear as one of the villains of the piece while Rumania, which is internally a Stalinist state, should, because of its independent foreign policy, appear to be on the side of the angels.

Some Hungarians go so far as to say that it was only by participating in the invasion that they could exercise some moderating influence on Moscow. They point to the fate of the Hungarian Dubček, Imre Nagy, who after taking refuge in the Yugoslav Embassy was promised safe conduct by the Russians only to be grabbed as he left the embassy by Soviet secret police and subsequently shot.

Meanwhile twelve years after the Budapest rising four Soviet Divisions are still stationed in Hungary.

They are invariably referred to in the Press as 'Soviet forces temporarily stationed in Hungary'.

Just on the outskirts of Budapest one can see one of their watch towers. The troops are kept out of sight as much as possible but Soviet officers often come into Budapest dressed in civilian clothes.

Still here, too, is Cardinal Mindszenty. The Cardinal, now seventy-seven, took refuge in the U.S. Embassy here after the entry of Soviet tanks into Budapest in 1956. He has not budged since. The Americans quartered him in two rooms on the first floor of their embassy building and these he occupies to this day.

He goes for a short walk in the courtyard every evening and sees his confessor regularly. Apart from that he receives twice yearly visits from the Cardinal Primate of Austria who brings him the latest reports from the Vatican.

The Vatican has made various efforts to persuade him to come to Rome and the Hungarians have offered him a safe passage but to no avail. He has strongly theocratic ideas of his role, similar to those of his opposite number in Warsaw, and among the conditions he poses for leaving the embassy is the restoration of church lands amounting to ten per cent of the arable land in Hungary. He has now become a considerable diplomatic nuisance to everyone, especially the Americans and the Vatican.

As a result of him taking refuge in the embassy diplomatic relations between the U.S. and Hungary were broken off and have only just been restored with an exchange of ambassadors between the two countries.

As for the Vatican, it would like to appoint a new Cardinal for this eighty per cent devoutly Catholic country but cannot do so while he remains entombed in the embassy.

Despite his confinement, he is said to be like so many other 77-year-olds, in very robust health. It looks as though he will be there for a long time yet and meanwhile the U.S. Embassy, now expanding, badly needs the office space he occupies.

Another missing person, as it were, is Rakosi, the one-time head of the Hungarian Communist Party, who had to flee Budapest under the protection of the Russians for fear of being lynched. A monster of evil and cruelty, he consciously models himself on Stalin, seeking to inspire fear in everyone. He is now in a remote part of Russia; in some kind of home the Russians must keep for failed dictators. The then head of the Secret

Police, Peter Gabor, however, returned to Budapest and now works in a clothing factory, being a tailor by trade.

Among the new professions thrown up by Communist Europe is that of 'compensator'.

Because most of Communist Europe is desperately short of foreign currency much of its trade is done by barter; and the 'compensator' is the Western businessman, usually with good connections in Eastern capitals, who arranges these deals and gets a cut of the heavy discount given by Communist governments on the price of their goods.

The Soviet Union itself uses the system often to obtain strategic materials through the satellite countries which are sometimes in a better position to obtain these products. The result is a kind of official contraband trade, the main passage of which is through East-West Germany. The discounts given are so heavy that they often bear no relation to the real value of the goods sold; and the result often is that one can buy Soviet oil or steel cheaper in, say, Budapest, than in the Soviet Union itself.

Another consequence is that the quality of the goods sold between Communist states is invariably inferior to what they try and sell to the West.

So it is that 'compensators', whose head offices are usually in Switzerland, swarm in every Budapest hotel lobby reinforced by heavy contingents of more orthodox businessmen from the West. These lead frustrating lives by day, but, come the evening, Budapest has everything to make them feel as though they were on a business trip in, say, Manchester or London. Plush restaurants, bars, night-clubs and, of course, squads of gipsy violinists envelop them in a warm embrace. Occasionally, when the violinists permit it, you can overhear a snatch of conversation as I did the other night between a group of British businessmen.

It was the part of a heated debate as to whether it was correct – the Duke of Edinburgh having apparently set the example – to wear decorations with dinner jacket or only with tails.

This is, after all, the land of the Gabor sisters and of the fabulous Kaldov and Balogh and countless other beautiful women and brilliant men. It would be astonishing, therefore, under any regime if Budapest were not a highly sophisticated city with considerable intellectual life.

In these matters it is way ahead of any other Communist capitals and it makes even Vienna look like a provincial backwater. One can go further – life in this exceptionally beautiful city, straddling both banks of the Danube, is, for the visitor, agreeable by any standards.

Though nationalised, Budapest restaurants still manage to operate as though the profit motive were still at work as, in fact, it is with a perfectly understood system of tipping which ensures regal fare and regal service. One has the feeling that if France ever went Communist something like the same respect for the customer and his stomach would survive.

For nothing is more useful for a dictatorship than an understanding of national weaknesses, foibles and passions. In Budapest, café life, good food, good talk and football figure very high among the necessities for a tolerable existence. This the regime has had the intelligence to understand and has provided for it with relative abundance.

In short, one feels the Hungarians, whose élite is the most intelligent of the world – despite the handicap of speaking Europe's most impossible language, or possibly because of it – will finish up by giving the world a Hungarianised version of Communism. It will be highly spiced and not unappetising.

Budapest, Friday, September 20, 1968

HOW MANY HOUSES SHOULD A GOOD COMMUNIST OWN?

To go to Belgrade is like throwing open a window on the stuffy Communist world. Here there was a rustle of ideas, accumulative and constant debate – a virile conscience which stamps the Yugoslav Communists as the only ruling Communist Party in the world which retains something of the idealism and sense of purpose of its revolutionary days.

The Yugoslavs are, in many ways, the early Christians of the Communist orthodoxy who are still wrestling with the devil. The devil takes many forms but, essentially, the debate is about how to retain a Socialist society while granting a measure of private property in the countryside, and a smaller one in the cities, and how to maintain an egalitarian society when the need is for incentives, which produce large disparities of pay.

For example, in the last week the debate came to the boiling point with a decree forbidding the ownership of more than one country house.

What apparently has been happening is that richer people in the cities had been buying up country properties and supplementing their income by subletting them. Similarly, a debate is now raging on the role of the Communist Party and the trade unions in the kind of Socialist society the Yugoslavs are trying to build.

Yugoslav Socialism is based on the idea of self-management, with the workers – through workers councils – running their own factories. What has been happening, however, in the more sophisticated factories is that the workers, conscious of the need for efficiency which bears directly on their own standards of living, have tended to elect the best among themselves as manager and leave the running of the factory to him.

If he makes a go of it – that is to say produces profit – he is retained, and if not he is fired and someone else elected in his place. As for the workers councils they meet regularly in such factories and then only to decide minor issues – such as the length of the Yugoslav equivalent of the tea break.

These tendencies are worrying the trade unions, which see their own role taken over by the workers councils, and is perplexing the Communist Party, which sees itself gradually being replaced by a new pragmatic managerial class. What is refreshing is that these are matters of keen debate in a society which still remains a Communist dictatorship.

Another refreshing feature of Yugoslav Communism derives, of course, from the very origins of the Communist takeover here.

Alone among the Communist rulers, Tito liberated his own country instead of being brought into Belgrade in the Red Army's baggage train. This has given the country an exhilarating independent spirit, which Stalin failed to break as far back as 1948 and which Russia's present rulers could only break if they were prepared to face a prolonged guerrilla war – which might well become the trip-wire of the Third World War.

There is a third, if possibly minor, exhilarating feature about Yugoslavia – and that is the almost Byronic links which bind it to Britain. Just as 19th-century Greeks associated their own struggle for independence with Byron, so Yugoslavs today – from Tito down – associate their own struggle with Britain's wartime support, and the remarkable men Britain parachuted to the partisans.

For this decision to switch support from Mikhailovitch's kittenish and conservative Chetniks to Tito's partisans, the credit goes to the Tory MP, Brigadier Fitzroy Maclean, whose reports from Yugoslavia convinced Churchill of the need to do so. As it happened, Fitzroy Maclean was in Belgrade last week – and as soon as Tito heard he was there, he summoned him to his island retreat of Brioni.

For Tito himself the Soviet invasion of Czechoslovakia is a major political defeat, and, in a sense, humiliation. Not only did he not believe that the Russians would invade but he thought he had convinced them in the course of an early visit to Moscow of the folly of such an action. The Czech Communists, he pointed out, were indeed split – but the surest way of uniting them would be to invade the country. He argued from his own experience in 1948, when a divided Yugoslav party united in the face of Stalin's threats.

As his policy of improving relations with Russia has failed, so his attempts to rally the so-called non-aligned world around a common policy have collapsed in ruins. With Nasser, for example, refusing to condemn the Soviet action, non-alignment is proved a sham.

Meanwhile, the Russians have mounted a propaganda attack on Tito which, in three weeks, has attained a pitch which it only attained in Stalin's day after three years. At the same time the Russians' obvious catspaw – Bulgaria – is now making sinister claims for the return of its erstwhile province of Macedonia.

Tito got away with it in 1948 for three reasons:

1. Russia's urgent economic need to partially demobilise after the war.

2. A tacit and then an open guarantee of support for Yugoslavia from Britain, France and the U.S.

3. Because the U.S. still had a monopoly of the Bomb.

None of these factors apply today.

What an astonishing life Tito has had: first, in his youth, a factory worker who joined the illegal Yugoslav Communist Party; then, picked out by Moscow as promising material, he was taken there for training and then sent back to reorganise the illegal Yugoslav party. He reorganised it so well that when occupation came the Communist cells that he had formed were a natural basis for his guerrilla army.

He is now seventy-six, in good health but beginning to show signs of age and there is no obvious successor. One of his great achievements has been to unite the five different nationalities which make up Yugoslavia around himself – so much so that Serbs tend to forget that he is a Croat and Croats are prepared to believe that he is a Serb.

Any successor would have the initial enormous difficulty of overcoming the handicap of his nationality, whatever it might be. Tito is, of course, an exceedingly vain man, with an almost comic love of uniforms and of luxury.

His wife, whom he married secretly a few years ago and who is of modest Serbian origin, was a startling beauty when she was an officer in the Partisan Army. Tito had a long struggle to persuade her to marry him, and she was put off by the style and panache with which he lived. She has now become rather stout, and Tito has imposed his taste on her. She manages to carry off a difficult situation extremely well.

A member of the former Yugoslav royal family is a familiar figure in the streets of Belgrade. He is 81-year-old Prince George, who would have been king had he not been forced to renounce the throne in favour of his younger brother after he had accidentally killed his batman.

Under the Regency of Prince Paul he was kept under house arrest, and was freed by the Germans. He refused, however, to occupy the royal palace they placed at his disposal.

He lives in a villa on the outskirts of Belgrade, half of which he rents to a Japanese trade mission. He has just written his memoirs, which are being serialised in a Belgrade daily and for which he received £4,000.

His relations with the regime are good, and he receives a pension as an ex-officer. A sturdy little man with a beak nose – characteristic of his family – and always wearing a beret and clutching a briefcase, he can be seen hopping on and off trams or, when strolling, solemnly acknowledging the salutations of passers-by.

Belgrade, Friday, September 27, 1968

164

INTERROGATED AND SEARCHED – FOR FORGETTING A TEN-MARK BILL!

'In his generous instincts, in his love of laughter, in his devotion to a comrade, and in his healthy, direct outlook on the affairs of workaday life, the ordinary Russian seems to me to bear a marked similarity to an average American. The two peoples have maintained an unbroken friendship that dates back to the birth of the United States as an independent Republic. Both are free from the stigma of colonial empire-building by force.'
General Eisenhower, 1945

This city is the culminating absurdity of the misbegotten Europe that Stalin and Roosevelt shaped between then in the concluding days of the War.

It stands in the heart of Europe, the divided capital of a divided country in the midst of a divided continent. As such, it is a fitting symbol of the diplomatic aberrations which produced the Europe of today.

Today, twenty-three years after the War, it is impossible to telephone from West Berlin to East Berlin, or the other way round. As for crossing from West Berlin to East Berlin, the passport, currency and Customs formalities are more formidable than those encountered at any frontier.

I returned from East Berlin late at night through Checkpoint Charlie. I had entered through the checkpoint, and the rules are that you must return through the same checkpoint. I had been warned, while in East Berlin, to collect all receipts and bills so as to account for money spent in the Eastern Zone. I produced them for the Eastern frontier guard who gravely added them up.

Then his face clouded: and he pointed out that ten marks – about £1 – were unaccounted for. What had I done with the ten marks? I tried to offer an explanation – that I had bought a round of drinks and forgotten to collect the bill. Not good enough.

I was then invited into his office for a lengthier interrogation, which finally concluded with my being asked to show the contents of my wallet and my pockets.

I felt like a character out of some spy thriller by the time I finally crossed through the gap in the Wall into West Berlin.

It is unnecessary to dwell on the contrast between the two zones – one prosperous, hustling and traffic-laden: and the other eerily quiet, still badly gashed by the war, and having something of the sullen look of an occupied city.

In fact, the gap between West and East Germany is being slowly reduced, and East Germany today is far and away the most prosperous country in the Communist camp with a standard of living far superior to that of the Soviet Union itself.

What is so chilling about East Berlin is the combination of German efficiency and Communist dictatorship. Lenin was dead right when he wrote that Germany would be the ideal testing-ground for Communism. Anyone in search of a good emetic can do no better than go to East Berlin these days and listen to official spokesmen defend the invasion of Czechoslovakia. One gets, of course, the same kind of speech in, say, Budapest; but somehow one senses that the person delivering it does not entirely believe in it.

In East Berlin, however, the spittle shows. The curious thing about East German participation in the invasion is the great blanket of secrecy that surrounds it. This is so heavy that there is now even doubt as to whether the East Germans were even allowed to participate in it at all.

In fact, I believe that they did send a token force into the German-speaking Sudetenland. This was an operation carried out in true Czarist Imperial style, based on the divide-and-rule principle, in which the Germans went into the Sudetenland: and the Hungarians, for example, went into the Hungarian minority area in Slovakia. The Hungarian Press, while I was there, made no bones about reporting the hostile reception they received from their fellow Hungarians.

The East German Press, however, has made no mention of its troops in the Sudetenland. In fact, I understand, their reception was so explosively hostile that their gallant contingent was removed after only eight days.

A suspicion remains in many minds that it was possibly the East Germans who insisted on the Russian invasion of Czechoslovakia. Whatever the truth of this, they are certainly the most enthusiastic defenders of the Soviet action.

This is not surprising, for whereas both East Germany and Czechoslovakia are industrially the most developed in the Soviet bloc, the East German regime is the one that would be most obviously imperilled by a liberalisation in Czechoslovakia.

It has a popular base of support which is no bigger than the driving seat of a Soviet tank.

Three impressions stand out from my tour of Eastern Europe – the first being that, with the possible exception of the East Germans, the Russian action in Czechoslovakia came as a complete and highly unwelcome surprise.

Everything in Eastern Europe was based on the assumption that a resort to force by the Soviet Union to impose its will on the satellites was unthinkable. The Russian action, therefore, upset a delicate equilibrium which was beginning to emerge as between the rulers and the ruled and relations between Eastern Europe and the West.

Internally, the promise was of steady liberalisation and externally of winding up the cold war.

Now both these concepts have been put in jeopardy.

The major advantage however is that one important delusion has vanished and that is that *détente* lies through better relations between the super powers. On the contrary it doesn't. The two super powers will pursue their policies of high-level agreement such as, for example, on the non-dissemination of nuclear weapons – but these agreements may only help to freeze the division of Europe and especially the division of Germany.

Only European powers can pursue wholeheartedly the policy of European *détente* and in this field Britain has a special and highly important role.

It is not a question of loosening ties with America but fulfilling a role which because of its super power status the U.S. is unable to fulfil.

The second impression is that everywhere among the satellites the standard of life is higher than in the Soviet Union. This reveals the antiquated quality of Soviet Imperialism which acts as a steady brake on economic progress among Eastern European countries which more and more identify such progress with increasing trade with the West.

The third is quite simply that the human spirit cannot indefinitely accept a tyranny as absolute and self-destructive as the Soviet one. In this case as so often in the past the Soviet incursion into Central Europe is a new incursion of barbarism.

I started with a quotation from General Eisenhower. In case it was thought that these remarks were made at some end-of-war banquet when the General was full of vodka, they do in fact represent the serious thinking of his political master at the time, Franklin D. Roosevelt.

It is now fashionable to deride the view that the Yalta agreements were the source of Europe's present plight. Two contradictory arguments are marshalled to this effect.

The first claims that the Russians broke the Yalta agreements by refusing to hold free elections in the satellite countries and the second that the partitioning of Europe after the war was merely the acceptance of *force majeure*.

Anyone who thought at the time that the Russians would allow free elections was clearly in no mental condition to direct the diplomacy of a great country and as for the second argument it is simply not true.

Czechoslovakia, for example, could have been easily liberated weeks ahead of the Russians if the American Third Army, which was only sixty miles from Prague, had not received orders from Washington to turn back.

Berlin, Friday, October 4, 1968

1969

THE LONG, BITTER RIFT BETWEEN THE GENERAL AND POMPIDOU

There was something almost laconic about the way General de Gaulle threw away power. It was rather like a player throwing away his racquet in disgust after a bad match at tennis. His bad match commenced with events of May–June last year when he muffed every shot and limped towards every stroke – all except the last, which was a smash hit.

This was when he left Paris at the height of the storm, the origins of which baffled and intrigued him to virtually repeat in miniature his famous flight from crumbling France to London in 1940.

Now, as then, like a good general, he was averting being imprisoned by events which he frankly confessed he could not control, to establish a base from which he could defend and finally re-establish a 'legitimacy' which he felt he represented, first against treason from London and now from Alsace-Lorraine if need be against a French relapse into revolutionary anarchy.

This was the sense of that astonishing escapade of his when, keeping his intentions secret even from his Prime Minister, he flew off to see his army chiefs; not to ask them favours but to tell them of his intentions and secure their allegiance.

Then, realising that nothing dramatic had happened in Paris during his absence, that the revolution had, in fact, shot its bolt, he returned to the capital the next day to make his electrifying broadcast announcing that he was staying and that he had ordered a General Election.

This last was a concession wrested from him only minutes before he made his broadcast by his Prime Minister, Monsieur Pompidou. Right up to that minute a quarrel had raged between them and had even reached an acrimonious pitch, with Pompidou insisting on a General Election which he was certain he would win and de Gaulle insisting on a referendum, which Pompidou was certain he would lose.

If de Gaulle had won that struggle, the May revolution would have claimed its victim not yesterday but ten months ago.

Ever since then de Gaulle has been off balance as though a victim of that 'shipwreck' which he called old age.

It is easy to say now that he called yesterday's referendum against the unanimous advice of all his staff and all his ministers in order to prove that he, and not Pompidou, was still the top man in France. There may be something in that; but there are other factors also.

Pompidou was scheduled for dismissal way back in March 1967. He was only saved by the fact that the Gaullists sneaked in by so narrow a majority in the elections of that year that they needed a good parliamentary boss to handle the situation and that, in any case, Couve de Murville, his chosen successor, had been defeated as a parliamentary candidate.

The rift between de Gaulle and Pompidou in fact preceded the events of last May. It was based on what might be called temperamental differences of ideology.

Pompidou is a liberal conservative; de Gaulle sees himself as a revolutionary who, as a nationalist, accomplishes the very reforms the Left has been clamouring for for generations and never been able to achieve.

De Gaulle believes that it is his mission to end the class war of France whereas Pompidou believes that enlightened capitalism has already rendered the very idea of class war an outdated 19th-century concept.

De Gaulle reproached Pompidou's conservatism for the May explosion. As for himself, he claimed not entirely without justice that he had been clamouring for reforms, especially university reforms, to no avail ever since the Presidential election of 1965.

To get de Gaulle in perspective one must recall something of his background. He is a man from Lille whose family were upper middle-class Catholics. The northern French Catholics differed from the southern ones in that they were familiar with the horrors of 19th-century industrialisation and were instinctively drawn to the earliest Christian Socialist movement.

His grandmother was an evangelical propagandist for workers' rights; his father defended Dreyfus against the French

Right. This was the atmosphere in which de Gaulle was brought up. A mixture of Catholicism, patriotism and social uplift.

His pre-war experiences in Paris and later in London developed these two latter aspects of his thinking. Peddling his military ideas in Paris based on the creation of a professional French armoured striking force he met with indifference on the Right, which was already knee-deep in capitulation, and political objections from, for example, Léon Blum, the Socialist head of the pre-war Popular Front government, who told him that though his idea seemed excellent, the Socialists would never support the creation of such an élite military force, in case it would turn against the workers.

Then came de Gaulle's hallucinating arrival in London after the collapse with virtually no one from the higher echelons of politics, army or the civil service to join him.

Two blistering hates which never left him developed as a result – against the political parties which had reduced France to its plight and against the whole French Establishment, the nation's so-called élite.

'The Left is against the nation and the Right is against the Republic,' he reflected sadly at the time.

Some time later, as the liberation of France approached, he noted that his colleagues whilst prattling of revolution were, in fact, preparing to return to the old political ways.

'I reflected then that among all these so-called revolutionaries I was the only serious one.'

His forebodings about the future proved justified.

Against his advice, the nation by referendum adopted a constitution which in effect restored the Third Republic, lodging both legislative and executive power in an all-powerful assembly. Ironically enough in view of the defence of the French Upper House by the French Left in the current referendum, at the time the entire Left clamoured for its abolition.

De Gaulle retired in dignity, referring to himself as 'the sidetracked leader'. He was replaced by someone called Félix Gouin.

What followed was what de Gaulle called 'the regime of parties'. This should be understood in its French context for it means and meant at the time quite literally that party caucuses against even the terms of the constitution could decide on the withdrawal of ministers without the Government even being defeated in the Assembly. What with that and ungovernable

171

assemblies, governments fell with the regularity of a guillotine working overtime.

It is interesting to speculate now on what would or would not have happened if de Gaulle had remained in power. I am convinced, for example, that neither the Indo-Chinese war (which broke out under a Socialist government) nor the Algerian war would have taken place.

Of course there could be no question for him after the war but that of re-establishing French sovereignty over the lost colonies; but once re-established, as his subsequent de-colonisation policy showed, independence within or outside the French union would have been negotiated.

In colonial policy as in foreign policy he zigzagged according to circumstances; but there was never any real deviation from course. As a man he divided his life into two rigid compartments – the de Gaulle of the history books and the family man.

As a political animal he could be both repulsive and fascinating. He had a deep cynicism about men and a deep pessimism about the future, which occasionally swept him away on cataclysmic visions.

His guile was, of course, notorious but – curiously enough – few statesmen have stated their intentions so clearly and followed the course of their ideas so resolutely.

He was no enemy of our country, for which he had a profound admiration and, certainly as far as the United States is concerned, he may have rendered it a greater service by denouncing the folly of the Vietnamese war than any other so-called friends did by condoning it.

In his family life and among close friends, mostly the very large family circle, he was both a gentle father and grandfather who displayed great sweetness of character.

His private life was scarred by the tragedy of his mentally-handicapped daughter, Anne, who died in her twenties and to whom he was devoted.

He consoled Madame de Gaulle at the time of the funeral with the words: 'Now at last she is like other children.'

Memories are short and people forget. It is not fashionable now to recall the Fourth Republic and compare it with the Fifth. Having lived under both I can honestly say that both as a reporter and a resident I felt more free and secure under the Fifth than under the Fourth.

It is not that the men of the Fourth were evil or corrupt or that

the Gaullist Party does not have its fair share of crooks or
adventurers (it might be noted in passing that the most notorious
of them long ago passed into the ranks of the opposition).

The politicians of the Fourth were by an overwhelming majority both honest and patriotic. It is simply that the uncertainties
the system generated and the impotence it imposed upon them
meant inevitably that the scum rose to the top.

I hope history will not repeat itself.

Monday, April 28, 1969

WELL, THE GENERAL WON'T BE BACK
FOR THE BIG DE GAULLE DAY . . .

I understand from sources close to the fairies at the bottom of
General de Gaulle's Irish garden that the General is propos-
ing to delay his return to France by as much as four days after the
second round of voting in the French Presidential elections.

This means that he will deliberately miss an important date
which is the subject of an annual Gaullist commemoration. This
is the anniversary of his famous appeal on June 18, 1940, made
from London to Frenchmen to rally to him and carry on the war
against the Germans.

Instead of being in Paris for that occasion the General will be
in Dublin. He has, in fact, accepted an invitation from President
de Valera to spend the last two days of his Irish holiday as his
guest and the guest of the Irish Republic. As a result he will not
be returning to France until June 19 and will avoid Paris by
landing at the military airport from which he left and driving
straight to his country home.

I must say I would give a lot to be present, with or without a
goblet of Irish coffee in my hand, at the sessions between these
two old men, both scarred by history and national self-
dedication and both the last of their breed of scholar-warrior-
politician.

Meanwhile I learn that the General did, in fact, before leaving
for Ireland write a warm personal letter to Georges Pompidou
wishing him success in his bid for the Presidency.

The letter makes it clear the the General regards Pompidou as the man best fitted to continue his work but as it does not explicitly authorise him to use it in his election campaign and is cast in such personal terms, M. Pompidou considers it would be an act of vulgarity to reveal its contents. As it is, Pompidou's position after the first ballot is so strong that even the temptation to utilise it has been removed.

Thus virtually assured of the Presidency, M. Pompidou can devote some of his time in the ten campaigning days still left to Cabinet making. It is essential from the point of view of national confidence that his new Government should be announced almost immediately after the elections. It is also essential that as the bulk of his support comes from the hard-rock Gaullist vote of forty-four per cent, whatever openings he makes to the Centre should not distort the essential Gaullist character of his Government.

I expect his new Prime Minister to be either M. Jacques Chaban-Delmas, the handsome present Speaker of the French Parliament, a moderate Gaullist with links with other parties, or M. Maurice Schumann, a veteran Gaullist from the London days, with a Left-wing outlook and close associations with the French trade unions.

The Foreign Ministry will be a key post and I expect that to go to a Gaullist despite reports that it has been promised to M. Giscard d'Estaing. M. Debré, the present Foreign Minister, will leave the post but I think his successor may well be the present Prime Minister, M. Couve de Murville.

Couve has no intention of leaving politics to return to his diplomatic career. He would not accept an embassy and nor would he accept anything but a key post in the Government.

Whatever happens he intends to remain fully active in the Gaullist Party.

Friday, June 6, 1969

1969

HOW TO WRITE A BEST-SELLER – FIRST
LIVE A LIFE OF CRIME

An extraordinary literary event has taken place in Paris over
the past few weeks with the publication of the memoirs of a
63-year-old ex-convict, Henri Charrière.

The book's title is *Papillon* (Butterfly), Charrière's nickname
in the Paris underworld in the twenties and, as the name suggests, he was a particularly dextrous and delicate-fingered safe-
breaker.

Published only four weeks ago, it has already sold more than
200,000 copies to a steadily soaring chorus of critical praise. This
week Charrière returned to France for the first time since 1932,
like some 19th-century fictional hero out of Victor Hugo and
Alexandre Dumas who is vindicated after nearly a lifetime of
banishment and exile.

All that is missing from his tale is a shipwreck or two and the
discovery of a treasure trove. This, however, he has found late in
life in Paris.

Coarse-featured, lean, with a copper-plate complexion, he is,
at the moment, dazzling France with his thick, South of France
accent, his racy, period Paris underworld slang, and his tallish
tales of deportation, escape and adventure in Latin America.

The son of a schoolteacher, he was orphaned early and quickly
became a delinquent. He then joined the navy, where he spent
most of his time in disciplinary camps. His first offence, he
claims, was due to his persistent habit of crushing his naval cap
into a special shape so as to give himself a rakish look.

Dishonourably discharged from the navy, he then drifted into
the underworld. Early in his underworld career, he was tempted
to set himself up as a pimp; but, by that time, he had married a
woman of strict moral outlook; and he was forced into a more
'honest' speciality – safe-breaking!

After some years of profitable work as a safe-breaker, he was
arrested, not for safe-breaking but for the murder of a well-
known Montmartre pimp. He denies this charge to this day, and
adds: 'Anyway, what does it matter? It wasn't as though I had
killed the Governor of the Bank of France.'

175

He claims he was framed, explaining: 'I was an easy target for a frame-up, picking the locks, as I did, of two or three safes a year.'

As a result of the murder, he was sentenced to life imprisonment on Reunion Island in the Indian Ocean, Devil's Island having, by that time, shut up shop.

There, he killed another prisoner who, he claims, betrayed his escape plans.

Finally, he did succeed in escaping from Reunion, after serving thirteen years. He was then thirty-six. He took refuge in Venezuela, of which country he is now a citizen; and where he worked in the mines, and for petroleum companies.

Later, he opened a luxurious restaurant in Caracas, which was destroyed by an earthquake. Charrière lost all he had and was covered with debts.

He read, by chance, of the extraordinary success in Paris of books written on her prison experiences by Albertine Sarrazin. He got hold of a copy at the local French Institute and decided he could do better. The result is a solid autobiography of 500 pages.

Comparing best-seller lists in France and Britain and the United States, all one can say is that Charrière's book is a far cry from *Portnoy's Complaint*.

Friday, July 4, 1969

1970

DE GAULLE'S FINAL STRUGGLE . . .

As he approaches his 80th birthday General de Gaulle can have the morose satisfaction that though power has slipped through his fingers the forthcoming publication of his memoirs makes him the hottest literary property in France, not excluding *Papillon*.

This week representatives of the Paris publishing house of Plon journey to the general's country home to collect the typescript of the first volume of his post-war memoirs and to sign a contract for its publication.

In many ways, quite apart from the sales his name ensures, de Gaulle must be any publisher's dream of an author.

The contract was not signed until the MS was delivered, and in his case it is always delivered well ahead of the promised date.

Nor is there any question of a publisher's advance against the work in progress.

The financial arrangements are in fact simplicity itself.

As was the case with his wartime memoirs so with post-war ones. The French royalties will go direct to the general while the foreign ones and all profits from syndication will go to the foundation created by Mme de Gaulle for backward children, in memory of the de Gaulles' daughter Anne who was herself so tragically afflicted.

International bidding for the memoirs has already started with, among others, Macmillans of New York offering 320,000 dollars for the American rights and Lord Thomson 75,000 dollars for serialisation rights of the first volume.

It is now a little more than a year since de Gaulle quit and in that short space of time he has become a legendary figure for the second time in his life.

Curiosity and interest in him in France is so considerable that the sales of books on de Gaulle have actually increased since he left office instead of being relegated to the remainder shelves.

So much so for example that the publication recently of the first two of a five-tome set of de Gaulle's collected messages and speeches, which have the particularly stiff price for France of £3 10s. a volume, have already sold more than 35,000 copies each.

What is rather more poignant, for the man clearly feels he may be working against time, is the ferocious energy de Gaulle has brought to the task of writing these memoirs.

Not only has the first volume been completed months ahead of schedule, but he is now well into the middle of the second volume.

At this rate the trilogy should be completed well within three years. It is, of course, this notion of working against time which has always plagued de Gaulle.

He was brought into the French Government, not only too late to avert disaster, but in the very midst of disaster.

He wasted thirteen of the best years of his life in retirement; in a sense, which he must feel keenly himself, he came back too late and too old. Now, too, with his post-war memoirs, he is working against a deadline which he cannot set himself.

It is this knowledge that death or senility might prevent its completion which gives the first volume an urgency and a breadth which it might not otherwise have had.

Originally, it was intended to deal with the events following his return to power in 1958 to the end of the Algerian war.

But it has grown into a much bulkier volume which constitutes in effect his political testament.

It is more than a recital of events as he saw them; it is de Gaulle's political philosophy and view of the world in its entirety.

Friday, July 10, 1970

DE GAULLE DIES AT SEVENTY-NINE

'France is a widow' says Pompidou

General Charles de Gaulle died last night of a heart attack – seated in an armchair, playing a game of patience and waiting for the television news.

The 79-year-old general, who quit as President of France in April last year, was at his country home, La Boisserie, in Colombey-les-deux-Eglises, 100 miles from Paris.

It was 7.30 p.m. His wife Yvonne was with him. Suddenly he slumped in his chair . . . his face became contorted with pain.

Madame de Gaulle summoned the doctor and the village priest.

This evening the General 'lay in state' in the drawing-room, dressed in the uniform of a two-star Brigadier-General, wearing one decoration – the Order of Liberation – and covered in the Tricolour.

The news of his death, just thirteen days before his eightieth birthday, came as a complete surprise to Paris this morning. It was just after five o'clock that Colombey's mayor passed the news to the French government.

De Gaulle's successor, President Pompidou, called an emergency meeting of the Cabinet and then appeared on television calling on Frenchmen to be worthy of the lessons given by the General. 'De Gaulle is dead,' he declared in a shaky voice, his face strained with emotion. 'France is a widow.'

Then followed another announcement about the funeral which will be on Thursday, private and at Colombey. De Gaulle had already decreed this in a 'last wishes' letter.

The letter, beginning with the words 'General de Gaulle' and dated January 16, 1952, read:

'I wish that my funeral be held at Colombey-les-deux-Eglises. If I die elsewhere, my body should be transported to my home, without the slightest public ceremony.

'My tomb will be there where my daughter Anne already lies, and where, one day, my wife will lie. Inscription: Charles de Gaulle (1890–   ). Nothing else.

'The ceremony will be set forth by my son, my daughter, my son-in-law, my daughter-in-law, aided by my secretariat, in such a way that it should be extremely simple. I do not wish a national funeral. No President, no Ministers, no parliamentary committees, no representatives of government organs.

'Only the French military service may take part officially, as such; but their participation should be of very modest proportions, without bands, fanfare or bugles.

'No speech will be pronounced either at the church or elsewhere. No funeral orations in Parliament. No seats will be reserved at the ceremony, except for my family, for my companions of the Order of Liberation, for the municipal council of Colombey.

'The men and women of France and other countries of the world may, if they wish, do my memory the honour of accompanying my body to its last resting place. But it is in silence that I wish it should be conducted.

'I declare that I refuse in advance any distinction, promotion, honour citation, decoration, whether it be French or foreign. If any such should be awarded me, it would be in violation of my last wishes.'

Village priest Claude Jaugey said today he hurried to a second-floor room and arrived to find the General stretched out on the floor.

He was dressed in a dark suit. 'De Gaulle was not dead,' he said, 'but seemed to be unconscious. He was suffering terribly.

'I gave him the last rites.' Madame de Gaulle, he added, reacted to her husband's death 'with perfect dignity, even nobility'.

Father Jaugey said that about nine o'clock some security guards asked him what was going on.

'They asked if anything was abnormal. I said "No",' the priest added with some hesitation. 'I lied.

I listened to the radio to see if there had been any leaks of the news. There was nothing, and I was pleased,' he said.

The church in the village of Colombey, which is in the Champagne region, is tiny, and will restrict the size of any planned ceremonies.

There are only 140 inhabitants – and yesterday started for them and the General like many they have passed together.

In the afternoon de Gaulle strolled under the tall trees in his garden. Then he went to his study in the tower that he added to his home and started work on his memoirs.

The first volume of *Memoirs of Hope* relating the history of his return to power in 1958 appeared a month ago.

He was half-way through the second volume. When he left his study yesterday afternoon he quietly sat down to play patience and wait for the television news.

Then came the heart attack.

Now his memoirs – the crucial third volume was to detail the events of May 2, 1968, and his subsequent defeat and resignation – will remain an unwritten secret.

Thursday, in France, will be a day of national mourning. Government offices, banks, businesses and schools will be closed.

President Pompidou and the rest of the Government will remain in Paris and attend a religious ceremony at Notre Dame as the Colombey funeral takes place.

There will be one corner of France where the name of de Gaulle will be fondly remembered . . . the home for backward boys and girls at Milton-la-Chappelle, near Paris, which is named after de Gaulle's daughter Anne, who died in 1948, aged twenty.

The Anne de Gaulle Foundation, as it is known, has been receiving the proceeds from the sale of the General's memoirs.

Tuesday, November 10, 1970

IT'S HIS OLD ENEMIES I FEEL SORRY FOR NOW

The tumult and the shouting die, the captains and the kings depart. Now everybody, and especially the French, will have to get used to living without even the shadow of de Gaulle. At this moment my special condolences go out to his enemies. What will they do without him?

For getting on thirty years now he accomplished the political miracle of uniting the French Left and Right in implacable hatred of himself. From his earliest days in London to his last days in Colombey no rumour concerning him was too fictional and no slander too gross for it not to find ready credence in some newspapers and salons in Paris.

His intentions were always questioned, his motives always doubted. The venom which followed him to the grave was so intense that it effectively prevented him from visiting Paris from the day he quit to the day he died.

He could not do so even to visit his publisher or members of his family because his mere appearance in the capital would have discharged a flood of reports that he was 'plotting'.

I recall, for example, with what disbelief amounting almost to hilarity a prediction I made when the General resigned was greeted. This prediction, based on slight knowledge of the man, was that once out of office he would maintain a stony silence and would not seek to interfere in any way in the Government's running of affairs.

I recall the panic that ensued when he left his home to go on an innocent holiday in Ireland. In the intervening hours between his departure from Colombey and the announcement of his arrival in Cork, Paris buzzed with confident predictions that he was mounting a *coup d'état*.

Why he should have run the risk of almost certain defeat in a referendum in order to mount a *coup d'état* was never sufficiently explained.

Thus there came about the bitter paradox of an elder statesman who on the meanest view had rendered some services to his country who was virtually an exile from his own capital. One reason obvious enough why he was detested by so many was that so many thought they could use him for their own purposes.

We thought so in the early stages of the war and came unstuck; the French Communists thought so in the latter stages of the war and after the Liberation but had to grind their teeth in frustration; sections of the French Right and big business placed high hopes in him only to realise that he was not their man; and finally the French army and the Algerian lobby thought they could use him to keep Algeria's part of France and everyone knows how they finished up.

Part of the disappointment engendered in his own friends who later became his enemies was the result of him not deceiving them but of them deceiving themselves.

Take his famous 'I have understood you' speech in Algiers after he returned to power. I heard it at the time and had no doubt as to its meaning. He was determined to set Algeria on the road to independence. I have the text of the speech in front of me as I write.

I find the statement of his intentions as blunt in print as they were in the spoken word. As I said earlier this is the moment to weep for his enemies. Think for example of Paris's famous satirical weekly *Le Canard Enchaîné*. What will it do, poor old thing, without its favourite villain?

I think I am right in saying that de Gaulle died not only a relatively poor man, but a man in very modest circumstances, despite the enormous success of his war memoirs he was, for example, in financial difficulties only a few years before he returned to power.

This suggests that the royalties from the memoirs went not only in part but very largely to finance the foundation for handicapped children in memory of his daughter Anne. He had refused all pension offers from the Government when he first quit in 1945, and a second refusal seemed so certain that no arrangements were made to pay him the pension due to an ex-President of the Republic when he quit last year. All that he accepted was a chauffeur and car plus office space and a small staff in Paris, and, of course, his pension as a retired officer with the rank of Brigadier-General. His domestic staff at Colombey consisted only of a cook, a maid and a part-time gardener.

He bought his property before the war when he was a Colonel intending to retire there when he left the army with no anticipation of a higher rank than the one he held. It is in a part of France where property values have always been low because it lies on the direct German invasion route of France.

De Gaulle's death of course means that his post-war memoirs will remain unfinished. There is, however, one literary consolation to his death. It is that André Malraux, the famous French novelist, former Minister of Culture and de Gaulle's closest friend, has long ago completed a book entitled *Conversations with de Gaulle*.

The book, however, was not to be published in the General's lifetime. Now of course it can go into print immediately and the manuscript is with de Gaulle's publishing house, Plon.

To get the full flavour of de Gaulle's impact on what might be termed 'governing circles' in London during the war I have turned to the diaries of that noted snob and sycophant the late Sir Henry ('Chips') Channon.

I find in his first mention of de Gaulle he refers to him as 'A certain General de la Gaule'. Later when he has learned to spell his name he writes 'Walking in St James after lunch with Sutherland I met de Gaulle strutting along insolently and we crossed over to avoid him. Nobody can stomach de Gaulle. His intolerable swagger and conceit infuriate everyone.'

A few pages later he gives details of a secret session at which Churchill addressed the House. 'Winston told much which surprised the House but which was no news to me. How the French hated de Gaulle and how the Americans refused to have anything to do with the Free French Movement, etc.'

Finally there is this delicious comment which leaves a nice savour on the palate. 'I lunched at the Ritz with Diana Cooper. We then went to a film, *The Liberation of Paris*. It was de Gaulle's great moment and yet somehow I thought he looked and acted absurdly. Diana whispered, "If Winston sees this he will have a stroke".'

Friday, November 13, 1970

1971

THE PRESIDENT IS *NOT* PLEASED
WITH DELON THE PATRIOT

Whatever is one to make of the story of actor Alain Delon and the holy Gaullist relic which he prevented from falling into infidel hands just in the nick of time?

The almost theological rumpus which followed this incident is still raging in Paris, although the outlines of the story are simple and undisputed.

It goes back to August, 1940, when General de Gaulle drew up his historic appeal for members of the French armed forces to join him in London.

It began with the words 'France has lost a battle, it has not lost the war.'

When de Gaulle had finished writing it, a secretary copied it and the original document was left lying about on the table. It was then in a moment of remarkable prevision that the impresario André Bernheim, who was in the room with de Gaulle and others, pocketed it.

He never made any secret about owning the document, and it was one of the showpieces in his Paris home.

It became known recently that M. Bernheim, who is seventy-one, intended selling his Paris house and with it much of his memorabilia. As a result he was visited by a young man with auctioneering connections who began classifying the huge quantity of documents and letters.

It was then that the possibility of selling the de Gaulle document arose – with Bernheim reluctant to do so, but the young man pressing him and suggesting that a discreet sale to a foreign buyer could be arranged.

On leaving Bernheim, the young man reported the news to an

auctioneer who in turn reported it to his friend and client, Alain Delon.

Delon's reaction was instant: this foul plot to sell this document to a foreigner must be foiled.

He then arranged for an Argentine friend to fly to Paris, pose to Bernheim as the agent for a rich Argentine collector and put down the equivalent of nearly £30,000 in cash for the document.

The document and money thereupon changed hands, the full story was revealed by Delon to *Paris Match*, and the document was then transferred with great ceremony to the keeping of de Gaulle's wartime order of the Companions of the Liberation.

A campaign of appalling vilification of M. Bernheim commenced. The unfortunate man, who was in New York when the storm broke, has now written to his friend, Col. Remy, the famous French wartime secret agent, telling him that the money 'was burning his fingers' and asking Remy to donate it to a charity of his choosing.

A man who was less than pleased to learn of Delon's *coup* was the President of the Republic, M. Pompidou. He has never forgiven Delon for the open letter which Delon addressed to him a year ago.

In this letter Delon asked M. Pompidou to call off police who, Delon alleged, were trying to implicate him in the Markovic affair. Delon suggested the police had also tried earlier to implicate M. Pompidou.

This police 'persecution' continues to this day, but it might be difficult to see how a man of such evident exulted patriotism as Delon could possibly have any connection with so sordid an affair.

Friday, January 1, 1971

THE APATHY THAT IS GREECE . . .

Apathy even more resoundingly than order reigns in Athens. To someone like myself, who has not been in Greece since the colonels took over more than four years ago, this apparent docility – or possibly more accurately resignation – comes as something of a shock.

One recalls the general strikes in Athens and Salonika and the massive demonstrations just before the colonels' *coup* and by contrast the Greece of today resembles a nation of sleep-walkers. The surprise is somewhat lessened, however, as one recalls the astonishing ease with which the colonels took over with only one casualty – and he, incidentally, an accidental one.

Nor did anyone move later when King Constantine attempted his counter-*coup*.

The sad fact is that though Melina Mercouri may hurl herself at the barricades in London, Paris and New York, no one is prepared to follow her example in Athens – not at any rate for the sake of the blue eyes of her politician father or those of any other politician, and least of all for those of King Constantine.

Of course there is an underground opposition but it is frag-mented and feeble and that part of it which is serious is almost entirely Communist; and the Communists, for a variety of reasons, are not prepared to show their hand yet.

It is interesting in this connection to note the excellent rela-tions the colonels have established with all the Communist neighbours and the fact that all of them, including the Soviet Union, accredit their ambassadors directly to the Regent and not, as the more squeamish Western countries still do, to the King in exile.

This situation points up a central feature of the colonels' rule which consists of a kind of double blackmail, one internal and the other external. To some of the Greek rich and the sophisti-cated upper middle-class who detest them, the colonels say in effect, 'If you think we are bad wait till you get the captains.'

To the United States they underline the ancient truth that countries which go whoring run the same risk as individuals, namely that of blackmail. This blackmail is now in full swing in Athens; for example, the Athens Press is currently publish-ing verbatim reports of Congressional hearings in Washington on whether the U.S. should continue to supply Greece with arms.

On the face of it this is an astonishing thing to do, for most of the witnesses are Greek emigrés who recount in great detail the iniquities of the regime. The political value of the evidence to the colonels lies, however, in the recurring accusations of U.S. interference in Greek affairs in the past and even to downright affirmations – incidentally false – that the colonels' *coup* was backed by Washington.

The clear implication of the publication of all this evidence is that if there is any more nonsense about stopping arms supplies then the colonels might be tempted to do some bean-spilling themselves, just as the clear implication of the cosy relations with Communist countries is that Greece, too, might be tempted to engage in some fancy footwork in its foreign policy – especially in relation to NATO.

Another beneficial result of this situation as far as the colonels are concerned is that it enables them to pose as the incorruptible defenders of Greek independence, unlike previous governments, which permitted themselves to be cuffed and bullied by Washington.

As from this week it has already become misleading to talk of the colonels. Instead I should speak of the Colonel, who is the Prime Minister, George Papadopoulos, henceforth to be referred to as 'Papa', a man of peasant origin and a native of Crete.

He served much of his time in Greek army intelligence. In a country which lays great store in oratory he is probably the worst public speaker Greek politics have ever produced.

He makes up for it, however, in shrewdness amounting to downright cunning, and great organisational ability. If there was any doubt that he was the boss he dispelled it this week in a Cabinet reshuffle by dispatching the two colonels who helped him seize power to govern distant provinces.

Before doing this, however, he engaged in an elaborate cat-and-mouse game with the so-called liberal opposition composed mainly of former politicians. To them he indicated that he was thinkng of broadening his government to include some of them and without exception they all rose to the bait.

One can hardly blame them. The regime had lasted far longer than any of them had expected and the prospects of both continued unemployment for themslves as well as the effect on the country if it were to be indefinitely deprived of their wise counsel provided the perfect occasion in which self-interest and patriotism could be deemed to coincide.

Having received their eager responses, Papa promptly reshuffled his government without including any of them. This is characteristic of the contempt he shows for the former governing élite of Greece, who are left alone if they keep their noses clean and restrict their activities to café conversations.

At the moment, Papa looks like being in the saddle for a long time. The Greek economy has expanded considerably, which it would probably have done in any case; patronage has been distributed in the classic Greek political fashion and on a liberal scale to his own supporters.

The monarchy is probably doomed and the country seems to be heading irreversibly towards a republic.

This is no bad thing in itself as the Greek monarchy never really took root and was always considered a symbol of foreign interference – in this case British – who of course first invented it and imposed it. Meanwhile pictures of the King and Queen are getting into short supply and it is only in the post offices of the more obscure islands that they are still on full display.

Occasionally, like some mute declaration of political neutrality, their pictures are accompanied by those of Our Lord and Papa himself.

Speaking of islands, I holidayed on the island of Patmos where St John the Evangelist wrote the Apocalypse and which is dominated by the huge grey stone 10th-century monastery bearing his name.

It is rocky, volcanic and bare and nothing much happened to it in the intervening centuries until the arrival there eight years ago of a young Englishman of taste, distinction and wealth – Edgar Millington-Drake.

Better known as Teddy, he bought for only £1,000 a splendid 17th-century house in the shadow of the monastery. Grandson of the first Earl of Inchcape he is also the son of the famous British ambassador to Montevideo who by his energetic diplomatic action at the time forced the German battleship *Graf Spee* to scuttle itself rather than face a hopeless battle against British warships waiting for it at the entrance to the harbour.

He is also a talented painter with a sense of humour which even extends to an amused tolerance when his pictures are hung upside down. Likeable, with a dry wit and urbane manners, he has brought to this rough-hewn island an air of distinction, splendid hospitality and an admirable display of how to live almost luxuriously without ostentation. So much so, that even his English butler merges almost imperceptibly into the Patmian scene.

While in Patmos, incidentally, the American aircraft carrier *Santiago* arrived and carried out a spectacular helicopter operation dropping air-conditioning units for the monastery – badly needed to preserve some of its precious manuscripts dating back to the ninth century.

Athens, Friday, September 3, 1971

1972

THE SECRET SADNESS OF
MAURICE CHEVALIER

Maurice Chevalier had all the world as a friend but lacked friends. As a corollary of this, he loved everybody and nobody. It was this paradoxical condition which he had not noticed for the greater part of his life which cast a kind of miasma of sadness over his last years.

So much so, that it was towards the end of his life that he most wanted to get married.

This is a so-far-undisclosed aspect of his last years. The woman he wanted to marry is a painter, divorced, aged thirty-eight, and with one child. Her name is Jeannine Michels. They met at a cocktail party in Paris twenty years ago, and for the last ten years Chevalier had been pressing her to marry him. The difference in their ages, however, was too great by that time, and his proposals were affectionately but firmly rejected.

Chevalier was always a great womaniser but his relations with women, as indeed with everyone else, were always flawed by his huge ego. It was the ego of the great artist who loved only himself and his public.

Everything else, apart, possibly, from his devotion to his mother, was subordinated to this craving for idolatry.

It is significant, for example, that his great romance with Mistinguett broke up not because one or the other had become bored with the affair, or had an eye on someone else, but over a question of billing. Chevalier wanted his name displayed as big as hers, and when this was refused, he left for London.

This self-centredness clouded his personal relationships even with his closest intimate, the former light-heavyweight champion of the world, Georges Carpentier.

Nothing indicates this better than the extraordinary dedication written on an early volume of his memoirs which Chevalier presented to Carpentier in the thirties. It reads: 'To *our* Georges from *their* Maurice.'

It was this which led a famous French writer to say that Chevalier was worthy of entry into the French Academie, because no writer had ever said more about himself in so few words.

He once made an extraordinarily pathetic confession to me. He said: 'My mother was the great passion of my life – apart from her, I don't think I know what love is.'

Of course, this was only one of the sacrifices he made for his career and his art. No one was such a perfectionist as he, and his whole approach to his work was rather like that of a dedicated athlete. He practised moderation in all things, including sex, and especially drink, which he held in special awe and equated in the light of his father's sad history with failure and poverty.

His ambition never wilted. He took seriously the half-jocular idea that he might become a member of the French Academie and to his last days believed that it would happen.

He also had ambitions to become a kind of French Will Rogers. He was always impressed with Rogers' transformation from a comedian into a home-spun philosopher and columnist. One aspect of Chevalier which was striking and exceptionally appealing was his dignity. It was the dignity mixed with a certain modesty of the craftsman.

Chevalier was so profoundly French that even his high regard for money, rather than alienating him from his countrymen, endeared him to them. Here, it was rightly said, were the peasant roots breaking through the Paris asphalt.

How rich was he? Including his Paris real estate investments and his huge earnings in the United States in the thirties which he left intact he was probably a sterling millionaire six or seven times over.

Of this, so far as it concerns actual money in France, the French State in the absence of a direct heir will collect anything between fifty-five and sixty per cent.

The rest will be divided up between his two nephews, both Paris butchers, his immediate entourage comprising two married families who have lived with him for the past ten years, one occupying itself with his business affairs, the other with his domestic ones, and the teenage son of Madame Michels.

Anything left over will go to various theatrical charities including the maintenance of his villa in Cannes which he donated as a home for old-age actors several years ago.

His U.S. fortune must be considerable and he was lucky in that he became a dollar earner not before the Wall Street crash, but just after. From that time on, after the worst in Wall Street was over, he left his American earnings in the U.S. over a six-year period stretching into the late thirties.

It is, of course, characteristic of him that this huge and complex fortune should be administered not by high-powered international lawyers but by a modest solicitor in the village near Paris in which he lived, Marne-la-Coquette.

One final note on Chevalier – it now sounds unreal to recall that he was refused a visa to the U.S. in 1954 because of his alleged Communist sympathies.

No Communist he, of course, but a man who was subjected to a heavy Communist blackmail after the liberation of France to make the right noises.

Friday, January 7, 1972

CRACK-UP IN DRUG CITY?

Walking down the Canebière, Marseilles' main thorough-fare, has always been for me an exhilarating experience. Not only do the sights and sounds suggest that one is on the threshold of Africa and Asia Minor, but the very smells have a distinctive and almost symbolic quality.

The predominant smell which hits you at every street corner is a combination of drains and saffron, the one reminding you of the famed Marseilles underworld, and the other of an equally famous Marseilles speciality, bouillabaisse.

One tends to forget what an extraordinary mixture of peoples inhabit this city of nearly 1,000,000, and if there is one criticism I have to make of that excellent film *The French Connection* it is that it did not make enough of the cinematic possibilities of Marseilles.

To have done so would have explained a lot about why it is such a citadel of criminality, and why it is today the centre of the drug traffic.

As a racial melting-pot, Marseilles is the nearest thing in Europe to New York. It is at one and the same time the biggest Algerian city outside of Algeria. It is the most important Corsican city in France, more important than Bastia and Ajaccio put together.

It is the biggest centre for those Europeans who fled Algeria after independence. It has an Armenian population, dating back to the First World War, of 25,000. It has a Jewish population of 30,000. It has a black African population touching 100,000, and finally it has big Yugoslav, Spanish and Italian colonies.

Yet on the face of it, Marseilles is a remarkably peaceful place. Muggings are rare, and the visitor can walk abroad at night without being worried about footsteps coming up behind him. Prostitution is rife and open, tolerated by the police as a means of recruiting informers. The place teems with small hotels with names like Comfort and Relax, which suggest neither.

In short Marseilles tends to look like a port city, like so many others, with a dash of Mediterranean ebullience and variety.

This is, of course, deceptive, a tribute not so much to the police as to the well-structured discipline of the Marseilles underworld. It is one major reason why Marseilles has been chosen as the place for transforming opium smuggled from Turkey into heroin, and then smuggling it into the U.S.

Not only were the hoodlums available in Marseilles but so were the highly trained chemists able to produce the raw product into heroin. Oddly and ironically enough, the chemists were recruited originally – before the underworld started – to train for the sweet-smelling perfume industry which flourishes in the South of France. Their skills in the perfume laboratories were ideally suited with a few adjustments to the drug laboratories.

Nobody knows exactly how many heroin laboratories are now functioning in the Marseilles area but the amount seized over the past year and a half (two tons) indicates that until recently ten at least were functioning full time.

This number is now possibly down to six as a result of recent arrests and may even be as low as four. Whatever their number it is clear that they are now working overtime to fulfil orders from their wholesalers in New York in anticipation of a drastic reduction of supplies from Turkey due to the American agreement with Turkey to buy the entire opium crop.

At this moment, therefore, the American and French narcotics agents, who have now worked hand in hand for some time, are facing the exciting prospect of racing against time as the traffickers try to build up their stocks as fast as possible while at the same time trying to find an alternative source of supply to Turkey.

As this race enters into what might well be the final stage it is clear that the advantage is shifting steadily to the police. Word is now out that the Americans are offering 50,000 dollars for information leading to the capture of a fully functioning laboratory. This is still chicken-feed to the profits the trade can bring to an even modest accessory but with the heat on in the way of police harassment a certain temptation presents itself to back out of the whole business.

This is really the beginning of a crack-up in the Marseilles Mafia. Actually there is no such thing as an individually directed Mafia but four and possibly five gangs for whom the profits from the drug trade have been so huge that any rivalries have been set aside.

The profits are of course fabulous. In no other illegal operation can a mere waterfront spiv spin into the millionaire class almost overnight. To give you an idea: 10 kilograms of raw opium fetches 350 dollars (£145) on the Turkish black market. The stuff is then processed in Syria or the Lebanon into one kilo of morphine base fetching 700 dollars (£290).

In Marseilles the same kilo of morphine can be sold for 1,200 dollars (£500). When converted into pure heroin in Marseilles the fetching price is 4,000 dollars (£1,666) a kilo. When it finally reaches New York its price per kilo is between 12,000 to 30,000 dollars (£5,000 to £12,500) depending on the state of the market.

In those circumstances bribes offered to informants are almost derisory.

The most encouraging arrest made in Marseilles recently was that of a veteran Corsican gangster, Jo Cesari, who had trained himself to become a super transformation chemist. His final product was so good that it was bought without question and preferred to other sources of supply by the New York wholesalers.

Cesari had been arrested as long ago as 1965 when he was caught red-handed operating a laboratory in a villa outside Marseilles. His sentence was relatively light – six years – and what with good conduct remission and bad health he was released in 1970. He was given the usual rest period by the underworld of about a year and then was put back to work again.

He was re-arrested a month ago in similar circumstances to those which led to his first arrest but this time he was in no doubt as to what faced him. The minimum sentence he could hope for was twenty years. He preferred to commit suicide in his cell and his body was cremated at Les Baumettes prison while I was there, amid much wailing and weeping from his huge Corsican family.

The Cesari suicide produced all the inevitable doubts as to whether it was actually suicide or whether he was done away with to prevent him talking too much. My own conviction is that he did indeed commit suicide. But whether suicide or not, his death points up the urgent need for the French to change their law in the matter of giving immunity or relative immunity to those arrested in drug cases as against any information they may give.

In Cesari's case, if he had been allowed some hope of a reduced sentence if he turned state's evidence, not only his suicide might have been averted but new trails might have been discovered.

French law, unlike American law on the subject, is adamant that there can be no remission of sentence in exchange for information. In dealing with a traffic as complex and organised as the drug traffic this is surely fatuous and there is every hope that the French will soon change this law.

One cannot visit Marseilles without discovering a feeling of almost awe for the American Narcotics Bureau agents who have been working there for ten years and whose activities naturally expose them to the ever-present danger that they might be found floating face down in the Old Port one of these days.

They operate in the riskiest possible fashion, disguised as hippies, mingling with the underworld and ever-present targets for underworld vengeance. Their major achievement has been after many bitter words to alert the French to a danger which the French themselves were slow in realising.

As for theories about high political protection for the drug traffickers in Marseilles, this strikes me as utter hooey. No politician, not even a Marseilles politician, would dare to get himself involved with anything quite so sinister as the drug traffic.

While the Marseilles underworld flourished on contraband cigarettes or the illicit manufacture of Marseilles' favourite drink, Pastis, there was no reason why there should not be an official nod and wink in exchange for votes produced.

Drugs, however, are different. As an American official in Marseilles told me: 'If we had proof that these people enjoy political protection what do you think we would do with the proof? We would go straight to Pompidou.'

Marseilles, Friday, April 7, 1972

VIETNAM: IF PEACE COMES . . .

Two considerable shadows, both based on unpredictables, are hanging over the latest and probably last phase of the Vietnam peace negotiations in Paris.

The French, who have access to both sides, sum up the unpredictables as follows: the first is the unpredictability of President Nixon's reaction to the prospect of having to eat so many brave words so recently uttered so soon.

The second is whether Hanoi will not be tempted to snatch total victory, which now appears to be within reach, rather than victory on a short instalment plan which any realistic negotiations would undoubtedly offer it.

This would risk, and even positively invite, the Presidential wrath, but how this would reveal itself other than by a gratuitous flattening of Hanoi and Haiphong it is difficult to see.

Sources close to the Americans here, however, hint darkly at the possibility of American marines landing north of the Sixteenth Parallel.

However, those here who know (and there are many) the mentality of the Hanoi leaders claim that they are more likely to go after a direct rather than a deferred victory whether, in fact, serious negotiations begin or not or even under cover of such negotiations.

French experience in Indo-China and elsewhere shows fairly conclusively too that, once serious negotiations begin, there is a panic rush among those who were once either your supporters or neutral to what will be revealed as the victorious side.

In short, it is hard to the point of impossibility to control the dynamic of such negotiations among people who will be living in fear of their lives and properties as a result of its outcome.

In those circumstances, even with the best will in the world in Hanoi to seek a negotiated peace – that is to say ordered victory for itself – the situation may soon arise where there will be no ordered power left in Saigon with which to negotiate.

Add to a disgusted and panic-stricken civil population in Saigon the tens of thousands of deserters from the South Vietnamese Army and you may soon have a situation in the South in which there is nothing left to negotiate about, except the safe evacuation of what remains of the U.S. expeditionary force and the release of American prisoners in Hanoi's hands.

Hopefully, however, Hanoi may be wary of humiliating President Nixon too much and will stop its advance at Hue while a government to its taste is formed in Saigon.

What the French fear most about the outcome whichever way it goes and whatever the degree of humiliation suffered by the U.S. are the effects of this defeat on the relations between the two super powers, not only in the Far East but also in the Middle East and even in Europe.

It is felt that the confrontation between the two will now become a direct one rather than through intermediaries – north and south in Vietnam, Jew and Arab in the Middle East and so on.

It is a sombre prospect as the sombre Vietnam tragedy draws to its close. If Europe's voice had been stronger during that period and if European statesmen had said out loud what they thought privately of the American adventure in Vietnam, the Geneva peace conference on Vietnam might have been reconvened long ago.

Friday, May 5, 1972

1973

SIGNING FOR PEACE

The 30-year-old Vietnamese War drew to its end appropriately enough where it began when all four parties to the war signed a peace agreement in the former Hotel Majestic today.

The four signatories were the Foreign Secretaries of the United States, Hanoi, Saigon and the Provisional Revolutionary Government in South Vietnam – the Vietcong.

The war began effectively when the French tried to re-conquer their former colony towards the end of World War II and continued on an immensely more massive scale than ever when American forces for ten years attempted to avert a Communist take-over of South Vietnam.

Today's peace-signing ceremony in the ornate salon of the Majestic Hotel where formal peace negotiations had been going on for four years was brief, frigid and self-conscious.

There were no handshakes between the representatives of the warring parties and the only gesture which relieved the atmosphere of severity was when all the delegates to the signing stood up when the handsome Madame Binh, Foreign Minister of the Vietcong, entered the salon.

The signing ceremony itself – lasting only a little more than twenty minutes – involved a marathon of signatures involving some 120 accords – most of them bilateral ones between Washington and Hanoi.

The four delegations sat around a circular baize-covered table, floodlit by an immense chandelier. There was an oblong table at the side to accommodate the ambassadors of Canada, Poland, Hungary and Indonesia – all of which countries will be providing the four-nation force to supervise the ceasefire.

The United States was represented by Secretary of State William Rogers; Saigon by its Foreign Minister Tran Van Lam;

Hanoi was represented by the North Vietnamese Foreign Minister Nguyan Duy Trinh.

This afternoon's special session involved only the Americans and the North Vietnamese, who were signing special protocols relating to, among other things, the defusing of U.S. mines in North Vietnamese waters.

A depressing drizzle of rain greeted the delegates when they arrived at the Majestic for the ceremonies. The Avenue Kleber pavements were thronged with Left-wing demonstrators waving Vietcong flags and chanting: 'The Vietcong will conquer!'

On entering the hotel the delegates passed through lines of Republican Guards in full regalia.

The hotel, which was a Nazi headquarters during the war and has been the property of the French Foreign Office ever since, was lavishly decorated with precious tapestries from the State collection for the occasion.

The American delegation was seated first; then came the North Vietnamese, who were seated opposite the Americans; while the Vietcong faced the South Vietnamese.

A complex system was devised for the signing so as to avoid Saigon and the Vietcong coming together officially.

The ceremony today stipulated that the ceasefire in Vietnam will come into force at midnight GMT. It will be followed by a peace conference in one month's time which will be underwritten by Britain, France, China and the Soviet Union.

Neither of the two men who negotiated the settlement – Le Duc Tho or Henry Kissinger – were present at today's ceremonies.

Despite the optimistic statements made on many sides, there is considerable scepticism in Paris as to the durability of the settlement.

Earlier, Mr Rogers called on President Pompidou – largely out of politeness – to thank him for the role that France has played as host to the negotiators; but he also unruffled some ruffled feathers that have been stirred up between Paris and Washington in the course of the last phase of the negotiations.

Many U.S. diplomats have accused the French privately of leaning over backwards in order to favour Hanoi in the negotiations. As a result, there is a distinct possibility that the forthcoming peace conference will be held not in Paris, as the French hoped, but in Vienna.

The South Vietnamese delegation protested later to French authorities against the demonstration which booed its leaders in front of scores of television cameras.

Saturday, January 27, 1973

PABLO'S MYTHICAL MILLIONS

The months following Picasso's death will be filled with legal disputations over the disposal of his fortune and tremors of the world's art markets over the disposal of 1,400 Picassos in his possession when he died.

As to his fortune, I have come to the conclusion that it is more fabled than real. There is certainly no trace of such a fortune in terms of investments and one can only come to the conclusion, after examining such evidence as there is, that Picasso's famed indifference to money was not feigned.

This lack of evidence as to the existence of the vast fortune is not really as surprising as it may seem, for there is an enormous difference in price levels between what Picasso received for his paintings from his dealer and their spiralling costs as they changed hands from buyer to buyer over periods sometimes as long as fifty years, or even more.

It is this which amateur assessors of his fortune tend to overlook when they make him a millionaire ten, fifteen, or even twenty times over.

The people who made the big money out of Picassos were not Picasso himself or even his dealer but they were shrewd collectors and in later years shrewd art speculators or millionaire investors.

Ironically enough, a great deal of Picasso's personal fortune was spent throughout his life in buying back Picassos at prices several times the amount for which he originally sold them.

For virtually his entire productive life and over a period covering 64 years his dealer was Daniel Kahnweiller, who is still alive and whose business interests have passed in recent years to his sister-in-law who owns the Leiris Galleries.

This Picasso–Kahnweiller connection survived every vicissitude and is a remarkable tribute to the loyalty and trust each man placed in the other.

One such vicissitude came with the outbreak of the First World War when Kahnweiller, a German, was interned and his entire collection including dozens of Picassos was auctioned and sold for knocked-down prices by the Custodian of Enemy Property.

Not even Kahnweiller's internment, however, induced Picasso to switch dealers.

At the moment, however, what is agitating the art market is the possibility that in order to meet heavy death duties the Picasso family will be forced to throw some of Picasso's Picassos on to the market.

In that case of course a sharp fall in Picasso prices can be anticipated. However, I think that the French Government has a trump card to play here.

It can absolve the family from death duties in exchange for its agreement to allow most if not all of the Picassos to remain in France and be housed in a special Picasso museum.

Such an agreement is already foreshadowed in the French Government's consent to Picasso being buried in the private grounds of his 16th-century Château de Vauvenargues, near Aix-en-Provence.

The château itself would make a magnificent setting for such a museum and any surplus could be distributed among French national art galleries which are notoriously poor in Picassos.

Such a solution is clearly facilitated by the fact that Picasso died intestate; and as for his great masterpiece, Guernica, as well as other paintings with a strong Spanish connection, they could go to Spain – in accordance with his known wishes – after Franco's death.

Such a solution would be both wise and just. For, after all, if it was France's privilege to harbour Picasso, it was also Picasso's privilege to live there.

He never showed the slightest inclination to live anywhere else than France. Apart from one absurd incident over his wartime Paris studio, which the Government allowed to be sold, every conceivable consideration was given to him.

Apart from a sense of personal loss that I feel at the death of Picasso – he was after all my second favourite subject after de Gaulle – I can't help feeling attached to the memory of a few brief meetings I had with him.

The first was in 1956 when he was celebrating his seventy-fifth birthday and I arrived on the scene bearing an unlikely gift for him from a former mistress.

She was Dora Maar who lived with him during the thirties.

Mlle Maar, who is still alive, is a fervent Catholic and the present she sent this gnarled old atheist was a devotional book by a Dominican priest.

I had a moment of apprehension on delivering it, feeling that Picasso might receive it with a touch of facetiousness.

Not a bit of it. His eyes positively gleamed with pleasure as he handled this paperback book.

Another woman in Picasso's life was Françoise Gilot, mother of two of his children, and a talented painter in her own right.

There was respect but no idolatory in her attitude to him. I remember one of her remarks about Picasso which struck me as being profoundly true. She said: 'That man has too much of everything. He is more than a painter, he is extremely clever. He can open people like a box. He loves laying traps for them. He adores the game of life.'

I remember, too, her remarks to me about Picasso's attitude to money. 'He knows the price of a packet of cigarettes and after that he thinks in millions. Anything in between he finds very expensive.'

It was she, too, who made a searching analysis of Picasso's Communism. 'Picasso is a Communist,' she said, 'only because the Communists seem to him to be the most uncompromising enemies of Franco.'

Friday, April 13, 1973

1974

VICTORIOUS GISCARD PLANS
CABINET SURPRISES

Conservative France has had the fright of its life as a result of yesterday's presidential elections. It now remains to be seen whether it will profit from it.

The margin by which M. Giscard d'Estaing won from the combined Left was only 400,000 and the Left rolled up its highest vote ever. Fortunately Giscard is young enough and intelligent enough and sufficiently aware of the country's social problems to embark on a programme of major reforms.

Of course the Left enjoyed considerable and almost unprecedented advantages in this campaign. It was asserting itself after sixteen years of uninterrupted Gaullist rule and a desire for change was almost overwhelming. The combined forces opposing the Left were in disarray and deeply divided.

Furthermore Giscard as Finance Minister for the past six years could be plausibly blamed for the country's problems with inflation and rising prices. Finally the Left, including Communists, was united as never before and could count on a range of votes spanning discontented Gaullists to Trotskyists and Maoists.

A great deal now depends on how Giscard goes about his task in the next few days and weeks. There is for example the composition of the new Government that he will form and the electoral promises which he will have to carry out in the immediate future to head off the threat of industrial unrest.

No one knows who his new Prime Minister will be, but it will certainly not be someone chosen from within the ranks of his own party, the Republican Independence.

It may well be a Gaullist like M. Olivier Guichard, Minister

for Equipment in the outgoing Government and former ADC to General de Gaulle.

This would help Giscard to make his peace with the Gaullists who are still bruised by the defeat of their candidate in the first round of the elections.

Observers here, however, consider that Giscard's choice of Prime Minister as well as of the Cabinet will contain surprises. It is conceivable and some consider it even likely that he will appoint a high civil servant of distinguished record and Left-wing views to the Prime Ministership.

There is also the question of who the new Foreign Minister may be. Here Giscard is walking a tightrope and it may well be that in the interests of both continuity and peace with his Gaullist allies he will hold on to M. Jobert for the post.

There is also the possibility that Giscard will make overtures to certain Socialists to join the Government. In any case, the tone of his victory message with his lavish praise of his Socialist Communist-backed opponent, M. Mitterrand, hailing him as a statesman and as a man with a role to play in France's future, not only struck a new note in French political history, but indicated the efforts he will try to make to try and detach the Socialist Party from its Communist allies.

In short, appeasement of the Left will be the key note of his policy in the next few weeks. This will involve the almost immediate granting of an increase in old-age pensions and an increase in the basic wage. He is also committed to reducing the minimum voting age from twenty-one to nineteen. This is a dangerous gambit for if the voting age had been nineteen in the present elections, the Left would have won comfortably.

On paper, however, the prospects for the Left look gloomy. Once again they have failed to make it and once again the chief cause of the failure was the alliance with the Communists.

The only Communist reflex still operates in France. Now this alliance as well as the rejuvenation that M. Mitterrand has carried out of the once moribund French Socialist Party is put at risk by the talents, skills and youth of the new President of the Republic.

At forty-nine, Giscard can look forward if all goes well to an uninterrupted seven-year term and then stand for re-election with all the advantages that an incumbent holds in such a situation. In other words, there is a distinct possibility that the

French have elected a President not for seven years but for fourteen.

This makes the Left's defeat even more serious than the results show. They fought this election in exceptionally favourable circumstances and under an exceptionally gifted leader. M. Mitterrand, however, is fifty-eight and there is the problem of whether he will be able to maintain his control of his own party and his own political prospects into the early Eighties.

One problem which Giscard will not have to face and which Mitterrand would have been confronted with is relations with the existing Parliament. Mitterrand would have had to dissolve it, while Giscard can work perfectly well with the present assembly.

No less than 300 of the present MPs supported him during his current election campaign. He therefore has a clear majority in the present House which includes 181 Gaullists.

The Gaullists are divided as to what attitude they should adopt to the new President with most urging support and participation in his new government while a considerable minority would prefer to support the Government but not participate in it.

The rapid progress France has made in the past fifteen years produced their own special social tensions and these were reflected in yesterday's vote.

The industrial working class and the new managerial class want and are determined to get a bigger slice of the cake that France's industrial growth has produced.

The Interior Ministry today announced near-final returns in the French Presidential Election. With 26,400,000 votes counted, standings were: Valéry Giscard d'Estaing, 13,214,000, 50.7 per cent; François Mitterrand, 12,842,000, 49.3 per cent.

Monday, May 20, 1974

1975

BACK IN THE FAMILY – AMAZING
JIMMY GOLDSMITH

With a single financial operation executed in Paris this week Mr Jimmy Goldsmith has finally been admitted as a full member of what might be described as the great Jewish banking aristocracy. The achievement is not without its ironies as well as having about it a certain historical logic.

What Mr Goldsmith has done is to secure a seven per cent holding in the Rothschild bank in Paris and a seat on its board. He has achieved this by selling the Rothschilds his seventy per cent share in the Paris Discount Bank, a deal which among other advantages has netted him a cool £4½ million profit.

With his entry onto the board of the French Rothschilds, however, Mr Goldsmith also achieves entry into a family circle composed of cousins who between them control the three major investment banks in Western Europe.

They are, apart from the Rothschild bank in Paris, the Lambert Bank in Brussels and the Oppenheim Bank in Cologne.

Goldsmith, too, is a cousin of all three but up to recently he has been a distant cousin both literally and metaphorically whom the other three have held at something like a wary arm's length.

This is not the first time, incidentally, that the Rothschilds have had to flex a knee-joint to the family upstart. They had to do so two years ago when in order to raise cash they were forced to sell Goldsmith their holdings in his French food company.

Goldsmith's astonishing financial rise has never been due to any financial help from his famous cousins. In fact, the only money he has ever received from a Rothschild was a little-known bequest from his godfather the English James de Rothschild.

It was for £5,000, the rest – £1 million – after death duties went to charity.

Sam White's Paris

For Goldsmith, what has happened now must be an occasion to savour with a not-so-secret smile. His own family relationship with the Rothschilds began and ended with the early beginnings of the Rothschild financial dynasty. In the very early beginnings of the Rothschild Bank one of Goldsmith's ancestors acted as Paris agent for the Rothschilds in Frankfurt.

At the time the Goldsmiths bore a double-barrelled name – Goldsmith-Rothschild. After that they became the poor cousins completely out of the Rothschild fold. Now, several generations later, a Goldsmith is well and truly back inside it.

For Goldsmith to be on the board of the Rothschild Bank is, I imagine, for him, with his strong sense of family history, more a revival of the family fortunes than a novelty.

This, I feel sure, he feels is as it should be and as it should have been a long time ago. Meanwhile fortune continues to smile on Goldsmith and in more ways than one.

Recently he was presented with a son who will rejoice in the splendid Old Testament name of Zacharias.

Politically, however, he had a disappointment with the downfall of Edward Heath. It is little known that the two men greatly esteemed each other, so much so that Goldsmith had become in recent years a respected adviser on European affairs to the Tory Shadow Cabinet.

Had Heath remained leader of the Tory Party it is not inconceivable that Goldsmith might have been tempted to undertake a political career in Britain. I do not see him, however, getting on so well with Mrs Thatcher. Goldsmith is something of a misogynist with strong views on a woman's place.

Friday, February 14, 1975

SAY 'NON' AND YOUR FRENCH
WILL BE PERFECT!

There is a growing feeling in European capitals and especially in Paris that it may be no bad thing if Britain votes 'No' in the coming referendum on the Common Market. This is a feeling that is growing in business and industrial circles, among politicians and even within the Common Market bureaucracy in Brussels.

So far it has found little or no expression but it is the secret hope of many – and again especially in Paris – that the British will apply de Gaulle's original veto boomerang-fashion on themselves.

This hope is based on two factors – first, a highly unflattering view of Britain's economic prospects and, secondly, deep suspicion of Britain's political motives in seeking to stay in the Community.

The two combined add up to a view that is the reverse of British anti-Marketeers. As one commentator put it recently: 'The real case for Britain leaving the Common Market is not what it would do for Britain but what it would do for the Common Market.'

The result is that there is a growing hope that Britain itself will solve the problem by voting 'No' and growing apprehension among hitherto stalwart supporters of British entry as to what will happen is she votes 'Yes'.

Even among the most optimistic the view is taken that if Britain's marriage to Europe is sanctified by the referendum it promises to be a very stormy marriage indeed. Quite apart from the fact that Mr Wilson has already stamped on the idea of Europe moving towards financial or political union, no matter how tentatively, more immediate problems are posed by his determination to keep one foot firmly in the Atlantic camp.

Thus, for example, on the issue of energy talks with the producer countries, Britain has lined up with Washington and not with the rest of the Common Market.

It is not surprising, therefore, that the late President Pompidou's warning made at the very last Cabinet meeting over which he presided almost exactly a year ago is being recalled here. In it, he said: 'The arrival of a Labour Government in Britain will bring about a profound change in the British attitude to the Common Market. We will find a Britain which will seek to be both inside and outside the Common Market at the same time and our relations will become difficult as a result.'

It is not surprising, however, that the old Trojan horse theory is being wheeled out again, this time by no less a figure than France's leading political pundit Professor Raymond Aron.

According to this theory Britain will enter the Common Market simply in order to wreck it. All this is fairly hilarious because it suggests that British opponents of membership of the Common Market are being naive and are misreading Mr Wilson's real motives.

Even more hilarious is to reread now the text of General de Gaulle's famous Press conference in which he spelt out his reasons for vetoing Britain's entry. All the reasons he gave are precisely those now being used by British anti-Marketeers and indeed the whole speech might have been written for him by Mr Douglas Jay.

I throw it out as a suggestion that it might be a good idea for the 'Keep Britain Out' movement to distribute de Gaulle's speech, for it states the British anti-Market case more effectively than any other I have yet seen.

I do not wish to strengthen the prospects of a 'Yes' victory in the June referendum by suggesting that an audible sigh of relief will go up in France if Britain votes 'No'. What I say is that it will not be all tears and gnashing of teeth if this should happen.

And if by any chance it does I hope that the anti-Marketeers will have the decency to propose that a statue to de Gaulle be erected at some suitable site – say the entrance to Dover Harbour.

Friday, April 4, 1975

THE CURIOUS DEATH OF CARDINAL DANIELOU

He died in a call girl's flat – and now the official record is revealed

With two of its most notable ecclesiastics found dead in circumstances which suggested that they frequent prostitutes, the Roman Catholic Church in France and the Catholic faithful in general have had more than their fair share of troubles and troubled emotions over the past six months.

Now comes a book by one of France's most prominent political commentators, Raymond Tournoux, which sets out among other revelations the exact circumstances of the death of the most prominent of the two churchmen, 69-year-old Cardinal Jean Danielou (the other dignitary was Monseigneur Tort, Archbishop of Montauban, and both men died of heart attacks on premises occupied by prostitutes).

M. Tournoux is a long-established master of the art of instant history and, as in so many other cases which he has handled with scrupulous skill, his account of the death of the Cardinal is related with a minimum of sensationalism and a maximum reliance on the texts of official documents.

In this case the documents are the dry, routine police reports of what the police found when they were called by a Madame Santoni to her three-roomed flat near the Etoile to find the Cardinal dead and the measures they took to inform the Church authorities and to remove the body.

At the time when the news of the circumstances of the Cardinal's death leaked out the Church authorities took great pains to dream up a version of his death: he was said to have a parish priest's sense of mission regarding proselytising among the most hardened of sinners and it was also said that the Cardinal carried on him a large sum of money indicating that he may have been trying to buy off a blackmailer on somebody else's behalf.

This was a mistake that the Church was not to repeat in the case of Archbishop Tort six months later.

As for Madame Santoni her identity was quickly established through police records. She was a procuress and her husband was in prison on a charge of living off her immoral earnings. Then came, in Tournoux's account, the police reports which he gives in full and which are couched in the usual police evidence style. Each report is signed by the relevant police officer or officers.

From the first police report, giving the identity of the dead man and stating that the Archibishop of Paris, Cardinal Marty, had been informed, the drama builds up in to an extraordinary stage set.

At the centre of the scene in the small flat's dining-room is the massive body of the Cardinal lying on the floor between the settee and the table, wearing grey trousers, blue jacket and a white shirt open at the neck. On the table is a black raincoat, a beret, a pair of glasses and a briefcase. Madame Santoni explains the background: the Cardinal's last visit to her was three months

213

ago and he telephoned her that afternoon telling her that he was on his way to see her. The flat is a fourth floor walk-up and the Cardinal arrived breathless and shortly after collapsed.

Within an hour of the police informing the Church authorities of the Cardinal's death the minute sitting-room of Madame Santoni's flat began to fill up with Church dignitaries until it looked almost like an annexe of the Vatican. Among them the police report noted 'was a priest who was obviously not French.'

The police report then goes on to note that yet another person entered the thronged room. It was a woman and the report notes that 'she is well known to the police of the 17th Arrondissement as a prostitute having the Avenue Carnot as her beat.'

So there is the scene – cardinals, bishops, archbishops, two prostitutes and the police busily taking evidence. Of course the first duty of the 'priest who was obviously not French' after leaving the scene must have been to report his first impressions to the Pope. This not even the enterprising Tournoux has been able to get his hands on.

All further investigations into the circumstances of the Cardinal's death were from then on stopped in their tracks on Government orders. As for Madame Santoni, she has disappeared.

All we know for certain was that the Cardinal was in the habit of visiting her and that he died on her premises. The Cardinal was France's leading Jesuit and politically a man of the Right. He had many enemies in the Church, especially among the Left-inclined Dominicans. Tournoux claims that the Dominicans have long known that the Cardinal's name figured on a police list as a frequenter of call girls.

Friday, April 18, 1975

WHY BARDOT SLEPT ALONE ON HER WEDDING NIGHT

Such has been the pace of the revolution in morals and manners in recent years that the memoirs of so young a man as Roger Vadim published here this week already have about them the sepia-tinted quality of a Victorian portrait album.

Vadim, now forty-seven, is of course chiefly famous as the discoverer (some would say the creator) of Brigitte Bardot and in the process of making her a star, he also married her.

The story of this courtship, both professional and amorous, is the highlight of a book which covers also his two other marriages (Catherine Deneuve and Jane Fonda) and his career as film-maker.

The story is told with wit and charm as anyone who knows Vadim would expect, and the sub-title, 'Memoirs of the Devil', recalls Vadim's reputation in the Fifties as a shameless exploiter of sex in his films. All this makes one smile a little when one realises that all the scenes in such films as *And Woman Was Created*, which worried censors at the time so much, would now pass either unnoticed or be the cause of considerable hilarity.

Contrary to the legend, it was not Vadim who 'discovered' Bardot, but a friend who spotted her and snapped her in the street and sold a photograph to a woman's magazine which published it with a caption indicating that she typified the teenage French girl of the time.

It is interesting to note that at the same time Britain was displaying an interest in Diana Dors, and I will refrain from making comparisons in the matter. Bardot was sixteen at the time and living in middle-class splendour with her businessman father, her mother and sister in the genteel Paris suburb of Passy.

The approach to give Bardot some screen tests was made through her parents, and they agreed, although off the set their relations were strictly chaperoned by either one or both the parents, or when they were away by a grandmother or by Brigitte's sister – the role incidentally which filled her with resentment not only at the time but in later years.

This apparently strict supervision was easily circumvented and Bardot and Vadim became lovers. On those occasions her father used to wait for her impatiently on the terrace of the Bardot flat awaiting her return from school or her ballet class, and was always relieved to find that she came home unaccompanied.

Vadim was welcome in the family's home, although M. Bardot disapproved both of his apparent Bohemianism and, even more, of his apparent lack of money.

At the time, she appeared to Vadim, who was seven years older, as an adolescent well in advance of her years. It was only later that he discovered that he had a child on his hands. It was in

most ways an enchanting child, but in other ways a self-centred
and cruel one. He considers that the years have not changed her
and that she remains essentially a child.

'She is forty now,' he writes, 'and she still has not put her nose
outside the artificial world of a child, a world which obeys her
whims and of which she is the centre.'

He adds this cruel comment: 'Viewed from this angle, much
about her is explained – her fears of having children and the total
lack of maternal instinct, for example.' He describes their marriage and their hilariously funny wedding night. After their civil
marriage they returned to the Bardot home for the night only to
be told by M. Bardot that a camp bed had been set aside for
Vadim in the sitting-room and that he would not be able to sleep
with his daughter until after the wedding in church the following
day.

Brigitte threw a tremendous scene, but her father remained
adamant. Bardot, according to Vadim, saw marriage as a kind of
splendid cake labelled 'Happiness' which one could eat day and
night, winter and summer, awake or asleep.

He realised that before long her childish illusions about
'happiness' would lead her to blame him for any shortcomings in
her envisaged state of permanent bliss.

The end came quickly in the course of making her first main
film and meeting her first leading man.

Friday, May 16, 1975

ENTER THE INVISIBLE MEN – OFFICIAL!

The list is short but it is too long and it is discreditable. It is the
list of crimes which have never come to court because of the
political pressure on the judiciary. The most notable example of
course is the Markovic affair.

It is now seven years since film star Alain Delon's Yugoslav
bodyguard Stefan Markovic was found murdered and four years
since the ex-gangster François Marcantoni was charged with
being an accomplice in the murder. The charge still stands but
Marcantoni remains free technically on bail – in short he remains

in a kind of judicial limbo, neither guilty nor innocent but simply untried.

In those circumstances it is becoming increasingly difficult to believe that lack of evidence rather than fear of evidence involving prominent people is the major reason why Marcantoni has not yet been brought to trial.

Now comes the hearing before the Paris appeals court tomorrow on an issue connected with another almost equally notorious case which should provide the French judiciary with an excellent opportunity for a ringing declaration of its independence from the State.

The case, now ready nearly eighteen months old, concerns the break-in by Secret Service agents at the premises of the Paris satirical weekly *Le Canard Enchaîné* and the attempt to instal in its offices highly sophisticated bugging devices. The men were interrupted in their work by a member of the staff who happened to be passing by and was intrigued to see the lights on so late at night.

The case, needless to say, became instantly a kind of minor French Watergate. Since then many of the agents have been identified by various witnesses, including the caretaker of the building, and some have been photographed and named in several journals.

The examining magistrate investigating the case, M. Bernard, has been fruitlessly trying to have them appear before him and to submit to identification parades. Now, after a year of stalling both by the Ministry of the Interior and the Ministry of Justice, a Paris court will decide whether the Secret Service men can or cannot be cited as witnesses in a case involving criminal charges.

Up to now the Government's case for refusing permission for the men to appear before M. Bernard is that they are counter-espionage agents whose physiognomy constitutes a national defence secret. Exaggerating? Not a bit of it – this is textually what the responsible Ministers have been saying in their occasional communiqúes on the matter.

Thus, as one commentator puts it, they are in effect invisible men and as such cannot or should not be seen. This rules out any possibility of them appearing before the examining magistrate and therefore any possibility of charges being brought against them. Furthermore, this view rules out even the possibility of an administrative inquiry into the case for even that would involve a confrontation with witnesses. Secret Service men are therefore, according to the official view, not only invisible but also untouchable and thereby by definition above the law.

It is of course a dangerous view which can lead from minor Watergates to major ones. It is now up to the appeals court to decide whether the law is a mere extension of Government power or whether it exists independently of it.

Meanwhile, what has happened to the Secret Service men involved in the Canard 'plumbing' operation? Altogether they number eleven and all of them have been widely dispersed in far-flung outposts of what is left of the French Empire, including such hell-holes as Djibouti in the Red Sea.

I imagine that those who once sported beards or moustaches have now shaved them off and those who didn't have grown them since.

Of course we manage these matters better in Britain, what with the Official Secrets Act and the stonewalling Ministerial answers: 'It would not be in the public interest to disclose . . .'

Friday, May 30, 1975

DELON IS HOPPING MAD – BUT WHY?

For the umpteenth time in recent years film star Alain Delon has uttered a lionesque roar of rage claiming once again that he is the victim of an organised plot to destroy him morally and professionally and once again he warns his tormentors that he is ready to fight back by every available means.

What is making him so mad? It is the seemingly age-old mystery of who killed his one-time bodyguard, the Yugoslav Stefan Markovic, whose body, dumped on a rubbish dump near Paris, was found in October 1968.

Arrested shortly after and charged with being an accomplice in the murder was a former gangster and friend of Delon, François Marcantoni. The charge still stands and Marcantoni, who has been free on bail for the past six years, has still not been brought to trial.

Obviously this is a situation which cannot continue indefinitely and this week it emerged that there were two conflicting views in the French judiciary as to whether he should be tried or the charges against him dropped. One is the view of the examining magistrate in the case, M. Jean Ferré, who wants the trial to proceed, and the other is that of the public prosecutor, Maître Pierre Bezio, who thinks the evidence insufficient and recommends that the charge against Marcantoni should be dropped.

A judicial tribunal will shortly decide on the issue. The Markovic affair has of course been political dynamite ever since the names of M. and Mme Pompidou – he was at the time the potential successor to General de Gaulle as President of the Republic – slipped into the dossier as alleged friends of Delon and his ex-wife Natalie.

It remains political dynamite of an even more dangerous kind because in the intervening years Marcantoni switched lawyers and replaced an apolitical lawyer with a highly politically orientated one whose very name invokes controversy. He is Maître Jacques Isorni, the famous defender of Pétain who has been at war with the regime ever since.

Isorni makes no bones about his line of defence. He has told me and he has told others that he will involve the Pompidous and other prominent figures in allegations of promiscuity with film stars. The fact that he is possibly talking rubbish does not alter the certainty that it is rubbish which will get headline treatment if repeated in a court of law.

The way French trials are conducted he does not have to produce evidence or show that it is relevant to his client's defence – he merely has to allege it.

We now have to return after this necessary detour to the recurring rages of Alain Delon. I must say I find the reasons for his latest outburst a little hard to understand. It is provoked by a leak of a summary of the report by a public prosecutor giving his reasons why he thinks the charges against Marcantoni should be dropped.

Maître Bezio argues cogently that not only is the material evidence against Marcantoni insufficient but the motives for the killing alleged against the accused seem to him to be highly implausible.

The most persistent theory as to the motive is that Marcantoni acted to protect Delon against blackmail. However, as Maître Bezio points out, Delon is virtually immune to blackmail. This he points out is because he has been astonishingly frank both about his past and about his present. He has never hidden, for example, that he has bisexual tastes.

Some readers may recall the remarkable interview he once gave on BBC television to a French journalist in which he spoke in an uninhibited fashion about his private life and morals. Maître Bezio therefore pours ridicule on the suggestion that photos in Marcantoni's possession could have tempted him to blackmail Delon.

He concludes that without the motive of removing a blackmailer Marcantoni could not have had motive for murdering Markovic. In short, in clearing Marcantoni the public prosecutor indirectly clears Delon of any complicity in the affair.

Friday, September 12, 1975

1976

GOLDSMITH: THE TWO-FAMILY FAMILY MAN . . .

Lucky Jimmy! I refer to Jimmy Goldsmith for whom the strains of big business are adequately compensated for by harmonious family life in Paris and London.

As is by now generally known, Goldsmith maintains two separate homes and two distinct families, one in each city, and both appear to be a considerable solace to him.

As far as I know, the two women concerned are content with the situation as it exists. The two women are his French wife Ginette, the mother of two of his children – a boy and a girl – and Lady Annabel Birley, recently divorced from her husband Mark Birley and sister of the Marquess of Londonderry.

She is also the mother of two Goldsmith children, again a boy and a girl. It is a remarkable situation made even more so because there is no attempt at concealment (no 'Tycoon's Secret Love-nest Uncovered' situation here) and again, as far as I know, no question of divorce.

Goldsmith himself is known to be resolutely opposed to divorce – it would constitute the break-up of a marriage which has lasted more than twenty years – and as neither Mrs Goldsmith nor Lady Annabel appear likely to press him to do so, it now looks as though the present situation will continue for the lifetime of all concerned.

Roughly speaking, of the twenty years Goldsmith has been married to Ginette he has shared ten with Lady Annabel. The normal pattern of his life is that weekends are spent with his family in Paris in their Left Bank mansion which was once the property of Cole Porter, and weekdays are spent with Lady Annabel with her children from her first marriage and those from Goldsmith.

The two women have never met since this dual relationship was established but strong links have been forged between the children of the two families. Thus, for example, the eldest son from his marriage, Zacharias, now sixteen, is godfather to Lady Annabel's youngest son, Manes, aged two.

Similarly Isobel, who is the daughter of Goldsmith's brief and tragic marriage to the late Isobel Patino – she died after delivering her daughter – is godmother to Lady Annabel's youngest daughter Jemina (the Old Testament names are incidentally an indication of the pride Goldsmith, who is himself only half Jewish, takes in his Jewish antecedents).

An odd feature about this odd set-up is the change it has worked in Goldsmith himself.

From being very much a ladies' man he has become a steadfast family man albeit a two-family man.

An interesting question is how all this may affect his future. He is only forty-two and he has ambitions of a kind that can only find fulfilment in politics.

Is British political life yet ready to accept a man who finds himself in this curious matrimonial situation?

This dualism in Goldsmith's private life runs like a thread through his history. He has both British and French nationality and, though his father was a distinguished English Jew, his mother comes from Catholic peasant stock from the Auvergne in Central France. His father, though related to the great banking families of Europe, had little personal wealth and Goldsmith grew up considered rich by some and poor by his relatives.

Similarly, there could be no greater contrast than that between his two marriages – his first to a Patino heiress (he renounced incidentally all financial benefits from this connection) and his second and present one to his former secretary, the daughter of an employee on the Paris Metro.

The contrast is equally striking between Ginette's family background and that of Lady Annabel. I should think that if there is any renunciation to be done, in furtherance of a possible political career, Goldsmith is much more likely to renounce his French passport than to renounce his wife.

Friday, January 30, 1976

TWENTY-SEVEN YEARS OF YOUNG JIMMY

Not to put too fine a point on it, Jimmy Goldsmith, the prospective peer, is not everybody's cup of Bovril, a beverage which incidentally when he bought it transformed him from a still somewhat flimsy City figure into a man of solid worth.

One reason why he is not universally popular is that he still has something of the bumptious undergraduate about him. To someone like myself, who has known him well for twenty-seven years, what is so striking about him is not how much he has changed over this period, but how little.

Under the now balding head and stooped shoulders, there still lurks – and all too often breaks out – the brash youth I knew at the age of twenty.

His tastes remain the same, his most intimate friends are the same, the schoolboy mischief still sparkles occasionally in his eyes and the machine-gun-like monologues which sometimes sound like rapped-out commands, remain unchanged. He still drinks as little as he did as a young man and he still wolfs his food. He still bounds up and down from his chair in conversation and he still chews his handkerchief in moments of high excitement.

The only changes that old friends can detect in him are that he now no longer comes home at dawn and that he reaches compulsively for someone else's cigarettes while never carrying any himself.

An important key to his character lies, I think, in the situation the Goldsmith family found themselves in after the War. After Goldsmith had left Eton following his now legendary £8,000 racing treble *coup* and had completed his military service in the British army, he returned to the family home at the Scribe Hotel in Paris to find the family fortunes sadly depleted.

His early life had been spent in luxury but he now found that although his family was related to the great banking families of Europe, like the Rothschilds, the Oppenheims and Lamberts, he was very much a poor relation.

His father Major Frank Goldsmith was by no means a rich

223

man and there were no prospects for the young Jimmy of a significant inheritance. Such money as his father left went wholly to his mother and he probably had to borrow from her and his elder brother Terry, now a well-known ecologist, to get him out of some early financial jams.

It should be noted at this stage that having earlier achieved notoriety as a profligate gambler and seemingly worthless playboy, traditional paths of progress through his family's banking connections were barred to him. The Rothschilds, of whose bank he is now a director, would not hear of him.

There is of course the legend that he benefited through his daughter from the Patino fortune, following the death of his first wife Isobel Patino. It is not true. Goldsmith did not get a penny from that source and he always insisted that any money emanating from his daughter's family should in due course go to her.

After Isobel's death he might have been expected to make another brilliant marriage; instead he married his secretary, the daughter of a retired French railway employee.

Now that he has built up the Cavenham food empire into one of the most formidable combines in the world, which makes a profit of about £30 million a year, I detect a shift in Goldsmith's business interests. His main investments are moving steadily from Europe to the United States. This has been especially marked during the past year. Control, however, will remain firmly in London and Paris.

To say that Goldsmith is an unconventional figure is to put it mildly. His private life is lived out in public. He might have tried to tidy up his matrimonial situation but he appears impervious not only to public opinion but to the effect it might have if he wished to enter politics.

It amounts to an almost aristocratic disdain. Whatever may be said about it, it at least has the benefit of lacking any trace of hypocrisy.

Friday, May 21, 1976

GISCARD AND THE ROYAL TOUCH

Writing on this page on the eve of President Giscard's State visit to London I suggested that probably the best and possibly the only card we had to play in negotiations with him was the Queen.

I never realised then the full truth of what I was saying half ironically: the fact is that Giscard and his wife and the entire French party have returned to Paris in a positively lyrical state about the British Royals.

So much so that if the visit can be pronounced an outstanding success which, for the time being at any rate, has transformed Anglo-French relations, then the credit must go almost entirely to the Queen with side credits to the Duke of Edinburgh and notably enough to Princess Margaret.

Of course the Giscards were ideal guests for such an occasion, being themselves a cultivated and debonair pair who could respond to all the subtleties of the Royal treatment they were receiving. Giscard brought a natural dignity to the proceedings both in his appearances and in his speeches which no other foreign State visitor to London has been able to match, apart from Giscard's own even more distinguished predecessor, General de Gaulle.

Indeed there were striking similarities between the two visits, even down to similar passages in the two speeches to the two Houses of Parliament, and it is to be hoped that this one will have a happier sequel.

What, by accounts reaching here, the Queen succeeded in doing was not only to charm Giscard but to impress him with her air of relaxed sense of position and authority. There was always a subtle interplay between the formal and the informal which greatly fascinated the French.

Another thing which impressed them was, of course, the well-drilled splendour of the ceremonial occasions and the careful planning of every detail of the visit, even down to the choice of a present for the President.

Who was to know, for example, that Giscard's favourite gun-dog had recently died and that he would have been on the look-out for a new one if the Queen had not presented him with Samba, a black Labrador from the Royal kennels?

What Giscard realised on his visit was something de Gaulle realised long ago and that is that whatever the vicissitudes of Anglo-French relations there is always a great fund of sympathy and affection for France within the Royal Family. Even in the worst Anglo-French days following de Gaulle's two vetoes on British entry into the Common Market, the General always maintained a warm personal relationship with the Queen as he did with her father during the War. It was not a bad way of taking at least some of the poison out of a poisonous situation and limiting the long-term damage that it might do.

This long-term damage has been considerable, especially affecting the officials of both countries and has been greatly aided by the traditional anti-French clottishness of the British Labour Party. It was therefore a particularly happy circumstance that some of the glamour of the visit and the new friendliness it generated should have rubbed off on a Labour Prime Minister.

As for Europe and its future there are now no serious grounds for disputation between the two countries, both of them taking the realistic view that there are no short cuts to and indeed no likelihood in the foreseeable future of bringing about the supranational state dreamt of by the Common Market's founding fathers.

Indeed what is happening is that we are moving towards the opposite – a directorate of the Common Market so dear to General de Gaulle's heart of its three leading powers: Britain, West Germany and France.

Friday, July 2, 1976

FRANCE'S CREDIBLE DETERRENT

An enormous theological dispute has broken out in France over that sacrosanct symbol of Gaullism – France's independent nuclear deterrent. The dispute blew up when the chief of staff of the French army, General Mery, published a learned thesis stating that from now on France must adopt a so-called 'forward' strategy deploying its tactical nuclear artillery on West Germany's eastern frontiers in the event of the Federal Republic becoming the victim of unprovoked attack from the eastern bloc. The uproar that followed still continues and the dispute has already claimed one notable martyr in the redoubtable figure of Vice-Admiral Antoine Sanguinetti, who was promptly put on the retired list by President Giscard as a disciplinary measure for his virulent press attacks on what he claimed was a new and most grave departure from Gaullist defence policy.

Sanguinetti claimed with considerable force in a series of articles in *Le Monde* and other publications including, oddly enough, the socialist *Unité* and the communist *L'Humanité-Dimanche* that the new policy signified that France was about to return in a stealthy fashion to NATO and to the unified – that is American – NATO command from which de Gaulle has rescued her. His reasoning was that in effect the new policy meant that France had accepted the American thesis of a graduated response to a possible Soviet aggression and that this in effect meant an undeclared reintegration with NATO and a consequent loss of independence in the vital matter of decisions concerning her own survival. It also meant, the Admiral claimed, the loss of all credibility of the French deterrent, for the aggressor would feel that by reducing western Europe to rubble with tactical atomic weapons he would render the use by France of its strategic atomic force all the more unlikely. Meanwhile the two super-powers would be effectively 'sanctuarised' by the balance of terror that exists between the two, and only Europe, deprived of independent French atomic protection, would be devastated.

According to the Admiral, therefore, the correct strategy in the event of a conflict should be the immediate threat of an atomic response based of course on an early evaluation of the Soviet threat – whether in short it was a mere foray which could be met with conventional weapons or the harbinger of a full-scale invasion. This is, of course, classic Gaullist doctrine, and the Admiral's viewpoint met with instant approval from such Gaullist stalwarts as the General's former prime minister, M. Debré, and his former defence minister, M. Messmer. It was also greeted with delight by the French Left, especially the communists, who, from having been the fiercest opponents of de Gaulle's successful attempt to build a credible French deterrent, have now warmed to the idea to the point where on defence matters they are hardly distinguishable from orthodox Gaullists.

The communists have long been baying that Giscard plans a French return to NATO, and the Admiral's words were honeyed ones to their ears. What especially irritated them about General Mery's declaration of policy was that the potential enemy was clearly designated as coming from the east whereas in de Gaulle's day defence was based on the '*tous azimut*' theory – that is, repelling attack from any quarter. Oddly enough the theory was not as dotty as it sounds. It was enunciated at the time of the Vietnam war when de Gaulle had serious fears that NATO countries might be involved in a generalised Far East conflagration. It also served, again at that time, his diplomatic purposes. It never, however, interfered with close co-operation with NATO after France had left the integrated command structure, a co-operation which, needless to say, exists to this day although it is now much closer and much more relaxed.

Does this herald a future return of France to the NATO fold? Not on your life. There is about as much chance of that as of France landing a man on the moon. To revert to de Gaulle and NATO, however, it should be remembered that France, while withdrawing from the military organisation, remained a member of the Atlantic Alliance, with all the obligations that that entailed, including the defence of any one of its allies if it were a victim of unprovoked attack. Nor did de Gaulle take these obligations lightly. He disapproved of the Vietnam war, which he considered to be a gigantic folly, but he fully supported the United States in the Cuban confrontation. Indeed his support for Kennedy's stand was the promptest of all America's allies. It is interesting to note in this respect that among all the Gaullist voices raised against Giscard's allegedly new defence policy there is one discordant one – and that a voice of quite exceptional distinction. It is that of a man who served as chief of staff under de Gaulle and who to boot is de Gaulle's son-in-law, General de Boissieu. Privy to de Gaulle's military thinking both in his official capacity and in regular family contact with him, the General, who is now Grand Chancellor of the Legion of Honour, says that far from there being anything new in what his successor has written it is all old hat to him.

What General de Boissieu is saying in effect is that the

so-called new defence policy is in fact the open declaration of the secret instructions given by de Gaulle himself to his military commanders when he was president. If de Gaulle was opposed to President Kennedy's theory of a 'graduated response' to an aggression, that was not because it involved the forward defence of West Germany but because it cast doubts on American readiness to use tactical nuclear weapons. General de Boissieu goes on to say that the West Germans naturally fear that a tactical nuclear battle would develop on their own soil and that it is therefore necessary to reassure them by insisting that their allies would unleash such weapons as close as possible to its eastern frontiers. Such, he says, was the plan approved not only by de Gaulle but also by Pompidou and by successive ministers of defence, including M. Debré and M. Messmer.

The basic credibility of the French atomic deterrent is now not in question. It can inflict from its underground silos, from its submarines and to a lesser extent by delivery from its Mirage IV, what de Gaulle called 'unacceptable damage' to a potential aggressor. What is in doubt is its credibility to its major ally, West Germany. That is to say whether France will defend West German territory with the same readiness as it would its own. It is this doubt that the Mery declaration seeks to set at rest and to spell out publicly. Those who in France now argue that the sole objective of the French nuclear deterrent is to secure the 'sanctuarisation' of French territory are treading on very dangerous ground indeed. They are not only putting in doubt French treaty obligations, but they are opening a Pandora's box of doubts and uncertainties in West Germany.

The entire political and diplomatic efficacy of the French deterrent lies, as de Gaulle once said, in that unlike the American one it finds itself not on the other side of the Atlantic but in Europe. For the French to refuse to extend the protection of its deterrent to the West Germans would condemn French diplomacy to sterility. Above all, it would open the temptation to the West Germans to defy all the risks and break their own treaty obligations by setting out to create a nuclear arsenal of their own. What the critics of General Mery, and by implication of President Giscard, are doing is to preach a kind of doctrine of national nuclear neutrality.

The best defence, or rather the best assurance that the bombs should remain in their silos or on their submarines and in their hangars, is that the potential enemy should be in no doubt that in the event of extreme danger to France or its allies the President will be a man of sufficient character and courage to press the button.

The Spectator, *July 17, 1976*

WHAT KRUSHCHEV SAID TO THE ACTRESS

Simone Signoret is I suppose the only actress in the world whose autobiography can be read for political rather than say prurient or purely gossipy reasons.

This is because her own and her husband Yves Montand's love affair with the French Communist Party dominates the décor like a large four-poster bed in a bedroom farce.

This is certainly the case where Madame Signoret's curiously titled autobiography, *Nostalgia Isn't What It Used To Be*, devotes considerable space to her and her husband's ideological rough and tumbles with leading figures of the French Left and even, in one uproarious scene outside France, with almost the entire Politburo of the Soviet Union.

It was on this occasion, at a banquet to mark Yves Montand's singing tour of the Soviet Union, that Krushchev let his hair down and told the couple in the presence of other members of the Politburo of some of the horrors under the Stalin regime.

This was in 1954, some years before his secret report to the Party Congress, but the pair apparently kept the information to themselves.

Actually, as she confessed rather grudgingly, Simone Signoret owes her survival during the war and the beginning of her film career to three people who were condemned for collaboration. Herself half Jewish and with a father who had fled to London to join de Gaulle, she was able to remain in Paris throughout the occupation because of a friendship with a famous actress, Corinne Luchaire, and Corinne's father, the newspaper magnate Jean Luchaire, who was executed after the Liberation.

In full knowledge of the facts concerning her, they gave her a job on one of Luchaire's publications, and a home. As for the

230

woman who launched her in films, she was the most famous actress of them all, Arletty, also arrested for collaboration after the war.

Because of all this she herself might have found herself in trouble after the occupation but she had already been converted to Communism, met Montand and, even more important, the poet Louis Aragon. Aragon was the great recruiter of Rightists and artists of all kinds for the Party at the time, and his intervention no doubt saved her, as it did for others including, for example, Maurice Chevalier.

The price of a clearance for Chevalier was that he should make appearances at Communist rallies. Like so many others Madame Signoret is somewhat disenchanted with Aragon now, accusing him of having failed to come to Montand's aid by using his influence with the Russians to cancel a scheduled Montand tour of the country which embarrassingly coincided with the Soviet suppression of the Hungarian revolt. As a result the tour took place, with Montand refusing to cancel it himself.

Apart from politics Madame Signoret writes vividly of the agony of playing Lady Macbeth before an English audience. She speaks excellent English herself but not of the kind required to play Shakespeare. She says: 'I saw the audience speaking my lines at the same time as I did and much better than I did.'

Friday, December 10, 1976

231

1977

STILL A WONDERFUL TOWN

There was a time when to speak ill of Paris was to brand oneself as a barbarian. Times have changed. Today from the Glenda Slaggs and the Lunchtime O'Boozes to the highest reaches of the British intelligentsia the cry goes up that Paris is both a clip joint and a cultural desert, an architectural eyesore and a gastronomic poor relation to Soho. 'Paris,' a prominent British intellectual told me the other day, 'is in danger of pricing itself out of civilisation.' Shades of: 'Storm in Channel – Continent Isolated.'

From all these views I beg to differ. For me Paris is easily the most agreeable capital in the world to live in. I would define it simply as a city where a civilised man can still lead a civilised life against a civilised background and consider it not as a feat of escapism but as something amounting to total immersion. It still remains a city manageable in size, easy to get about in and easy to get out of, with each area retaining an individual character. And it still remains lived in for the greater part by the people who actually work in it. This of course makes an enormous difference to life as compared to cities like London and New York which each day gorge and disgorge millions of commuters leaving only a desolation of office blocks behind them. Nothing like this needless to say happens in Paris and this is particularly noticeable at weekends when London becomes a graveyard and Paris a playground.

All this of course I realise is old hat but it still continues to make an inestimable difference to the quality of life between Paris and London. There is one other European city which might rival Paris both in beauty and in its closely-knit character and that is Rome; but Rome is essentially a provincial city which has lost its provincial charm. With its noise and its traffic problems, it is now scarcely habitable. It has a further handicap: it is not big enough to absorb its expatriate population, especially the Americans. These latter are of an exceptionally mediocre and pretentious quality with the result that one tends to meet more bores in bars in Rome in the course of an evening out than one would meet anywhere else in a month. Away with Rome then as with Berlin and Vienna, both of which have lost their status as great capitals.

Having said all this I now realise that I stand exposed to the full counterblast of the Paris detractors. They will talk of the architectural horrors perpetuated in Paris in recent years, such as the Montparnasse skyscraper and the complex of skyscrapers to the west of Paris looming over the Arc de Triomphe, to say nothing of the desolation created when the central markets of Les Halles were uprooted and moved out of the city centre. That these protests should be particularly vociferous across the Channel is probably an indication of our own uneasy conscience over the much vaster vandalism perpetrated in London. The vandalism in Paris has been limited in extent and has at any rate spared the centre of the city and its historic and architectural sites.

Here the Seine continues to flow past the same landmarks and under the same bridges. It still remains impossible for building promoters to lay their hands on such delectable pieces of real estate as the unused Gare d'Orsay. In short, anyone who was visiting Paris for the first time in say fifty years and planted himself in the middle of the Concorde bridge would see to right and left in front and behind him the same unspoilt magnificent views. As for the Montparnasse tower, admittedly it does not please me and would please me even less if I had a flat, say, overlooking the Luxembourg Gardens, but at least it does not dominate the city like for example the even more hideous Post Office Tower in London. As for the other object for protest and outcry, the skyscraper complex at La Défense, here not only does it not disturb me but I approve of it wholeheartedly. It is situated well away from the centre of the city and is in itself an interesting and rather beautiful architectural creation.

On the question of Les Halles and the uprooting of its famous pavilions suddenly discovered to be notable works of art, here I have even less sympathy for foreign critics than over the *affaire* of La Défense. Once it was decided to end Les Halles' role as Paris's central food market, then it seems to me there was no point in keeping the pavilions on the site. There is a large element of hypocrisy in the whole debate over Les Halles: for decades the very existence of this market in the heart of Paris was considered evidence of French backwardness, but once the decision was taken to remove it and put the space to new and largely non-commercial use there was this huge outcry. It would seem that in the eyes of foreign critics Paris can't win: if it modernises itself it is guilty of vandalism and if it doesn't, of backwardness. For those *nostalgiques* for the days of Hemingway and *A Moveable Feast* it should be pointed out that the cost of maintaining Paris as a city for foreign expatriates to live in was precisely to keep France as a backward and basically agricultural country.

Despite the enormous changes of the last twenty years the essential human quality of Paris still remains. It still remains, as I pointed out earlier, a lived-in city, a city of Parisians while London is ceasing to be a city of Londoners and New York has long ceased to be a city of New Yorkers. It still remains too an 'open' city where a citizen's rights include those of being able to get a meal or a drink at any hour of the day or night and as the whim takes him. All this too is a city with a still solidly implanted tradition of good food and service. All this adds up for me to my idea of what a city should be: where a civilised man can partake of civilised pleasures in a civilised manner and in a civilised setting.

I must admit – and it remains a constant regret with me – that I am the least qualified of men to get the most out of Paris. My French remains incorrigibly bad, my taste in food and wine does not rise much above the standards of La Coupole and my feeling for the French cultural scene is exceedingly feeble. Yet I like it here and carry my self-inflicted frustrations lightly. None of the awful misadventures which befall colleagues when they visit Paris seem to befall me despite my give-away accent or at least not with anything like the same regularity. So much so that I cannot recall the last time I was cheated by a taxi-driver. I hear dark tales of Paris's cultural decline but I notice that at the moment sixty-eight theatres are playing to full houses and that two new Jean Anouilh plays are running. I note too something like twenty times more books are sold in Paris than in London and that a learned political essay by President Giscard has sold well over a million copies. I note too that so many art shows are listed that it would take one a fortnight working an eight-hour day to take them all in. All this makes me puzzled at the current

Francophobia that reigns in London. Could it be bafflement and bewilderment at the fact that the French have made a better fist of running their country since the war than we have? Could it be resentment at our relative decline in relation to the French?

The Spectator, *January 1, 1977*

LIVING WITH POMPIDOU'S BABY

Sufficient ink has already been spilt on the Pompidou Cultural Centre which President Giscard will open on Monday to establish that architecturally it is a highly controversial pile of glass, steel and tubular trimmings.

General opinion is divided between those who think it looks like an oil refinery and those who think it is a Meccano set version of an oil refinery. The result has been one of the stormiest debates that Paris has witnessed regarding a new landmark since the erection of the Eiffel Tower.

As the subsequent history of what was deemed a monstrosity at the time showed, Parisians and the world in general learned to live with (and love) Eiffel's creation: so they will no doubt learn to love what is already half affectionately known as 'The Pompidoulium'.

For once the French cannot be accused of cultural chauvinism in the matter of choosing an architectural style: the building was the choice of an international jury and the joint winners were a British and an Italian architect, Richard Rogers and Renzo Piano. It was daring of the two architects to submit such a revolutionary plan for a museum, daring of the jury to choose it, and magnificently daring on the part of the Paris authorities to accept it without demur.

For let this be said – the museum's location is almost as controversial as its design. It has been built on the so-called Beaubourg Plateau, lying between the Marais district and the now uprooted site of the old Paris Central food market Les Halles. This is one of the oldest areas in Paris, housing the famous Gothic church of Saint-Merri and with buildings which look like stage sets for dramatised versions of Victor Hugo's novels.

To make way for the Centre, the homes of hundreds of small shopkeepers, artisans and restaurateurs had to be demolished. Those who stayed on had to endure two years of hell while the building was under construction.

Now that it is completed, a whole new population is moving into the locality – enterprising West End gallery owners who are opening branches in the vicinity, the owners of smart new restaurants, souvenir shops and so on, all hoping to make a killing from the Centre's tourist potential.

Actually the Centre was banking on a turnover of 10,000 visitors daily seven days a week, including public holidays, all between the hours of 10 a.m. and 10 p.m. This is twice as many visitors as the Louvre gets.

To meet the huge cost of its construction (more than £100 million) and the high cost of its staffing and maintenance (more than £15 million a year), there will be an admission charge for entry and additional charges to see special exhibitions and musical and theatrical events. However, for £5 a year one can become a member and enjoy free entry and free access to everything that is going on.

For this year alone no less than 150 special shows are scheduled. Its opening art show – apart of course from its permanent one – will be devoted to Maurice Duchamp, one of France's greatest surrealist painters.

Oddly enough, this grandiose art centre came after and not before the most ambitious of France's Ministers of Culture, the late André Malraux, had left the scene. President Pompidou, a man of deep culture himself, could claim its sole paternity.

He was, as it happens, greatly distressed by the philistine image he had created for himself by allowing the growth of skyscrapers in and around Paris. Anxious to efface this image, he set great store on his idea of a cultural centre and the plan for it was finally bulldozed through Parliament after his death by his disciple, the former Prime Minister M. Jacques Chirac.

As Pompidou was a patron of modern art, the collection very largely reflects his tastes. To stock it the authorities raided the existing museum of modern art for Matisses, Dérains and Van Dongens. Max Ernst and Kandinsky are also well represented and there is even a Pollock.

A notable feature of the Centre will be the institute of

musical-acoustical research and co-ordination which is built underground and will have as its director the composer-conductor Pierre Boulez. It was precisely the lack of such a centre in Paris which drove Boulez into exile in New York and winning him back is something of a triumph for the Paris musical world.

Another outstanding feature will be the library, a badly needed addition to the over-crowded and dated Bibliothèque Nationale. This occupies three floors on the left side of the building and will be the most up-to-date reference library in France. A notable feature is that forty per cent of its books will be from foreign sources and some will be accompanied by a French translation where it exists.

There will be no attendants and visitors will have direct access to the volume they are looking for. Theatres and cinemas complete the ensemble and there will be a special area reserved for children.

There will also be a studio for amateur painters where they can experiment with material provided by the Centre on white enamelled walls with tutors available for advice and criticism.

To revert to the building itself, it is essentially five huge concrete slabs encased almost entirely in glass and supported by a network of vertical and horizontal pipes – the large vertical ones filled with freeze-proof water to lend weight and to supply the fire-extinguishing system.

Despite a seeming pretentiousness, it looks like being a fun place. There is an excellent restaurant on the top floor providing fifteen-franc meals and the view from the top is sensational. One sees from it Notre Dame, the Panthéon, the Invalides, the Eiffel Tower and the Sacré-Coeur on the top of Montmartre.

Friday, January 28, 1977

HOW DID HE FIND THE TIME?

Novelist Georges Simenon's claim to have made love to 10,000 women in his life-time has disappointed his French admirers. They expect a higher degree of plausibility from their favourite author's imaginings.

What does not surprise those who know him well here, however, is that his sexual boastings should at last have reached the public prints instead of being the secret of a few close friends, one of whom is the extremely attractive publishing executive Mme Thérèse de Saint-Phalle.

She tells me that she has spent many a long hour discussing Simenon's strong sexual appetites and his confessions to her went something like this: as in the now famous Zurich interview Simenon claimed that he had his first sexual experience at the age of thirteen.

This did not surprise Mme de Saint-Phalle, who is a happily married woman with two children and whose banker husband also began his sex life at that not so tender age.

From then on the account varies markedly from the Zurich one. According to her, Simenon told her that up to the age of thirty-five he needed to go to bed with three different women a day.

'How did you find the women?' she asked.

Simple, he replied, they were servants – a cook, a chamber-maid and a secretary.

After thirty-five, he continued, his powers waned and he was content with only one woman a day.

And now at the age of seventy-three – though some claim he is older by a decade – he lives happily with his Italian maid, aged forty-five, to whom he is entirely faithful. He is by now divorced from his rather terrifying French-Canadian wife, who is the mother of his last three children.

The only time I had occasion to observe Simenon closely and over several hours was some years ago at his villa near Cannes. I must say there was no hint of sex in the offing at the time and Simenon seemed more preoccupied with changing his typewriter ribbon than changing his sleeping partner.

He was then starting work on the 167th novel published under his own name and his 436th book if you include those he has written under a dozen different pseudonyms.

From the appearance of his study one might have thought he was planning to go on a long and complicated journey. The large table was littered with maps, railway and bus timetables and the telephone directories of half a dozen countries.

At the telephone his wife was busy cancelling all appointments for the next eleven days, the scheduled time it took him to produce a new book. A last-minute detail was to arrange a medical check-up for Simenon, who is something of a hypochon-driac and worries about his blood pressure. (An interruption for illness would snap his concentration so completely that the novel would probably be discarded.)

Beside him, as he consulted maps and timetables, was a tray full of some thirty newly cleaned pipes and an orange-coloured manila envelope. It was on this envelope that he was plotting his new novel.

On it he had already written the name of the town in which the action took place, the names of the leading characters taken from telephone directories, and their family histories and profes-sions.

This, Simenon assured me, was all he knew about the book on which he would start work at 6.30 a.m. the following day and finish the first chapter in time to join his wife and children at breakfast at 8.30 a.m.

The afternoon was filled with correcting his wife's typed copy, a solitary long walk, a short nap and a drive around the Riviera countryside.

Throughout the period of gestation, he told me, he identified himself entirely with his chief character. He would be surly and aggressive during this creative time and it was a happy day for the household when the book was finished.

But not much time for sex during this tight eleven-day sche-dule I would have thought. His wife, who was both his secretary and business manager, was an unsmiling woman and would not, I am certain, have put up with any nonsense.

Friday, April 22, 1977

WHERE THERE'S NO WILL . . .

The case of Picasso's heritage, which was thought to have been settled last spring, has been reopened at the instigation of Picasso's widow Jacqueline. It is a painful decision for every-one concerned – except perhaps the lawyers involved who, if matters prolong themselves for a further few years, might find themselves becoming very nearly the chief beneficiaries from Picasso's fortune.

The dispute as to who should take what and how much from the paintings Picasso left behind him, to say nothing of his properties and his bank account, has already dragged on for four years and now – in the face of Jacqueline's renewed intransigence – it looks like dragging on for a few more.

To be fair to this proud somewhat imperious woman, who looks younger than her fifty-one years, she has had a lot to put up with from the haggling over the estate from both the legitimate and illegitimate branches of Picasso's family.

There is, for example, Picasso's stated wish – he made no will – that his collection of other painters' work should go to the Louvre, a donation which will no doubt exempt his estate from death duties.

This donation would come out of Jacqueline's share of the estate, but instead of agreeing to a lower estimate of its value the other litigants succeeded, with rival expert advice, in almost doubling the value: this was on the principle, no doubt, that the less there was for Jacqueline the more there would be to share out among themselves.

Similar if somewhat less serious irritants were introduced into a dispute over the château of Vauvenargues in the grounds of which Picasso is buried. The children and grandchildren of his other marriage and his two famous liaisons with Marie-Thérèse Walter and Françoise Gilot are demanding free access to it and an option on its purchase should Jacqueline ever want to sell it – a suggestion which she regarded as an insult.

With pride and sentiment as well as cash becoming involved, the issue has become more complex than ever. Altogether, apart from Jacqueline, the people involved in the case are three illegitimate children and two legitimate grandchildren from his first marriage to the Russian ballerina Olga Khokhlova.

They are disputing the fortune which, in paintings and other works alone, is legally estimated at one billion, one hundred and fifty-four million francs (nearly £136 million).

Then there are three properties in the South of France and a bank account. Picasso always refused to invest his money and the only estimate that can be given of his bank balance is by the size of his tax bill. This is now known – he paid 15,000,000 francs in tax (about £1,750,000) for the year 1972.

Under the agreement reached earlier this year, Jacqueline

would have got a third of the fortune, the two children from his legitimate son's two marriages another third, and the three illegitimate children the remainder.

Friday, August 26, 1977

LENIN: FRANCE IS STILL LISTENING . . .

No country in the world was more profoundly affected by the Russian revolution, sixty years old this week, than France. The effects continue to this day.

The events in Russia were quickly followed by a split in the French Socialist Party with a majority breaking away to form the Communist Party. With it began the long alienation – which remains unbroken – of a major portion of the French working class from the nation. The consequences have been appalling.

It has meant that a voting force, varying between six and four million, has never – except for a brief period after the Liberation – had any effective role in the government of the nation and has existed in a kind of political ghetto. Thus at least twenty per cent of the voters have been to all intent and purposes disenfranchised.

Throughout these sixty years there has been no way in which a parliamentary democracy could come to terms with the Communists and no way, as the recent split on the French Left shows, in which the Communists could come to terms with it.

Furthermore, and much more seriously, not only do the Communists bar themselves from power but they bar the Left as a whole from power.

The old French political adage remains almost as true today as it was before the War – the Left can't win without the Communists and can't win with them.

This has meant that French democracy remains in a permanent state of imbalance with a constantly crippled opposition. How has it come about that the flame lit in Petrograd sixty years ago by Lenin & Co. has had such long-lasting consequences here? After all, the Communist Party never became a mass party in Britain – and in Germany, where it was once powerful, it is

242

now in the Federal Republic reduced to little more than a sect.

One reason, probably the major one according to the historian Max Gallo, is that many Frenchmen saw the Russian Revolution as the logical continuation of their own, which had produced not only Napoleon but also the abortive Paris Commune of 1871. The Red Terror was equated with the terror which followed their own revolution and was excused on the grounds that 'who wishes the ends must approve the means'.

What is astonishing is that despite all the horrors of the past, despite all the spectacular somersaults of Soviet and French Communist party policies, despite the now general disenchantment with the Soviet Union, the Communists should still be able to count on the support of the French industrial working class.

What is even more remarkable is that the Party has played no significant role in pioneering social reforms. It was not a member of the Popular Front Government of 1936 which introduced paid holidays; it was the Pétain Government which introduced family allowances; it was de Gaulle who introduced large-scale nationalisation after the War; and it was the past three Presidents, de Gaulle, Pompidou and Giscard, who introduced a flood of reforms – some of which were not even thought of by the Left – which have made France one of the most socially advanced countries in the world.

Recently there has been a spate of books by ex-Communists all shedding new light on the Party and its history. The most notable is an autobiography by Charles Tillon, who led the mutiny of the French Black Sea Fleet against the French intervention in the Russian civil war. He was a Party member for fifty years and is a former member of its ruling Politburo.

His is a terrible story of suffering and courage, of chicanery and double-crossing, of appalling blunders and epic steadfastness. He tells, for example, the story of Marcel Gitton, a member of the Politburo in charge of the Party's underground operations, who, at a critical moment – when the party was declared illegal after the Hitler–Stalin pact – was revealed to be a police spy.

He tells, too, of the Party's attempt to establish good relations with the German occupying forces while Hitler and Stalin were still allies, and how it succeeded in receiving temporary permission to publish the organ, *l'Humanité*. Throughout there is the enigmatic figure of the Czech Eugène Fried, Moscow's agent in the party, who master-minded its policies and saw to their application, and who was later to be liquidated by Stalin.

Friday, November 11, 1977

1978

CAN THE MAYOR KEEP ON DANCING?

There are two dynasties on France's famous Côte d'Azur: the Grimaldi one in Monaco and the Médecin one in neighbouring Nice.

The Grimaldi dynasty is, of course, an ancient one but taking into consideration that – unlike the Grimaldis – the Médecins have to face regular elections, the latter is by these standards fairly ancient too. For fifty years now the Médecins, father and son, have been running the fair city of Nice both as its mayors and its chief representatives in Parliament.

Only a few years ago, Nice without a Médecin at its head – the family name, incidentally, gives it some claim to descent from the Italian Medicis – would have been as unthinkable as Nice without the Promenade des Anglais. Now, sadly, it looks as though the dynasty is crumbling and might collapse in the general elections next March.

The present head of the family, handsome 49-year-old Jacques Médecin, is not only the Mayor of Nice and its MP but also Minister for Tourism in the present government. He therefore enjoys not only the added advantage of Ministerial prestige but also that of holding precisely the post which can look after Nice's important tourist interests at the highest level.

Yet something seems to have gone wrong with the magic hold of the Médecins over Nice. In last year's municipal elections, for example, Jacques Médecin came within a few hundred votes of being defeated – and being defeated by a Communist at that.

The result of that vote is being contested and a court will hand down its verdict on alleged irregularities after the March elections. Meanwhile, in these elections too, Médecin faces defeat – this time at the hands of a Socialist. What then has gone wrong for Médecin in a city of placid ways and easy-going cynicism?

245

Sam White's Paris

It is, furthermore, a city dominated by a single newspaper, *Nice Matin*, a publication not given to asking nasty questions or wavering in its loyalty to both Prince Jacques of Nice or Prince Rainier of Monaco.

Médecin has been attacked for some of his associations. The satirical journal, *Le Canard Enchaîné*, has been waging a campaign against Médecin along these lines for the past year and the matter is now being brought to court in a pending libel action.

Another reason for Médecin's decline is that the population of the city has changed with the influx of retired people on modest pensions from Paris and other cities. A third concerns ugly rumours of speculative building.

Finally, Nice is in many respects even more expensive than Paris and this has precipitated something like a crisis in the hotel industry as well as dissatisfaction among hotel staff.

Then too there is the ecological factor – a speculative building boom which has wrecked one of the most beautiful coastlines in the world, transforming it into an unbroken wall of cement dotted with sea-polluting marinas.

The result is that the ecological vote, rated at five per cent by opinion polls in France as a whole, stands at fifteen per cent in Nice.

Crucial to all this is the building boom. It has corrupted everything: life, the administration and the population in general. If building permits are granted to the big promoters how can they be refused to owners of an acre of land whose expectations of a comfortable retirement are based on this prospect? There is considerable corruption at all levels, and with corruption has come an influx of gangsters.

Enormous fortunes have been made out of real estate and bribery is rife. A square metre of land on the outskirts of Nice represents something of a fortune in itself, with the result that the city – whose population now stands at 400,000 – finds it too expensive to build needed workers' flats or even an extra post office or two. For lovers of Nice such as myself this is immensely sad.

It looks as though someone will have to carry the can for the mess, and it looks like being Médecin. There is only one hope for him and that is that the greatly reduced French colony in Monaco, which can now vote in Nice, may come to his rescue.

Friday, January 20, 1978

AN ILLUSION SHATTERED

This time Giscard came clean. In what was generally acknowledged to have been the most effective speech he has ever
delivered since becoming President, he spelt out clearly what
would be the consequences of a Left victory in the French
general elections in five weeks' time. The speech, delivered last
weekend in a Burgundy township, was much anticipated since he
had promised to indicate to the French what their President
thought would be 'the good choice' for the nation in the coming
elections. Nobody doubted what the President would consider to
be 'the good choice', everybody doubted, however, whether he
would express it with sufficient clarity and force to rule out any
possible collision between himself and a victorious Left next
March. In the event, he told the French that, if they insisted on
playing with fireworks, then they were not to count on him to
play the role of some super-nanny running around administering
first-aid and otherwise limiting the damage. He would be powerless, in other words, to prevent a victorious Left from im-
plementing the full common programme to which the two major
parties of the Left, the Socialists and the Communists, remained
committed.

It was a much needed, even dangerously belated, clarification.
Until this speech was made, there had been a great deal of
confusion over what would be the powers, even indeed the
functions, of a President with four more years of his office still to
run in the face of a freshly-elected hostile parliament. Giscard,
by his repeated statements that he would stay no matter what the
outcome of the elections, had merely added to the confusion.
The main effect of these statements was to reassure the electorate that, with Giscard at the helm, it was safe to vote Left. The
result would be a few spectacular social reforms stopping far
short of the full programme of the Left, with Giscard holding the
ultimate powers to block. It was an illusion which has played an
important role in giving the Left such a spectacular lead over the
existing majority in the public opinion polls. The question before
last Friday's speech was whether Giscard would continue to
maintain this illusion or break it.

He broke it with a bang. The real fact is that, despite all the nonsense talked about the Fifth Republic constitution creating a kind of presidential monarchy, ultimate power under it lies not with the president but with parliament. If parliament wills, the president must bend – or resign. If the Left wins, it will be able to enact every piece of legislation that it has promised to enact – and the president could not block it. The president however would still retain one important weapon – and only one – that of the right to dissolve parliament at a time and on an issue of his own choosing. It is an important asset but one not to be squandered lightly: having been used once it cannot be used for another year. But, as Raymond Aron points out, this is not as impressive a weapon as it sounds; with a triumphant Left baying for the president's resignation, an early dissolution could be positively welcome.

The most likely outcome of a victory of the Left, then, would be to reinforce the new majority, force Giscard's resignation and bring about early presidential elections. Certainly the Socialist leader, François Mitterrand, would attempt as soon as possible to use a parliamentary triumph as a springboard for a presidential one. In short, the idea that Giscard would be allowed to retreat quietly to the Elysée and bide his time there until the inevitable disaster ensued is an illusion – and it is an illusion which until recently he himself has been inclined to share. Certainly as far as Mitterrand is concerned, his strategy will be not to make things easy for Giscard but to oust and replace him with himself as quickly as possible. Thus Mitterrand, and not for the first time in his chequered career, has come full circle. From being the Fifth Republic's fiercest enemy, after having described its constitution as a recipe for dictatorship, he now not only covets its highest office but sees it as a vehicle for his own ambitions – and not just for those of de Gaulle, as he was fond of declaring in the past.

The presidency, by giving him national stature, will give him the whiphand not only over the Communists but over his own left-wing supporters, but then Mitterrand's whole career invites irony. A Socialist who shunned Socialism in his heady youth, he was, after all, busy being a minister in ten different post-war governments – he came to Socialism rather late in life. His public declarations are Marxist, his private ones disclaim fidelity to that doctrine. Abroad, among his fellow statesmen of the Socialist International, he boasts that his greatest achievement has been to cut the French Communists down to size while at home he was responsible, before the recent split, for handing some thirty major towns to the Communists in last year's municipal elections. Meanwhile, paradoxically, the split on the Left, far from weakening it, has actually strengthened it. All its component parts – the Socialists, the Left Radicals and the Communists – are doing better divided than they ever did united.

This has led to yet another switch in Communist tactics: instead of scenting defeat for the Left, they now scent victory. As a result, they are demanding that Communists be represented in the anticipated Mitterrand government after the elections. Mitterrand is already committed to inviting them to join his government, but they are insisting that they will not join in any junior capacity but will demand some of the major posts. Their weapon in forcing Mitterrand's hand will be the agreement that will have to be reached immediately after the first round of voting as to who will stand down in favour of whom in the second and decisive round. So there goes another illusion shared by almost everyone only a couple of weeks ago – that whatever else the split on the Left entailed, its major consequence would be the definite exclusion of Communists from the next French government. Mitterrand's offer to invite them to join a Socialist-led government despite the recent disagreements was not meant to be taken seriously. Unfortunately his bluff is being called on this point too.

As Raymond Aron points out: 'Cynically, Mitterrand is moving to the left just because the Communists accuse him of moving to the right. He is now accepting certain measures which he rejected with indignation when the Communists first proposed them. If after the first round the Communists, as a price for standing down in some electorates in favour of the Socialists, demand such and such ministries and such and such new nationalisations, one wonders if Mitterrand, driven by an appetite for power and conscious of the fact that this is his last chance of achieving it, will still have the courage to resist. We shall see. Meanwhile it is interesting to recall that when Mitterrand met President Carter recently he told him that if the Left won in March it would come to power in an atmosphere of crisis.' He can say that again.

The Spectator, *February 4, 1978*

SEVERAL DAYS IN MAY

Coming as it does on the heels of the defeat of the left in the March general elections, the tenth anniversary of May '68 could not have come at a worse time for those congenital Peter Pans who still seek to draw inspiration from it and hope earnestly for a repeat performance. Today's climate is different for, paradoxically, as apparently boundless prosperity has given place to austerity, the mood for such frivolities as those of ten years ago has evaporated. To rail against the consumer society now would be to mock the unemployed, of whom the young form the largest single element. Not only are the young no longer in the mood to man the barricades but as the March elections, in which the voting age for the first time was reduced to eighteen, showed, the majority of them are not even prepared to vote left. No one should forget that the troubles of May '68 were started not by students living in hovels in the Latin Quarter but by the sons and daughters of a bourgeoisie which had prospered mightily under de Gaulle; many of them went home after a night's rioting to good suppers and clean sheets in elegant flats in the sixteenth arrondissement.

And when of course they returned home bearing the bruises of battle and told tales of police brutality, horror and indignation swelled in parental breasts to the point that the government soon realised – and it was to add to its helplessness in the situation – that public opinion (and bourgeois public opinion at that) was decisively on the side of the students. And there was more to public opinion than just the thought of the *fils de papa* being clubbed by a copper as though he were some vulgar working-class type. It was not only a time of unprecedented prosperity for France but a time when de Gaulle's prestige stood at its highest. He had settled the Algerian war and was now playing host to peace negotiations between the U.S. and North Vietnam in Paris. Now if there is one man the French bourgeoisie hated and still hates, it is de Gaulle. There was the colonial lobby which could not forgive him for Algeria and the whole decolonisation process which he had instigated; and there were the Vichyites who could not forgive him for his wartime 'treason', the post-war purges, and the inclusion of communists in his first government. And there was big business which profoundly distrusted him.

All these elements on the classic French right had long ago reversed their famous pre-war slogan 'rather Hitler than Léon Blum' into something which literally became their battle cry as the troubles developed: 'rather Mendès-France than de Gaulle.' And if the students could wipe the self-satisfied smirk from de Gaulle's face, then bully for the students. Needless to say, this view was shared in Washington, Bonn and London – especially the latter, still smarting from two successive Gaullist vetoes on British entry into the Common Market. The only solace the general could find was in eastern Europe, and there he insisted on going, at the height of the riot, on a long scheduled visit to Bucharest, against the entreaties of his prime minister M. Pompidou.

At this point one should say a word about the relations between de Gaulle and Pompidou. The two men were at loggerheads before the storm broke and remained at loggerheads almost throughout. De Gaulle had a bee in his bonnet about worker participation – a project which left Pompidou not merely cold but aghast. De Gaulle had long ago decided to replace Pompidou with Couve de Murville, but the general election of the previous year had produced a government majority of only one and it became imperative that he stick with Pompidou. A complicating factor was Couve's inability to win a parliamentary seat. He had stood for two of the safest conservative seats in the country – and this is an indication of the bourgeois hatred of de Gaulle – and had been soundly beaten in both. Now, with the student riots sparking off what looked like becoming a general strike, de Gaulle, egged on by André Malraux and other left-wing Gaullists, could not resist the temptation of blaming Pompidou for his obstinate conservatism in matters of social policy. It was this which led to the bitter battle between the two over the question of a referendum or a general election as a means of overcoming the crisis.

De Gaulle wanted a referendum which would embody his reformist ideas, while Pompidou saw that as a certain loser and favoured an election. In the end, in dramatic circumstances as we shall see later, Pompidou won both his point and the election too. Just as de Gaulle was to be absent during a critical period in Bucharest, so Pompidou was absent during an even more critical period – the very beginnings of the crisis – in Afghanistan. He did

251

not consult his ministers on his return but only his Chef de Cabinet, Michel Jobert. He promptly decided that serious mistakes had been made in the handling of the situation during his absence. The universities and especially Nanterre should not have been closed because of the rioting, the police should never have been allowed to enter the Sorbonne – although they did so at the urgent request of the rector – and twelve students should not have been held for trial for carrying weapons and attacking the police. He went on television that evening to announce that the universities would be reopened, the police withdrawn from the Sorbonne and that the charges against the arrested students would be dropped.

The result of these gestures of appeasement was the opposite to what had been hoped. That very night saw some of the worst violence yet, as the rioters went on a rampage of 'victory' celebrations. From that point on, too, the rioting became more serious in character – better organised, almost professionally led, with strategic points besieged and public buildings like the Odéon theatre seized. All the techniques of street fighting had been considerably perfected; the manufacture of Molotov cocktails had become something of a cottage industry; a communication system between rioters had been developed with dispatch riders guiding them away from areas where the police forces were strong to points where they were weakest. Also the Paris underworld had decided to join in for what there might be in it for them, and the streets were full of roaming armed gangs of hoodlums from St Denis and Belleville.

Meanwhile if the streets were uncontrollable the strike itself was taking on the proportions of a national catastrophe. Here the old French tradition of anarcho-syndicalism had come to the fore to match the anarchism of the students. It had nothing in common with the student agitations, held itself aloof from them and the student slogan: 'Students, workers – the same battle' remained an empty one from beginning to end. What had, however, happened was that the apparent ease with which the students were bringing the government to its knees lit a spark, first among the young and largely unorganised workers, which quickly spread. Not having initiated the strike movement, the union leaders and especially the communist ones could only follow in a desperate attempt to control it. On 16 May there were only 300,000 strikers; by the next day the number had doubled and two days later it stood at two million. It quickly mounted to six million and finally reached nine million. Many of the strikes were 'sit-ins' involving the forcible detention of managers, and while the factory gates remained closed to the police they also remained firmly closed to the student agitators.

At this point something sinister was beginning to develop in the mood of the country's élite. It was a mood strangely reminiscent of the one in 1940 when the regime was threatened by the onrush of panzer divisions and not by student rioters and strikers. It was, in short, becoming frankly defeatist at all levels – cultural, journalistic, political, in the administration and even among some elements in the government. Gaullists were rare on the ground and coats were turned with what one might almost describe as practised dexterity. The regime had had it and the time had come to come to terms with those who were most likely to be the country's new rulers. Film directors, actors, painters and a host of writers suddenly disovered that they had always been men and women of the left. I remember Madame Pompidou, who had a host of friends in these circles, telling me with some bitterness how her telephone fell silent during that month of May. The idea that de Gaulle ought to be dumped began to gather force even among Gaullist ministers though not, I should add, with Pompidou himself. The press suddenly began to take a strangely emasculated appearance with many familiar by-lines missing, and new unknown ones taking their place. *Le Monde*, needless to say, became the students' spokesman and major apologist, trumpeting unsubstantiated claims of students killed and of police brutality.

Its circulation soared from less than 400,000 to over 800,000. Like the rest of the Paris press, however, *Le Monde* was subject to the most dangerous of all forms of censorship – an unacknowledged one which left the reader in ignorance of its existence. The censorship was exercised by the printing unions, and a newspaper that was particularly badly hit by it was *Le Figaro*. There the entire political staff of the paper was 'blacked' by the unions and its most distinguished political columnist, Raymond Aron, was only allowed to appear if he refrained from writing about current events. *Figaro* did not protest publicly about the censorship at the time nor has it acknowledged it since – leaving it to M. Aron to spill the beans in his famous pamphlet on the May events, *La revolution introuvable*. Against this background the talented young imitators of Goebbels had a field day planting stories of tortures in police stations, of dead bodies mysteriously disposed of by the police and finally a daily toll of those allegedly killed in the rioting. This reached a grand total of seventy-three killed when in fact the six weeks' rioting did not produce a single fatality in Paris – which in itself provides a fitting commentary on the student slogan 'CRS = SS'. In fact not only was the government itself hesitant about using force – it allowed, for example, the rioters to build six-foot high barricades while forbidding the police to intervene – but Paris was fortunate to have at the time a prefect of police, M. Grimaud, noted for his humanity and restraint in the use of force.

This, and not police violence, provided the true setting for the almost daily and nightly displays of posturing vainglory on the part of the students and their leaders. Having been an eye-witness on both occasions, some of the Paris scenes reminded me strangely of the rioting *Algérie française* students of Algeria and their simulated clashes with the police. Fortunately at this point elements of farce began to creep into the situation; Jean-Louis Barrault beating his breast at the Odéon before audiences largely composed of boozy *clochards*, and telling them that of course his heart was with the students and that they were welcome to the theatre of which technically he had custody; Sartre trying to win recognition as the spiritual father of the student revolt and being greeted with cries of 'Go home, papa'; a succession of television celebrities including a particularly notorious rugby commentator confessing their sins and asking for forgiveness, and pilgrims from afar included, as I remember, a humble Stephen Spender paying homage to this new fount of revolutionary wisdom. It was all beginning to take the form of a bloodless version of the Chinese cultural revolution.

However, there were more important figures jostling to take the centre of the stage, among them M. François Mitterrand and M. Mendès-France. They had originally come to a pact between themselves to have nothing to do with the student rioters. However, as the situation deteriorated, both independently decided that they had a national role to fulfil in the crisis. For Mendès-France it was largely a matter of being seen and being acclaimed at student demonstrations. For Mitterrand it was an occasion for live political action. He therefore announced that the time had come for the formation of a provisional government of which he generously offered the prime ministership to Mendès-France. He himself, he solemnly announced, would be a candidate for the presidency of the republic. That this procedure was totally unconstitutional and seditious did not seem to cross his mind. Now back to Pompidou and de Gaulle. The latter had appeared to have retreated into the shadows in a mood of the bleakest despondency while the former virtually constituted a one-man government. He seemed to be holding at least five different cabinet posts at the same time, while simultaneously engaged in a marathon negotiation with the trade unions in an effort to get a return to work. He never flinched, never tired, seemingly never slept and never lost his temper.

The trade union talks went on unbroken for thirty-six hours, with Pompidou shifting from dossier to dossier and from detail to detail like some kind of chess master playing against twenty different opponents. His tactic never varied – the communists, frightened about being outflanked by the extreme left, and worried about the intrigues of Mitterrand and Mendès, were his objective allies. And so they proved to be up to a point. There was a moment when the communist leadership was torn between the temptation of toppling the government and frustrating its enemies on the left. It became intense when the communist boss of the CGT, Georges Séguy, having secured massive wage increases, was howled down at the Renault works when he presented the terms of agreement for approval. It was a mysterious business and remains a mysterious business to this day. Finally, however, the communists chose a return to work – largely because a return to work was already beginning in as spontaneous and uncontrolled a fashion as the strikes themselves had broken out. It was now the moment for the last most carefully staged and most spectacular act in the drama.

I refer, of course, to de Gaulle's famous disappearance on 29 May. For once the general had been reduced to a subsidiary role, not merely at a loss for words but unable to choose the right ones. In the middle of the crisis he had made a television appearance which not only failed to catch the mood of the country but had seriously aggravated its anxieties. It was, in short, a disastrous flop. On that particular day, with the rejection of the Pompidou–Séguy agreement at the Renault works, the situation had suddenly taken a turn for the worse. A large demonstration was scheduled for that day which would take the marchers within a short stroll of the Elysée Palace. It was also the day for the weekly cabinet meeting. This was the morning that the general chose to ring Pompidou and tell him, just as ministers were beginning to gather for the cabinet meeting, that he was cancelling it and that he himself was about to leave Paris to spend the night in the restful air of his country house at Colombey-les-deux-Eglises. He ended with what for him were strong words rich in emotive feeling: 'I embrace you.' His departure was as carefully arranged as his words were carefully chosen. First a convoy of cars loaded with the de Gaulles' personal luggage – very much more than they would need for an overnight stay – and containing, too, their personal servants, set out for Colombey.

Then more luggage was loaded in one of the two helicopters composing the presidential flight. In short, the impression was carefully given that de Gaulle was leaving the Elysée not for a night but for ever. This was the conclusion Pompidou came to and the helicopters had no sooner taken off than he ordered the French television to stand by for an important declaration that he would make that evening. After two hours and still no sign of the general arriving in Colombey, panic set in. Where was he? It was only four hours later that it was discovered that he had flown to the HQ of the French army in West Germany, commanded by the ever-faithful General Massu in Baden-Baden. What happened in Baden-Baden is now a fairly open secret and is as revealing as the deception practised in the departure from Paris. For Massu's benefit de Gaulle played out the part of a broken man facing an imminent revolution, who was seeking refuge with an army which might very soon be called upon to restore his presidential legitimacy. Would the general and his wife be staying the night? Certainly, and the luggage was duly unpacked and beds made ready in the Massu residence. Then two hours later after a hearty lunch, the general announced that he would be going back to Colombey that evening and then back to Paris the following morning. The bags were duly re-packed and re-loaded and the general and his wilting wife took off again.

The general must have returned to Colombey well pleased with his day's work. He had pulled off a triple bluff. First by his carefully staged departure he had created an apparent void into which he invited his enemies to show themselves by stepping into it. Secondly he had assured himself of army support for the constitutional head of state. And thirdly he had delivered a shock to public opinion of such a resounding nature that even the left was thrown off balance, being more concerned at what de Gaulle was up to than what it could do itself. It provided the fitting background to his final speech which rang down the curtain of the May '68 psycho-drama. 'I stay' were the key words of that speech, but it was a speech that was not finally framed without a last tussle with Pompidou. In the end Pompidou got what he wanted – a general election not a referendum. As is now history the general election was won with the biggest single-party majority in the history of the republic.

The Spectator, *May 13, 1978*

THE MYTHS OF OCCUPIED PARIS

Come August, and a dismal chain of anniversaries set in for the French, lightened only by that of the Liberation of Paris. Lightened did I say? That is hardly the word, for the mood now encompasses an irresistible urge to scratch at the sore of how Paris behaved during the occupation. The romantic glow has faded from this City's liberation and has given way to a more realistic not to say a downright cynical view of the event itself and the four years that preceded it. It is as though the original romantic version, fostered by the Left at home and abroad, of France as a nation of heroes betrayed by a few scoundrels has given way to the reverse – of France as a nation of collaborationists redeemed by the acts of a handful of heroes. It is this latter view, of course, which was so successfully propagated by that masterpiece of skilful distortion, the film *Le Chagrin et la Pitié*, the authors of which had sharp personal and political motives for pouring scorn on their countrymen. This August, however, has seen the annual debate over the events of thirty-four and more years ago take on a more passionate note than ever with renewed pleas by Colonel Rémy for some kind of 'historic compromise' between de Gaulle and Pétain. This has been an old hobby horse of Rémy's, and he is in an excellent position to promote it, having been one of the first resistance leaders in occupied France and one of the first to join de Gaulle. His argument, which does more credit to his Christian heart than to his head, is that France at the time needed both a sword and a shield – with de Gaulle of course providing the first and Pétain the second.

It is an argument which might have had a certain plausibility, if the shield itself had not turned into an anti-resistance sword and if Pétain had not promulgated anti-semitic decrees improving even on the Nuremberg ones. Rémy's theory is enthusiastically supported by Alfred Fabre-Luce, an old-time apologist for Pétain among whose arguments is that fewer Jews were deported from France than from any other of the occupied countries. One reason for this which seems to have escaped Fabre-Luce is that it was easier to round them up in smaller countries like Holland, but undoubtedly he is right that the Vichy version of the Nuremberg decrees was more loosely applied, until the last days of the war, than elsewhere and his own survival as a half-Jew is, as far as he is concerned, a satisfactory proof of this. It is somewhat less so for those who did not have the right family or political connections. One last point emerges from the debate, and this is provided by Raymond Aron, not usually found among the apologists for Vichy. He argues that the French collapse in 1940 was a blessing in disguise, because it averted the kind of casualties which France after the blood-letting of the first world war simply could not afford. This was, of course, the basic reason for the pacifism of all political parties in France before the war, from left to right, and it became a fully national pacifism with the signing of the Hitler–Stalin pact when the Communists called a halt to their anti-Hitler crusade.

All this brings us back to the question of how Paris behaved during the occupation – an issue, which nags at one like the reputed infidelities of a favourite mistress. To supply some new answers to this, *Paris-Match* over August devoted four special issues to Paris under the occupation and I have supplemented this with a reading of the second volume of Simone de Beauvoir's memoirs which largely cover this period. It is interesting to note for example that, though Paris was hungry during this period, to the point where some people may have been tempted to denounce their grandmothers for a good black market châteaubriand, culturally it was undergoing a considerable renaissance. It was the golden age of the French theatre and the French cinema, launching a torrent of talent such as Paris has not seen before or since. For the single season of 1940–41, no fewer than 110 plays were running in Paris of which thirty-five were new ones, while in the year of Stalingrad eighty-three films were made, many of them ranking as classics. Playwrights like Guitry and Cocteau, Giraudoux and Sartre, Salacrou and Anouilh, either consolidated their reputations or made them during the occupation. Then there were film directors like Clouzot and Becker and Bresson and performers like Danielle Darrieux, Gérard Philipe, Serge Reggiani and literally tens of others who achieved the greater part of their fame during this period. The same was true of the minor arts such as the music hall – the voice of Piaf haunts this period – and jazz, in which France almost gained world ascendancy during this time.

At this point it is useful to turn to one of the articles in the *Paris-Match* series entitled 'I Amused Myself Greatly During the Occupation'. It is written by a woman who was nineteen in 1940, a great beauty who had the great fortune or great misfortune to become the mistress of one of the French collaborationist high-ups. The article, peppered with name-dropping, is a picture of occupied Paris as seen from Maxim's. It is, as may be imagined, highly amusing and very revealing. There its famous head-waiter, the more than portly Albert (saved from a grisly fate after the liberation by the intervention of the restaurant's British shareholders), dispensed his own form of social justice by relegating wartime profiteers and Germans in uniform – including Goering – to lesser tables while keeping a table ostentatiously empty reserved for Aly Khan. Apart from the absent Aly, the main dining-room was reserved for the literary and cultural élite, the titled, the German Ambassador to occupied France, Otto Abetz and his staff, and the higher dignitaries among French collaborators. There, too, some had their favourite Jews whom they protected; Luchaire, the most prominent of the press collaborationists, for example, employed Simone Signoret as his secretary before launching her on her film career, while Guitry fought successfully for the release of Colette's Jewish husband.

There was also the animated table of literary celebrities, presided over by Florence Gould and there was Raimu and Paul Mor and Serge Lifar and Marie Bell and Alice Cocea and Drieu la Rochelle. Altogether, as the author points out, despite the absence of 'le smoking' Maxim's was never smarter than it was then. And then there were first nights, such as of Montherlant's *Reine Morte* at the Comédie Française or of Sartre's *Les Mouches* or the particularly memorable and sumptuous one of Claudel's *Le Soulier de Satin*, which with interruptions for air raids lasted seven hours. To cap it all there were the fantastic fashions which seemed to set no store by the textile shortages and which seemed to make every woman look twenty years

259

younger, to the dismay of their teenage daughters. Nobody who was in Paris in the days immediately following the liberation will ever forget the ballooning skirts of women cyclists or the legs painted to make it appear that they were wearing silk stockings or the mountainous headgear that they affected. Never did the couturiers have it so good, and never were the dictates of a Lucien Lelong and Coco Chanel or a Maggy Rouff more assiduously followed. All this makes Mlle de Beauvoir's account of the occupation years, as seen largely from the café terraces of Le Dôme and Le Flore, seem exceedingly pedestrian. All the more pedestrian because the resistance scarcely intrudes on her narrative. We are allowed to gather that Sartre is in some way connected with it, but what the exact nature of his activities were is left vague.

She does mention a trip they both made to the occupied zone to try and enlist the support of Gide and Malraux in a nationwide writer's resistance group, but she records failure in both cases. She records, rather bitchily, that Malraux received them in a rich friend's villa in the South of France where 'exquisite chicken Maryland was exquisitely served'. She records Sartre's theatrical successes at the time – he had two plays running during the occupation – but does not appear to be aware that lesser men were punished after the liberation for doing less than that.

One other witness is worth citing here – this time a German. He is the writer, Ernst Junger, who served on the Kommandatura in Paris throughout the occupation and extracts from whose diaries at the time are published in the *Paris-Match* series. Here is one extract dated 2 July 1944: 'The colonel in charge of propaganda organised today the movement of American airmen prisoners across Paris by rail. At the same time groups of Parisian riff-raff were rounded up, supplied with suitcases so that they would appear as ordinary rail passengers, in order to have them threaten the prisoners and spit on them. These scenes were filmed and photographed for the benefit of the French newsreels and press.' It is just this scene, taken from the German archives, which appeared in *Le Chagrin et la Pitié* without any indication that this was, or even might have been, a put-up job.

The Spectator, *September 2, 1978*

DEATH OF A POET

The death of Jacques Brel produced such striking outward signs of national mourning that one was almost surprised to see that the flags on public buildings were not at half-mast. It was one of those reactions which the French reserve only for their greatest men, usually for their most famous writers, and it was therefore especially striking that the object of such genuine veneration so accurately reflected in the black headlines and pages of commentary in the French press should have been a music-hall performer and a balladeer. And to make matters even more perplexing he was not even French but Belgian, and was not merely Belgian but Flemish Belgian where French is still considered a foreign, even an enemy tongue.

One jokes about French linguistic imperialism or their effort to protect even an enemy French from the inroads of 'Franc-Anglais' but the fact is that in Brel they discovered a pearl of a propagandist for their language in all its purity and subtlety. Uncharacteristically for the French, who like to carry their quarrels beyond the grave, the strife he stirred up with some of his anti-patriotic, anti-militarist, anti-clerical and anti-bourgeois songs was stilled during the days following his death while newspapers ranging from the far right to the far left vied with each other in praising him.

This reached an almost embarrassing point so that some commentators were bound to point out the contradictions involved in so much praise being heaped on him from so many disparate quarters. *Le Monde* finally called a halt to this torrent of eulogy by writing: 'Jacques Brel was a poet, a great poet. He was also a man with his contradictions, his sufferings, his loves and his furies. Now let him rest in peace.' Another writer, this time in the *Figaro*, was driven to protest at what was by implication his own newspaper's attitude which he described as 'an attempt to bury Brel in a dinner jacket'.

Politicians, always expert at body-snatching, also tried to get in on the act. Georges Marchais of the French Communist Party was quick off the mark by claiming Brel as his own. There was even a mass said for him by a priest who had become a close friend of his and who said of him: 'Brel certainly did not believe in things of the Church but he knew himself to be a child of God.' Leaving aside however all the exaggerations and intellectual burblings which his death provoked we get back to the essential fact concerning him as mentioned in *Le Monde*: 'He was a poet, a great poet.' As such he was in the great tradition of many French entertainers both past and present but he was superior to them in the quality of his lyrics. He never sagged into sentimentality and his imagery as well as his remarkable rhyming skill was wonderfully fresh and sharp. He made no concessions to his audience and he never sang down to them, whether he was performing in Paris's Olympia Music Hall or in provincial town halls. Nor did he have any of the physical attributes of a popular star: he was ungainly and had a distinctly horsy face.

We are therefore left with his basic asset – the quality of his songs, the quality of his lyrics. The remarkable thing therefore is that these should have had such a wide national appeal, cutting across all class and educational barriers. This can only lead to the conclusion that the French are as a nation better educated in the use of their own language than the British, for example, are in theirs. It is not merely a matter of contrasting the quality of the lyrics of a Brel or a Brassens with the banality of most English popular songs, although that is significant enough. It is basically that a French intellectual can communicate to a surprisingly wide audience and an English one to a surprisingly limited one. It is as though the French language well used is a unifying force while in Britain it tends to bear the stigmata of class distinction. Certainly it is my considered opinion that it is easier for Frenchmen of different classes and levels of education to communicate and to do so as equals than it is in Britain. It is, particularly, easier for writers who enjoy a much wider fame here than they do at home.

This, it seems to me, is one of the most interesting aspects of Brel's fame – that it should have been based on his use of the French language and on its enrichment. It should be remembered too that Brel was as well known in French-speaking Africa as he was in metropolitan France, making him something of a missionary in the cause of French linguistic imperialism – and a highly effective one. All in all Brel had reason to be grateful to his adopted country, and his adopted country had reason to be proud of him. They were a credit to each other.

The Spectator, *October 21, 1978*

1979

WHY FRANCE WELCOMED THE
SHAH'S ARCH-ENEMY

Whether by accident or design or possibly a combination of the two, France finds itself in the agreeable situation of playing host to a man destined to play a major role in shaping the future of Iran – the ageing leader of the Shiite Muslims, the Ayatollah Khomeini.

How exactly this came about is a matter of considerable speculation. It is four months since the Ayatollah settled down in a suburban villa near Paris, and proceeded – by means of revolutionary exhortations recorded on cassettes and flown to Tehran for nationwide distribution – virtually to take charge of the uprising against the Shah.

It was a situation which, it might have been thought, the French Government would find acutely embarrassing and which it might have been expected to put an early stop to, either by expelling the Ayatollah or by shutting him up. Instead, some five weeks ago it despatched an official from the Protocol Department of the French Foreign Office to the Ayatollah's residence to deliver the standard lecture on the discretion that the French authorities expected political refugees on its soil to show.

The beaming smiles on the faces of the Ayatollah and the members of his entourage as they ushered the official off the premises, indicated fairly clearly that the admonition had been made as the merest formality and was not to be taken as a serious expression of the French Government's displeasure.

Then, the other week, the Ayatollah's three-month tourist visa, on which he entered the country, was quietly renewed. By that time, of course, any danger of serious repercussions for the French in harbouring the Shah's deadly enemy had evaporated

263

with the Shah's own fatally declining power and it would have been sheer folly for the French to have acted otherwise.

This brings us to the central mystery of how the Ayatollah ever got to France in the first place. At that time the Shah's chances of survival were still reckoned to be fairly good, and the risks of grievously offending him by showing hospitality to the Ayatollah might therefore have been considered too great to take.

The Ayatollah, who has been in self-imposed exile for the past thirteen years, came here from Iraq where he had lived for some time. The official story is that he was expelled from Iraq, although it is difficult to see why that country should have taken this measure in view of its own enmity for the Shah.

Then, the story goes, the Ayatollah asked for asylum in Algiers. This was refused, although it is difficult to see why Algeria's rulers – also hostile to the Shah – should have done so. Then he arrived in Paris, where obviously carefully laid arrangements were made for his reception.

One suggestion is that the Ayatollah's move from Baghdad to Paris was made after soundings had been taken by the French in Tehran and the move received the approval of the authorities there. This is not as implausible as it sounds.

It must be remembered that at the time the Shah appeared anxious to see if he could reach some kind of compromise with the Ayatollah, and that no sooner was he settled here than a stream of official visitors and Iranian politicians began to arrive to talk to him. It might well have been felt in Tehran that from the point of view of negotiations with him, Paris was a more convenient centre than either Baghdad or Algiers.

It is therefore not surprising that the French feel they have brought off a considerable diplomatic *coup* by their kid-glove treatment of the Ayatollah. No doubt they hope that the pleasantness of his stay in France will be remembered when peace finally returns to Iran.

Friday, January 5, 1979

FRANCE'S GAMBLE WITH KHOMEINI

It would of course be misleading to compare the action of the French in providing a constraint-free refuge for the Ayatollah Khomeini with the action of the Germans in the first world war in transporting Lenin in a sealed train to what was then Petrograd. Yet the fact remains that in allowing the Ayatollah to use France as a base for the decisive phase of his campaign against first the Shah and then the Bakhtiar government, the French have made an immense contribution to his cause. There is in fact no parallel to the French action in giving a political refugee all the facilities for engaging in a revolutionary campaign against a friendly government. Yet these facilities were extended with a liberal hand during the Ayatollah's four-month stay in a village on the outskirts of Paris. His telephone service between his headquarters at Neauphle-le-Château and Tehran and, most important of all, the holy city of Qom, never failed and his daily orders and exhortations duly recorded beforehand and then re-recorded at the other end were distributed nation-wide the next day. His disciples were free to convert a village setting into something like a national shrine and his couriers could come and go without let or hindrance. It was almost as though his fourteen years of exile had already ended once he had set foot in France.

How did this astonishing situation come about? The answer is largely by chance and only partly by Quai d'Orsay machination. The Shah had paid heavy sums of money to the Iraqis finally to expel the Ayatollah from Baghdad – where he had spent the greater part of his exile – by a certain date. When the date finally came up the Ayatollah's intention was to move to Algiers. Unfortunately this coincided with Boumedienne's long coma which preceded his death, and no one in those circumstances in Algiers was prepared to take the decision to let him in. He therefore journeyed to Paris instead, equipped with an Iranian passport and the status of a political refugee. Although the French have never made any public statement to that effect they did in fact consult Tehran before allowing him to stay and Tehran gave its approval. There was an obvious reason for that – the Shah himself hoped to open fruitful negotiations with him and from that point of view it was preferable to have him in Paris than in Damascus or Algiers. That this version of events is true is confirmed by the fact that there has never been a peep of protest from Tehran regarding his presence here. From this point onwards the French began to pin their hopes on the Ayatollah, or at any rate not to make the mistake that Washington and London made, which was to continue a policy of outright support for the Shah.

It must be remembered that the French had no particular reasons to be enamoured of the Shah. Giscard himself felt an aristocratic disdain for him and he was cordially detested by the French-speaking bourgeoisie of Tehran, with whom the French embassy found naturally the majority of its closest contacts, as he was indeed by the majority of the Iran embassy staff in Paris. Furthermore he had given France many a rude commercial setback. In those circumstances they were among the first to become convinced that the Shah's days were numbered, and on the principle that it is an ill wind which does not blow someone some good they began to regard the Ayatollah's stay in France as something of a windfall. The Quai d'Orsay became quite intoxicated with the idea and began to see in their uninvited guest the guarantor of France's future in Iran. Meanwhile there were obvious immediate advantages to be gained from the Ayatollah's presence in France. It provided for example a kind of safe-conduct guarantee for the French in Iran as well as rendering French property immune from attacks by rioters. The Air France offices in Tehran, for example, were never attacked while other foreign airline buildings were.

Could it be possible that at this point the Ayatollah became something of a blackmailer, threatening French lives and property in Tehran with his rioters if the French sought to limit his freedom of action? It is not impossible and indeed there is good reason for believing that this is actually what happened when disenchantment with the Ayatollah began to set in among senior French Foreign Office officials. This disenchantment became clearly evident when M. François-Poncet, formerly the head of Giscard's Elysée staff, replaced M. Guiringaud as Foreign Minister.

Indeed M. François-Poncet recently confessed privately that he thought it was high time the Ayatollah displayed his talents elsewhere. The disillusion began to seep through as the French made efforts to engage the holy man in political discussions.

They found to their dismay that they were talking to a religious fanatic who really meant what he said when he talked of an Islamic republic. Gradually French hopes dwindled and finally expired as they realised that by talking like this he was either dashing his own chances or, if he succeeded, then he was a menace to all except the Soviet Union, which could be expected to pull some irons for itself out of the Iranian fire.

The view that the Bakhtiar government would pop like a champagne cork on the Ayatollah's return was hastily replaced by fervent hope that the government would survive. In short, by playing the generous host to the Ayatollah the French, instead of pulling off a diplomatic *coup*, have committed a major diplomatic folly. They might have hoped to play the role of mediators but it is unlikely that the army or Bakhtiar will accept them as such in view of their previous chumminess with their principal foe. Similarly, if the Bakhtiar–army alliance survives and consolidates it is unlikely in the extreme that the new rulers will be disposed to make France one of their favoured economic or political partners.

It now looks as though, apart from the temporary protection of its interest in Iran, France will lose rather than gain from its involvement with the Ayatollah. It will be a heavy price to have paid for having broken the traditional rules governing the right of asylum and the obligations of reserve and discretion which France normally imposes on those whom it admits as refugees.

The Spectator, *February 10, 1979*

SO IS THE PATIENT BETTER OFF IN FRANCE?

Which national health service functions better – the French or the British? The question has come under some discussion in Paris as a result of a financial crisis in the affairs of the one and seemingly growing chaos, spotlighted by the recent strikes, in the affairs of the other.

Fortunately, the presence in France of a small but growing band of British doctors who have had experience of both systems enables the layman to make a reasonably balanced comparison between the two.

When this is done it is difficult to escape the conclusion that despite its fabulous financial deficit – far bigger than that involved in the British service – it is the French system which functions better, both from the point of view of the doctor and the patient.

To put it simply: the French system functions better from the doctor's point of view because, although it means working exceptionally long hours, it enables him to earn considerably more than his British counterpart; earnings of £20,000 a year for a GP in the Paris area are quite common.

From the patient's point of view it is preferable because there is no shortage of hospital beds and even no waiting lists for even the most minor of operations. And the French patient has almost unlimited choice of doctors and specialists and is not, like the British one, limited to the kind of present-day version of the old panel system.

The basic difference between the two systems, however, is that the French patient pays his doctor directly and recovers the greater part of the sum later, whereas in Britain, of course, no money changes hands, with the exception of prescription charges.

Today some ninety per cent of French doctors belong to the NHS; the rest take only private patients. Those with the health service charge fees usually of fifty francs for a surgery consultation and sixty francs for a bedside one. A lot of form filling is involved in the reimbursement procedure both for the doctor's fee and the prescription (it amounts to seventy-five per cent of both) and the delay in repayment varies from one week to two. This system – aimed at discouraging people from seeing their doctor unnecessarily as well as of course saving the State some money – has, oddly enough, had the opposite effect and is, in the view of some, in danger of producing a nation of hypochondriacs.

It is not unusual for patients to consult four or five different doctors for the same ailment, with some of those consulted recommending a specialist and often getting a kick-back from the specialist's fee. It is often the case, too, that a doctor who does not prescribe medicines for what he probably considers to be an imaginary ailment runs the almost certain risk of losing his patient.

Furthermore, the pharmaceutical industry and chemists, who are the major profiteers from the French health service, play a direct role in encouraging doctors to prescribe unnecessarily and expensively.

A great many people seek their chemist's advice in finding a doctor and the chemist is only too well aware of the prescription habits of the doctors in his locality. In this connection another basic difference in the workings of the two health services should be noted – while the British doctor on the NHS will not care about losing a patient, in France the competition among doctors for patients is intense. This is because there are too many doctors in France and their numbers have been increasing at a positively alarming rate from the point of view of both the existing practitioners and the State.

The growing numbers add considerably to the costs of the health service. Not only is there greater density of the medical profession in relation to population in France than in Britain but the density is increasing at such a rate that today there are 194 medical students per 100,000 of population in France, compared with only thirty-three in Britain.

One reason is that in France there was no selection system for entry into university and therefore into medical schools – this problem is now being met by a form of indirect selection, simply by failing up to seventy-five per cent of medical students after their first year and barring them from repeating the course.

Meanwhile, France continues to spend more on its NHS than Britain and the increase has amounted to more than twenty per cent over the past five years, while the national prescription bill is five times as much as it was five years ago. All attempts to nationalise the production of drugs and medicines have repeatedly been foiled by the powerful pharmaceutical and chemist lobbies, the latter being particularly strong and influential in times of elections.

Now the runaway deficit in the services has become such that the Government has been forced to take action, and the highly popular Minister of Health, Mme Simone Veil, has seen her popularity somewhat dimmed as a result of the measures she has had to take. These have been to increase the patient's share of his contribution to his medical fees – and as lower-paid workers are spared these extra charges, the main burden falls on the professional middle class.

It should be pointed out at this point that while the patient pays something towards his health bill, hospitalisation for serious illnesses is entirely free. The hospital situation in France has been completely transformed in the past twenty-five years, so that from having a notoriously backward hospital system, France now boasts one of the most modern in the world and one which is certainly superior to that in Britain.

It also boasts, in the hospital at Ville Juif in Paris, one of the leading cancer research units in the world. There has been no let-up in hospital construction and modernisation for economy reasons and the only way to cope with a growing cost is to discourage doctors from hospitalising their patients when they could be cared for at home.

Many Paris hospitals have a permanent population of old age pensioners. The marvel is that in these circumstances hospital beds should be so readily available. This is a tribute to the scale of the building programme undertaken in recent years.

Friday, February 16, 1979

A RICH LADY'S LAST GOODBYE

I knew only one of the seven husbands of Barbara Hutton, the Woolworth heiress, who died last week – but the one I knew, her fifth, was absolutely shameless.

He was the playboy so-called diplomat, Porfirio Rubirosa, whose marriage to Miss Hutton in 1953 lasted only seventy-three days but won him a million-dollar settlement.

Her last one, to the Laotian Prince Pierre Raymond Doan Vinh, came to my notice when she paid him off in rather bizarre circumstances.

The couple had been staying at one of Morocco's most glamorous hotels – the Golden Gazelle – owned by a French aristocrat, the late Baron Pallenc. I ran into Pallenc in Paris shortly after Miss Hutton had left and he told me the story of her departure.

She had wanted to leave without her husband's knowledge and the baron had to organise her getaway. The crew of her private aeroplane were alerted the previous evening to stand by for a dawn departure. Meanwhile, the baron organised the staff of servants to pack and dispose of Miss Hutton's avalanche of luggage – packing and loading operations began at 3.0 a.m. to ensure that the prince would be soundly asleep at the time.

By 6.0 a.m. everything was ready for Miss Hutton to step into her Rolls-Royce and be driven to the airport. The Rolls was being loaded along with the rest of the luggage on to the aeroplane.

The Prince woke at ten o'clock, breakfasted in his room and then tried to phone his wife. It was then he heard that she had left that morning.

When he went to the reception desk he found an envelope for him from his wife. It contained two cheques – one was for three million dollars for himself, the other was one million dollars for his brother.

The Prince apparently took the situation philosophically and went off for a day's golf.

Friday, May 16, 1979

PICASSO'S PICASSOS

It is something of an irony that a major portion of Picasso's work spanning his entire life as a painter should now find itself in the hands of the French state as a result of a tax settlement which the facts of life have imposed on the painter's bickering heirs. Yet this is what has happened and it has transformed Paris at a stroke from impoverishment as far as Picassos are concerned to being the richest depository of his work in the world. Neither the Hermitage in Leningrad nor the Museum of Modern Art in New York nor even the Picasso Museum in Barcelona will be able to match the collection which will be housed in the Hotel Sale in the Marais from 1981 but which goes on show at the Grand Palais this week.

Up till 1947 there was only one state-owned Picasso in France, and that was a donation not by the painter but by the widow of one of the subjects of one of his earliest portraits. Picasso himself donated ten paintings shortly after to the Paris Museum of

Modern Art, but when the state itself showed a belated interest in acquiring Picassos, it was too late. Prices had rocketed to a point which no French museum could afford. Now comes this windfall of 229 Picassos, plus 149 sculptures, 85 ceramics and innumerable water colours and sketches. The collection is essentially that of the legendary Picasso's Picassos and many of them have not been shown in public before. They are the paintings that Picasso hoarded for himself, representing in many cases some technical or aesthetic triumph from which Picasso derived enormous, almost secret pleasure, and others which he had sold, regretted doing so and then bought them back from the original buyers.

The man largely responsible for securing this treasure for France was André Malraux who, as Minister of Culture, introduced a law enabling owners of works of art to pay their death duties in kind rather than in cash. The law was passed in 1968, and Picasso died five years later. In pushing this law through Malraux had the future of Picasso's Picassos very much in mind.

At first, following Picasso's death, there was no problem – the two heirs, the widow Jacqueline and the painter's son Paul, agreed to pay their death duties with Picassos and they went even further and made an outright gift to the state of paintings by Degas, Matisse and Cézanne which Picasso owned. Problems however arose when the circle of heirs expanded. First Paul died, leaving his two children as heirs. Then, after prolonged legal battles the courts decided that Picasso's illegitimate children should share in the fortune. They were a daughter from his liaison with Marie-Thérèse Walter and the two children of Françoise Gilot, Claude and Paloma. This had the immediate effect of raising the total amount payable in death duties, increasing it to roughly about a third of the estate. Apart from his many homes, Picasso's fortune consisted almost entirely of the Picassos still in his possession, and these, piled up in his various residences in empty rooms, cellars and lofts over the decades, presented a picture of indescribable chaos. Picasso had the habit of never throwing anything away, even the most trifling object down to a newspaper in which something had caught his fancy.

The first task therefore was to establish an inventory of what Picasso had left behind him and then to establish its value. A court-appointed assessor was therefore named – the famous Paris auctioneer Maître Maurice Rheims – who in turn recruited a team of six experts to help him. The totals they reached were staggering. The total value of the work that Picasso had left behind him was estimated at over £100 million and the number of Picasso works uncovered amounted to 1,885 paintings, 7,089 drawings, almost his total output of sculptures numbering 1,228 pieces, 3,222 ceramics and over 30,000 engravings. Basing themselves on these figures the court assessors estimated the death duties at roughly £29 million.

How to pay? Clearly the best way of doing so was to make the necessary donations to the state. To sell in order to raise the money would risk lowering the value of the remaining Picassos while, on the other hand, to place a considerable number of Picassos out of reach of the market would enhance it. A further obstacle arose at this point, and this was as to which Picassos would go to the heirs and which to the state. Were the heirs to choose first or the state? On this question, the authorities were firm – their experts would choose first and the heirs could divide up the rest among themselves. The result is that the state's share represents what might be described as a scholar's choice of Picassos – comprehensive and illustrating every phase of the painter's development.

An argument is now developing as to whether it would not be preferable to hold over the showing of the collection until its permanent home – the Hotel Sale – is ready to receive it in eighteen months' time. Then this great event would have, it is argued, its maximum impact. One can understand, however, the impatience of the authorities in the matter and their understandable pride in their achievement – an achievement in which scholarship, patience and legal cunning have all played their part. It is no mean feat to have settled among other things inter-family disputes sometimes amounting to downright hates in the six-year period since Picasso's death. Some of the terms of the settlement were very hard indeed for Jacqueline Picasso to swallow. She had to accept not only the loss of some paintings to which she was sentimentally strongly attached, but also the bitter pill of the legitimisation of children whom Picasso in his life-time had always refused to recognise. Now these matters are behind her, as are her husband's various feuds with various French governments. One of the most bitter of these arose from his expulsion from his studio in the Rue des Grands-Augustins in the mid-Fifties. It was at a time of great housing shortage in Paris, and the government decreed the requisitioning of all unused flats. Picasso's fell into this category, and he never forgave the French for allowing it to be sold. To such a point that years later he boycotted a retrospective showing of his work at the Grand Palais organised by André Malraux and refused the Legion of Honour. He also went back on a promise he had made to donate a large number of his works to French museums. Now, involuntarily, he has done just that, and on a vaster scale than he could ever have envisaged.

The Spectator, *October 13, 1979*

GISCARD AND BOKASSA'S DIAMONDS

Diamonds may be a girl's best friend, but they are at the moment a cause of great embarrassment to President Giscard. It is now clear – indeed he has made an oblique confession on this point – that Giscard accepted a gift of diamonds from Bokassa, the recently deposed ruler of the Central African Republic, when he was Minister of Finance in 1973. It was of course to be expected that, when the French finally got round to deposing their former protégé, there would be a number of scandals connected with their past close association with him. The association had been too intimate, too personal and had involved too many cover-ups for Bokassa's appalling deeds over too long a period – thirteen years – for there not to be. This was why the Socialists, in shrewd anticipation, had put down a motion for a parliamentary commission to inquire into the relationships formed between successive French governments and Bokassa shortly after the former 'emperor' went into exile.

Nobody, however, expected that the first scandal to break would take so crude a form as this. Giscard, after all, is no vulgar careerist but an aristocrat, and immensely wealthy at that, and one would have thought that, in this case, whatever lesser mortals might do, the gift would have been either instantly returned or equally swiftly contributed to a favourite charity. This was certainly the feeling in the National Assembly on the two days following the revelations in *Canard Enchaîné*, and it inhibited the reactions of politicians of all parties. They were wary of the possibility – indeed, in their view, the likelihood – that Giscard, having allowed the storm to rise, would then majestically dispel it by producing a document proving that he had disposed of the diamonds in either of the two above-mentioned manners.

Instead of which there was silence, followed by an ambiguous statement which amounted to a confession. The statement was brief but not to the point. It merely said that the exchange of diplomatic gifts when members of the government visit foreign countries 'never have the character nor the value of those mentioned in the press in connection with the Central African Republic'. One could only gather from this that the value of the thirty-carat diamonds mentioned in the *Canard* was considerably less than 100,000 dollars at which it valued them. What the communiqué did not mention was that when such gifts are exchanged in the course of foreign visits they are donated publicly. Giscard's gift, however, was not made in the course of a visit, nor was it given in the course of a public occasion. It was sent to him in Paris by order of Bokassa, and it is his letter ordering their delivery which the *Canard* reproduced last week. It was a private gift, and what was particularly unseemly about it was that it was given to a minister who was virtually Bokassa's paymaster. For who decided the size of French subsidies to Bokassa's budget, who paid his school-teachers, his army and his civil service? None other than the French Minister of Finance – in this case Giscard himself.

But there is also the matter of the three members of Giscard's family who have strong financial interests in the Central African Republic – Giscard's cousins François and Jacques, and his brother Olivier. All three, as well as two members of the government, have been accused by the *Canard* of accepting gifts from Bokassa. The politicians have remained silent, but the three Giscards have vehemently denied the allegations. There is no reason to disbelieve them, if only because no one knows what other documents the *Canard* has up its sleeve. It promises further revelations in its next issue, which is causing understandable apprehension in some circles and keen anticipation in the rest of the nation. For, side by side with the story of the diamonds, goes the story of the removal by French agents and French troops of Bokassa's archives from his palace to the French embassy in Bangui. Every French correspondent on the spot testifies to having witnessed these removals, and it was no doubt some stray breeze which has blown a document or two the *Canard*'s way. The Minister of Foreign Affairs, M. François-Poncet, has solemnly denied that the Quai d'Orsay or any of its agents was engaged in any such task. There is no reason to disbelieve him, just as there is no reason to disbelieve the eyewitness accounts. The fact is that the Quai is often deliberately kept in ignorance of what the government is doing in its former black African colonies. This has been the case even since de Gaulle set up a special department, quite separate from the Quai and often in rivalry with it, to deal with African matters. The result has been an endless stream of complaints from French ambassadors in these countries that not only are their reports ignored, but that often they are unaware of developments planned in Paris and not communicated to them.

The present head of this special African section, M. Journiac, reports like his predecessors directly to the Elysée and ignores the Quai. In those circumstances, it is easy for M. François-Poncet to deny what is in fact undeniable. He has not been officially informed of the removal of the archives; therefore, in his eyes, they have not been removed. What has been especially interesting to watch in this case, however, has been the behaviour of the media. Although all newspapers receive copies of the *Canard* twenty-four hours before it goes on sale, the Hersant press (comprising *Le Figaro*, *France-Soir* and *L'Aurore*) ignored it, as did television and radio. What gave the story its real impact was the treatment given to it in *Le Monde* on the afternoon of its appearance in the *Canard*. With what at first appeared to be the wildest recklessness, *Le Monde* splashed it on the front page, followed by two pages on the inside, and the whole capped by a front-page leader signed by the editor himself, Jacques Fauvet. It has since become clear, of course, that there was collusion on the story between the two publications, with *Le Monde* knowing well beforehand exactly what cards the *Canard* held. It is doubtful if *Le Monde* will ever be forgiven, while Giscard is president, for its alacrity in jumping on the *Canard* bandwagon, and there will be a renewed outcry in establishment circles for Fauvet's head. He is in for a rough ride during the two years of his editorship which remain before he has to retire.

There are two other pieces of evidence which deserve to be included here. First there is that of M. François Giscard d'Estaing, Giscard's cousin, who in an interview with the weekly *Le Point* says: 'It is possible that at some time diamonds figured among official presents. I seem to recall the president saying to me one day: "I am very embarrassed by such gifts. I must sell them and give the proceeds to charity".' The other comes from Bokassa's former French secretary, Mme Dmitri, to whom he wrote the note reproduced in the *Canard*, giving instructions for the diamonds to be sent to Giscard. She does not question the authenticity of the letter, but is quite definite that she never received instructions to send presents to Giscard's relatives. She says it was normal to offer diamonds to people of importance, since they were one of the few articles of value produced in the Central African Republic. She adds that the diamonds usually given were of modest value, and that the estimate given by the *Canard* of the value of Giscard's gift 'bears absolutely no relation to reality'. It may well be, therefore, that Giscard, having been given an estimate indicating that they were not of great value, and while still intending to sell them, simply put them away in a drawer and under pressure of work forgot about them. But if that is what happened, then why, in heaven's name, not say so?

The Spectator, *October 20, 1979*

A FRENCH LESSON IN LYING LOW

There is growing unhappiness here at the passive, indeed almost neutralist, role that France in particular and Western Europe in general are playing in relation to events in Iran.

This feeling is not shared by President Giscard, but it is one which is being voiced increasingly in Parliament and the Press. To those critics, France – to say nothing of the rest of Europe – is once again following the slippery path of appeasement which, unless swiftly arrested by a dramatic show of solidarity with the United States, will lead to the same disastrous consequences as in 1940.

Needless to say, those who take this view are being denounced like the anti-appeasers of the Thirties as 'warmongers' or, in more up-to-date terms, as 'nostalgics for the days of Empire'. In fact, they represent all sections of political opinion with the exception of the Communists.

It is significant, for example, that the most eloquent plea for solidarity with the U.S. in the present crisis has come from the Socialist leader, M. François Mitterrand, and this has been echoed by such usually stern anti-Americans as the country's leading Gaullists.

The French, of course, have a particularly sensitive conscience regarding events in Iran because of their kid-glove handling of the Ayatollah Khomeini during his five-month exile in France before his triumphant return to Tehran. At that time he was showered with diplomatic privileges and given all facilities to direct the mounting revolution against the Shah.

In reply to a question in the course of a TV interview the other day asking him if France does not now regret the privilege treatment it gave to the Ayatollah during his stay here, President Giscard made a revealing reply.

He said that if France had placed any restrictions on him then, 'who knows, it might be the French Embassy that was being occupied now and Frenchmen who were being held hostage.'

In short – appeasement has paid off, France has been spared. It is this remark which has brought the current debate to the boil with critics quick to point out that America's humiliation is not just America's alone but one which the entire West shares.

True, France is active in Tehran trying to bring the new regime around to a more reasonable state of mind but in general the tone of official comment has been similar to the line taken by Senator Kennedy – the Shah was wicked, the Americans made the mistake of bolstering a corrupt regime and the Iranian revolution is in Giscard's words 'a profound and understandable event'. All this is no doubt true but it is also true that many Iranians who helped to make the revolution feel as alienated from the reactionary regime that the Ayatollah has installed as they did from that of the Shah.

It is not surprising therefore that many are now recalling de Gaulle's behaviour in similar crises involving the Americans. A savage critic of American policies in Europe and elsewhere, he showed himself to be a surprisingly prompt and staunch foul-weather friend in times of trouble.

In two major confrontations between Washington and Moscow, he unhesitatingly supported Washington. The first was during the Berlin crisis in 1961 and the second, even more surprisingly, over Cuba a year later.

While the rest of the world was still debating the authenticity of photos showing Soviet missile installations in Cuba, de Gaulle was the first to give the Americans assurance of his full support for any action they might decide to take. This is because de Gaulle probably realised that his cherished ambition of 'Independence' for France had a price tag attached to it – a strong U.S. allied to Europe.

Friday, December 7, 1979

1980

THE GIANT WHO TOOK A
WRONG TURNING

They are burying Jean-Paul Sartre in Paris today with the kind of honours he always shunned in life.

I am writing this the morning before the funeral takes place at the historic Père Lachaise cemetery – that Panthéon of a burial ground – but it is already clear that it will take on that character of massive mourning with which France traditionally marks the passing of its greatest literary figures.

It will thus inevitably be compared with the funerals of Voltaire and Victor Hugo.

Sartre's political involvement was total and was rooted in the injustices he saw all round him. The result was his fierce championship of the most underprivileged sections of society – immigrants of all kinds and especially the lowliest of all, the Arab immigrant workers. His funeral procession will be swollen by tens of thousands of these.

Having said this, one pauses to reflect on his truly appalling political record. Politically he resembled in many ways Bertrand Russell in his dotage. Politically again, however, Sartre's dotage extended over nearly his entire active life.

He defended Stalin in the Fifties and even derided the earliest Soviet defectors in one of his plays. He fell for all the great ideological swindles of our time and especially the Chinese and Cuban ones.

He was convinced that de Gaulle was a Fascist who intended to use the army both to hang on to Algeria and install a Fascist regime in France. There was a period when he deliberately sought martyrdom only to find de Gaulle obstinate in refusing it to him. 'One does not arrest Voltaire,' de Gaulle remarked at a

Cabinet meeting at which Sartre's appeal to French conscripts to desert was discussed.

There was something distinctly distasteful about a man protected by his age and fame advising young men to embark on a course of action which would involve the risk of ruining their lives. It was at this time that de Gaulle wrote him a famous letter beginning '*Cher maître*' of exquisite politeness, exalted praise and gentle rebuke.

It was at this time, too, that his critics recalled that Sartre had two plays running in Paris during the occupation – an act for which lesser writers were held guilty of collaboration. Indeed, he was left unmolested during the occupation despite his efforts to set up a clandestine writers' anti-Fascist committee and it was during that period that he set up his headquarters in the Café Flore on the Boulevard St Germain and his long romance with Simone de Beauvoir commenced.

In her published memoirs of that period Mlle de Beauvoir devotes much more space to the praise Sartre was receiving in the Paris press for his two plays than she does to their resistance work to which indeed there is only one reference.

In his own autobiography Sartre gives a revealing picture of himself as a child. The coddled offspring of a bourgeois family, he was cross-eyed and ugly and found difficulty in getting other children to play with him. This may provide a Freudian clue to his later development.

He was sexually obsessed – neither he nor de Beauvoir were by mutual consent ever faithful to each other – and in politics he had something of the air of a wilful toy-breaking child.

Towards the end of his life it should be noted he confessed to disenchantment with most of his past political beliefs leaving only anti-racialism as the last fundamental of his faith.

His considerable literary fortune has long been disposed of with large acts of generosity to friends and the political movements he supported. As he most probably did not leave a will his continuing royalties will by law go to his adopted daughter Arlette el Kaim, a Jewess of North African extraction.

Friday, April 18, 1980

THE MOSLEYS ON THE WINDSORS

'It was the King who made the running throughout and if Mrs Simpson had left him she knew that he would follow'

I was intrigued to learn that Lady Diana Mosley has written a life of the Duchess of Windsor. She is particularly fitted for such a task not only because of her husband's life-long association with the Duke but because of her own close friendship with the Duchess which blossomed over a twenty-year period when they were near neighbours in the country just outside Paris.

Most intriguing of all, however, was the prospect of a book by the wife of Britain's lost leader about the widow of Britain's lost King.

The Mosleys and the Windsors have led strangely intertwined lives and they might just as conceivably have ended up ruling Britain together as in near exile in France. It was with these somewhat sombre thoughts filling my mind that I journeyed to Orsay, a town near Paris, to lunch with the Mosleys in their lovely château built for one of Napoleon's defeated generals and named appropriately 'Le Temple de la Gloire'.

Lady Diana retains all the marks of a classic beauty she has always been. We got down to battle immediately and in keeping with my earlier reflections it soon became apparent that Lady Diana equates her loyalty to her husband with loyalty to the Windsors.

Edward VIII, she said, should have been allowed to keep his throne and marry Mrs Simpson morganatically or otherwise.

It might have changed the whole course of history, she claimed, by preventing the Second World War. On this point Sir Oswald was more categoric – it would have prevented the war. He felt he knew this because although it was impossible for the two to meet after he had founded the British Union of Fascists, they had maintained a steady correspondence before and during the abdication crisis.

True, there were anti-appeasers like Churchill and Duff

Cooper among the King's advisers but they were balanced by himself and Lloyd George, to say nothing of the King's own strong aversion to war with Germany.

Every now and then Sir Oswald would growl: 'We should have told Hitler he could do what he liked in the East but not to touch France or move against the West. If he wanted the Ukraine as far as we were concerned he could have it.'

Gently Lady Diana shifted the conversation to the Duchess. Although she is one of the Duchess's few remaining close friends it is now nearly three years since she last saw her. During that period the Duchess's memory has gone and she has lost the use of her limbs. She only leaves her Paris mansion for short stays in the American hospital. Only her doctors, her round-the-clock relays of nurses and her lawyer, Maître Suzanne Blum, see her.

It is Maître Blum who with unbending strictness applies the medical rule against visitors. Like everyone else Lady Diana is struck with admiration at Maître Blum's total devotion to her client and charge.

She seems to identify herself with the Duchess to the point of attributing to her emotions she cannot possibly any longer feel. Hence, for example, her curious statements about the Duchess's alleged indignation over the recent British television film on the abdication.

Nothing fuels the indignation of this remarkable woman – still handsome, still the brilliant lawyer although she's almost exactly the Duchess's age – more than suggestions that her client might have gone to bed with the Duke before they were married. Lady Diana's comment on this was worth recording. 'After all, they had been together for some years before they were married and I must say I would have thought more of the Duchess if she had than if she hadn't.'

Maître Blum has also talked of love letters which, according to her, show clearly that the Duchess never wanted to become Queen. She says that she has placed these letters in the hands of an historian. Whoever the historian may be, it is certainly not Lady Diana.

The Duchess herself, according to Lady Diana, 'never gave a fig for titles', and the denial of that of Royal Highness only affected the Duke not her. He was doubly indignant not only because it was a slight on his wife but because it seemed to him a gross form of cheating.

He had been denied a morganatic marriage while he was King

only to find that he was morganatically married after he had abdicated. Lady Diana is emphatic – and there she agrees with Maître Blum – that the then Mrs Simpson had not wanted to marry the King of England or to be the cause of his abdication.

She wanted a divorce for Ernest Simpson's sake – 'Like all seemingly complaisant husbands, he had begun to look very foolish' – and in any case he had fallen in love with his wife's best friend whom he subsequently married.

Just how ludicrously impossible Ernest Simpson's situation had become was shown by the extraordinary interview he had with the King on the subject of his wife. Says Lady Diana: 'He behaved like a Victorian father talking of his wife as though she were his daughter and asking the King what his intentions were towards her.'

In any case, said Lady Diana, it was the King who made the running throughout and if Mrs Simpson had left him she knew only too well that he would follow.

He was, she says, quoting Shakespeare on Antony: 'Like a doting mullard.' What then did this latter-day Cleopatra have to reduce Edward to this mullard-like state?

Lady Diana seems to be as puzzled on this point as the rest of us. 'A certain freshness of approach, an ability while being perfectly respectful of avoiding any trace of obsequiousness. She made him feel valued for himself rather than for his position' is the best she can do.

It is extraordinary to reflect they both at this stage were middle-aged – he in his early forties, she in her late thirties – and she after her divorce from Simpson found herself for the second time in her life both homeless and penniless. Clearly Lady Diana's book will be on the idolatrous side and she is reluctant to speak of two episodes which spoil the Windsors' image.

The first is the Duchess's extraordinary escapade with the American homosexual and Woolworth heir, the late Jimmy Donoghue, which brought great misery to the Duke. She admits that it very nearly brought about a rift in their marriage but insists that it was an innocent relationship, Donoghue's homosexuality and the fact that he was nineteen years younger than her making him a perfect escort for a woman who liked night-clubs and late nights which the Duke did not.

It was the first time the Duchess lost her grip on her dignity and she fully merited Donoghue's crack when the relationship broke up and he was asked if he was still seeing her: 'No, I have abdicated.'

The other episode is the Windsors' wanderings in Madrid and Lisbon in the early stages of the war when the Germans were making indirect and later direct approaches to him to remain in Europe rather than take up the post of Governor of the Bahamas.

Important documents concerning these German approaches are still being withheld from historians. As for the transcripts of Hitler's talks with the Duke before the war during his notorious visit to Germany – of which I suspect Sir Oswald has some knowledge – these appear to have vanished.

Two other mysteries remain, one of which Lady Diana cannot clear up and another she claims she can. The first concerns Queen Alexandra's jewels which it is widely believed the Duke took with him when he abdicated.

All Lady Diana can say is that she never saw the Duchess wearing them and she adds disarmingly that she has never asked her. Now it is too late.

Then there is the matter of the Duchess's age, generally supposed to be two years more than her stated one. Not so, says Lady Diana, for she has found that the Duchess's Uncle Warfield planned a coming-out eighteenth birthday party for her which he cancelled because of the outbreak of the First World War.

I was interested to learn, too, that the Secret Service played a role in breaking up the Duke's affair with Lady Furness, pre-Mrs Simpson, by reporting to him her shipboard flirtation on a trans-Atlantic crossing with the late Aly Khan.

Altogether a rewarding lunch.

Friday, May 30, 1980

COMMUNISTS PAST AND PRESENT

Although operating in a free society, the French Communist Party continues to show the same impudent recklessness in re-writing and distorting its history as the Soviet Communist Party did and continues to do in coping with its own. Thus we are repeatedly asked to believe that events which quite definitely did take place did not take place, and that the party leader, Georges Marchais, far from being a voluntary worker in a German aircraft factory during the war, was a model of the spirit of resistance which, it is claimed, animated the party throughout it.

Being a mini-image of Big Brother has its problems; one of them involves a compelling need to re-write history every so often. When, usually because of a change of policy, unpleasant facts have to be admitted, then the admission – though made with much ceremonial sorrow – usually contains a few subtle escape clauses which enable the party to return to the original, falsified version without too much trouble. (A classic example is provided by the party's handling of the Stalin problem. Did the leadership know of Khrushchev's denunciation of him at the time? For ten years it has persisted that it did, then it confessed that it knew all along but that it withheld the information – mistakenly, it adds – for internal French political reasons. Should Moscow at some future date decide to rehabilitate Stalin, the French party could point with pride to its own reluctance to condemn him in the first place.)

Now the debate concerning the party's past has been revived again, and in a particularly acute form, with the publication of two books by two former communist leaders, Charles Tillon and Auguste Lecoeur, which focus on the party's wartime role, from the signing of the Hitler–Stalin pact to the German attack on Russia and the astonishingly rapid rise of Georges Marchais in the post-war years to the post of secretary-general. Both men are veteran revolutionaries (Tillon led the Black Sea mutiny of the French fleet in support of the Bolshevik revolution); both were active in the Spanish civil war. Both were former members of the Politburo, and both were major organisers of resistance to the Germans during the last war. Both men also fell foul of the then French party boss, Maurice Thorez, and of Stalin, and were duly purged in the middle Fifties, thereby opening the way to Marchais's rapid rise.

On the signing of the Hitler–Stalin pact, the Daladier government committed a grievous historical error. It declared the French party illegal, thereby provoking a reaction of solidarity within its ranks and healing an incipient split which the pact might well have brought about. Driven underground, the party continued to function with discipline and fortitude. The leadership, on Moscow's instructions, took up its allotted posts;

Thorez was spirited away from his army unit to which he had been called up and, akin to something like Lenin's voyage to St Petersburg in a sealed German train, travelled to Moscow via Germany. Jacques Duclos was told to remain in hiding in Paris and pick up the threads of the party organisation. Tillon and Lecoeur, among others, were dispersed to the provinces.

One of the Duclos's tasks was to continue publication of the underground version of the party organ *L'Humanité*, a four-page roneoed flimsy. The early issues carried the message that the war was an imperialist one, and clamoured for an early peace. De Gaulle was dismissed as an agent of the City of London. With the German occupation, *L'Humanité* called for fraternisation with the German troops, denounced terrorist acts against them, and for the first time raised the demand that the paper should be allowed to appear legally. The climax came with a formal request to that effect to the Kommandatura by a party delegation of three. The Germans strung them along, thereby encouraging more and more communists to come out of hiding before finally refusing on the grounds that Vichy would not hear of it. By the time the attack on Russia came, the Germans were able to swoop on a substantial number of communists, including two of those who had made the plea for *L'Humanité*. The third escaped and is still alive. Until four years ago, the party grimly clung to a denial that any such approach to the Germans had been made. Then it confessed that 'a tragic mistake' had been made, but added that 'the three comrades had acted independently and without the knowledge of Duclos'.

Then there is the curious matter of the letter addressed to François Billoux, who later became president of the communist deputies in the National Assembly, to Marshal Pétain. Dated 19 July 1940, the author offered to give evidence at the notorious Riom trial of Third Republic 'traitors' like Léon Blum, Georges Mandel, and Paul Reynaud. This, no doubt, was another 'tragic mistake', although so far still an unacknowledged one.

These are, however, past lies, past cover-ups. The biggest one, though deriving from the past, is very much of the present. It concerns the present secretary-general of the party, and a future candidate in the coming presidential elections. The fact is that there is a three-year wartime gap in Marchais's life which no official biographer has been able to fill and which Marchais has never been able to explain satisfactorily. All the evidence shows, beyond a shadow of a doubt, that he went to Germany as a voluntary aircraft worker and that he did not return to France until 1945. All this would be bad enough. What is worse is the party's persistence in denying it, and in the process having to fit him out with a totally fictional past as a refractory requisitioned worker who finally succeeded in escaping from Germany in 1944. He joined the party in 1947 and, according to the rules, he must have submitted a detailed autobiography to the party's control commission before becoming, seven years later, a paid functionary. According to Lecoeur, who was himself a member of that commission, no such report was ever presented to it. If it exists, the party has never revealed it. What is obvious is that the truth about Marchais's past must have been known to Thorez and Duclos at the time, to Moscow, and to successive French governments fully briefed on the subject by their secret service.

Not to put too fine a point on it, Marchais is clearly in the uncomfortable position of being open to blackmail regarding his past by both the Russians and the French. This brings us to the further point of his usefulness to both. His usefulness to the Russians is obvious, and his usefulness to the French government almost equally so. By destroying the 'union of the Left', and by splitting the left vote, he is now far and away Giscard's best electoral ally. It is this which makes nonsense of Marchais's repeated claim that the whole campaign concerning his past has been engineered by *le pouvoir* which wishes to destroy him as a credible presidential candidate. Giscard himself went directly to his aid by describing the attacks on him as 'scandalous'. Similarly the Ministry of the Interior continues to claim that the charge that Marchais was a voluntary worker in Germany is 'unproven' despite the evidence of its own vast dossier on Marchais elaborately proving it.

On its crudest level there is, of course, a two-way traffic in such matters – you spare me and I'll spare you. This was demonstrated in the Boulin affair, when Marchais came to the government's assistance by denouncing the press for fomenting an allegedly fictitious scandal. However, there is more to it than that, more to it than a mere reciprocity of silence arising from fears that, if too much light is shed on Marchais's past, he may be tempted to shed too much light on other people's from his own well-stocked dossiers.

The fact of the matter is that Marchais and the French Communist Party are now, and have been for the past two decades, a kind of institutionalised asset to France's rulers. They are part of the system, an essential cog without which the machine could not work as smoothly as it does. In every crisis, in obedience to Soviet policy, they come to the government's rescue. They did so, for example, in 1968, then again in the parliamentary elections in 1978, and will do so again in the presidential elections next spring. The fact that they are a self-styled 'revolutionary' party merely enhances their value to the system they seem to be hell-bent on overthrowing. They are essentially a party of opposition – and largely empty opposition at that – and not a part of government. Of course their present line may change, as it has often done in the past, but that will depend as always on a change of Soviet foreign policy. In that case, the other side of their advantage to the existing order will come into play – they will frighten more voters than they will reassure. The mystery is, therefore, how a party like that, seemingly doomed to eternal opposition and given to constant deception about its past in order to keep up with its violent switches in policy, can continue to retain the loyalty of a mass membership.

History is part of the reason. When the French Socialist Party split in 1921 between those who wanted to join Lenin's Third International and those who didn't, the majority voted for joining and broke away to form the Communist Party. This got the party off to a good start. It was as though the British communists had had a similar success at that period in splitting the Labour Party. It gave the French party an immediate nation-wide organisational base, and a national trade union federation. It also gave it a prestigious national organ, founded and edited by Jean Jaurès, in *L'Humanité*. Another reason is the historic alienation of the French working class from the nation, which naturally attracted it to a party which made a virtue of that alienation. (De Gaulle's famous term for the communists, 'the separatists', was not lightly used.)

Another explanation is the one put forward by Auguste Lecoeur. It is that the party's apparent retention of the loyalty of its members, through crisis and upheavals and ideological somersaults, is largely deceptive. In fact the membership is constantly changing, to a point where there are now many more former members of the party than there are actual members. In the present period alone, the party is not only losing a large number of its intellectuals but also of its working-class activists. These merely drop out without actually resigning. They signal their disenchantment by not paying their dues and by failing to attend their cell meetings. At the same time, there is no reason to disbelieve the party when it claims a large influx of new members. All this means that there is a constant renewal of the membership, with the new members understandably more credulous about falsifications regarding the past than the older and more disillusioned ones. Only the apparatus at the top remains unchanging, solidly rooted in its Stalinist past.

The Spectator, *August 23, 1980*

THE FRENCH JEWISH CONNECTION

The recent bomb attack on a Paris synagogue has aroused fears and emotions which are wholly understandable. It was not an act of blind or indiscriminate terrorism, like the outrages in Bologna and Munich which preceded it, but one which deliberately singled out Jews as a target. As such it inevitably revived nightmarish memories of an all too recent and hideous past. Yet the fact remains that, far from reflecting an upsurge of anti-semitism in France, it underlined the contrary. For the first time in this century anti-semitism has become almost undetectable in French public life. No political party defends it, no publications proclaim it and no one at any level has been elected to public office on the strength of it. There is no significant current of opinion to support it, and such minuscule neo-Nazi groups as exist lead furtive lives and exist, as one commentator put it, 'as fish without water'. This is, of course, in such striking contrast to the recent past, even the post-war past, that it is not surprising that President Giscard was stung to fury by foreign comments depicting France as a kind of anti-semitic haven. All this underlines the dangers of over-reaction, although these dangers unfortunately are already beginning to show themselves. Wild talk of forming Jewish groups and wild charges against the police are signs of the new mood. Talk of mobilising a Jewish vote against the Government in the coming presidential elections is another.

Then there is the fuel being added by the Israeli prime minister in equating anti-Zionism with anti-semitism, and accusing French policy in the Middle East of favouring the growth of the latter. Finally a witch-hunt is already under way which is associating everyone on the right with fascism and anti-semitism. In short it can already be said that, if one of the purposes of provocation is to provoke indiscriminate reaction, then the perpetrators of the bomb attack have already scored some kind of a victory. Matters have already reached the point where Giscard himself is now accused of being well disposed to anti-semites (his wife's father and elder brother, incidentally, died in a concentration camp), and an obvious slip of the tongue by the prime minister, Raymond Barre – 'an attack on Jews in which innocent Frenchmen were killed' – is being taken as an expression of his innermost thoughts. All this, it should be noted, before it is clear that the bomb attack was the work of local neo-Nazis. Indeed such clues as exist point to imported terrorists from the Middle East. Ten days before the synagogue bombing, there was a bomb attack on a Jewish institution in a provincial town. The perpetrators who were arrested turned out to be two Palestinians. The legendary terrorist, Carlos, is known to have carried out the bombing of the Jewish-owned Paris 'Drugstore' some years ago. Nothing would be easier than for Middle East terrorist groups to discard a left-wing mask for a right-wing one, when it suited them to do so.

Indeed the Jewish community here, itself undergoing some kind of a crisis of identity, is a perfect political target for Arab terrorism. Now the third biggest in the world, more than half of it is made up of North African Jews with the bulk of them *pieds noirs* from Algeria. It is split on the issue of Zionism, with the newcomers overwhelmingly pro-Zionist. If the split deepens, its overall support for Israel would be weakened. Furthermore if the scale of anti-Jewish attacks mounted, the community as a whole could be isolated from the rest of the nation – or so, no doubt, it is hoped. Here are possibilities for mischief on a grand scale.

Meanwhile, there is already considerable scope for mischief in the bandying about of allegations that the French police are soft on Fascists and that, of the 150 members of the most important neo-Nazi group, no less than thirty are policemen. It was of course to be hoped that the police had infiltrated this movement, but infiltration on such a scale seemed to suggest that it was the other way round. Made originally by two police trade union officials, the charge has since been steadily watered down. From being one of 'we know', it has become one of 'we heard'; from the claim that the Minister of the Interior was informed and did nothing it has become one of 'We assume the Minister of the Interior was informed'. And, finally, from claiming that they know the names, they now refuse to reveal them – even confidentially.

This does not mean that there are not disquieting elements in the French police; what it does mean, however, is that reckless charges are not the best way of extirpating them. Nor is it true that terrorist attacks against the left go unpunished while those against the right are quickly solved. In both categories there are almost the same number of unsolved crimes, including those of murder or attempted murder. The right-wing journal *Minute* has been bombed three times in recent years and the perpetrators have never been discovered. Similarly the flat of the mildly right-wing writer and academician, Jean Dutourd, was recently blasted: again, no arrest. Four prominent figures, two of the extreme left and two of the extreme right, have been assassinated in the past three years and in all four cases their murderers have not been found.

To revert to French anti-semitism, however, it is astonishing to reflect how vociferous it was as recently as the mid-Fifties, and how moribund it is now. It was in the Fifties, with the memories of the War still fresh, that fifty Poujadists, all more or less anti-semitic in outlook, were swept into the National Assembly. This was the period, too, when Maître Tixier-Vignancour, an avowed anti-semite, was not only a Deputy but something of a national figure who stood against de Gaulle in a presidential election. Anti-semitic feeling then rose perceptibly with the rise to power of Mendès-France. He became the target for the same squalid attacks as did Léon Blum twenty years earlier. It was shortly afterwards that the anti-semitic right in France began to enter into almost total eclipse. It is easy to see why now. It was not only that the national mood had changed from one of self-pity to self-confidence and optimism; the Six Day War and the approaching loss of Algeria also had something to do with it. The Six Day War killed off the legend of the Jews as a non-warrior race – a notion dear to the theoreticians of *Action Française* – while the Algerian war substituted the Arab for the Jew as the internal enemy. The paradoxical result can be seen to this day. The extreme right in France, or what remains of it, is now fiercely pro-Israel and equally fiercely anti-Arab.

Without going back to the Dreyfus case, when it was fatuously considered vital to the army's morale in the coming war with Germany that the treason charge should be fastened on a 'Jewish Frenchman' rather than, as it were, a 'French Frenchman', one should spare a glance at Charles Mauras and his own peculiar variant of anti-semitism which exercised such an influence in French intellectual circles before the War. The official doctrine of Mauras's *Action Française* regarding the Jews was not based on race but on *raison d'état*. Jews were to be denied political power simply because they were, according to his doctrine, themselves an alien political entity. They could escape their fate of being reduced to the status of second-class citizens by becoming Catholics. This many thousands of French Jews did, at a rate which resulted in a dramatically diminishing Jewish population – only checked and then, in even more dramatic fashion, reversed by the influx of North African Jews. Among the more notable converts of that period were Michel Debré's father, whose own father was a rabbi, Maurice Schumann, who was the spokesman for the Free French in London during the War, and André Maurois – the latter, incidentally, viewed with warm approval by the *Action Française*.

The last major flurry over anti-semitism that I can recall was when de Gaulle made his famous statement after the Six Day War that the Jews – he meant specifically the Israelis – were 'an élite, sure of itself and domineering'. It was the word 'domineering' that jarred. Nothing he ever said or did before or after dismayed his followers so much as that remark. He was clearly angered by the Israeli refusal to accept his advice not to attack and by the enthusiasm of French Jews over the swift victory. He later claimed that he intended the remark as a compliment, which might well have been the case. A few days later he invited the Chief Rabbi to the Elysée, and gave him his explanation and his profuse apologies. It must have been the first and only time de Gaulle apologised for anything he said or did.

The Spectator, *October 18, 1980*

A FASCIST TO THE LAST

At some point in the early Fifties, the late Frank Owen was
staying with me when he announced one morning: 'I'm off
to have lunch with Tom Mosley – come and join us.' After my
puzzlement over the 'Tom' had been cleared up – Sir Oswald was
'Tom' to his close friends – and the invitation refused, Owen had
to cope with my deeper puzzlement over such an unlikely
friendship on the part of one of the co-authors of *Guilty*. There it
is, said Frank, 'I like the man and I admire him. I never thought
of him as a fascist. I think it was just some kind of English
upper-class eccentricity which made him pretend to be one.
People like Michael [Michael Foot] and I never turned our backs
on him. Even when he was in Holloway we visited him regularly.' This indicates the kind of magic spell Mosley was able to
weave around those who came into contact with him in his earlier
years, and something of it remained evident right up to his death.
A new generation of hero-worshippers had come to sit at his feet
as passions over his fascist past subsided, and there was always a
steady stream of pilgrims to visit him in his aptly named gem of a
château 'Le Temple de la Gloire', where he and Diana Mosley
had settled shortly after the war. It must have required repre-
sentations at the highest level to have secured permission for the
Mosleys to settle in France, and so near Paris, at a time when the
French were still energetically pursuing their own fascists – and I
suspect that Churchill had a hand in it.

It was a tax exile as well as a political one, and it enabled
Mosley to save what was left of what was once a huge fortune
derived from Manchester ground rents. I got to know Mosley –
professional curiosity made me seek him out – late in his life
when the old magic still smouldered in the ashes, but when his
powers to bewitch and beguile were clearly far less. His circle of
close friends at the time was small, consisting mainly of the Duke
and Duchess of Windsor, the scientist and former half-
proprietor of the *News of the World* Professor Derek Jackson, a
few Anglo-American socialites and a few of the more estimable
shipwrecked survivors of the Vichy regime like Gaston Bergery,
a once shining light of the French left who had become a

Pétainist. The Windsors were particularly close both physically and sentimentally, for their weekend house was only five minutes' drive from the Mosleys. Their presence inevitably lent a court-in-exile air to this small community. The British embassy, for its part, had strict instructions to shun Mosley and members of its staff were under orders – they still were right up to the time of his death – immediately to leave any social gathering at which he was present.

Inevitably much of the conversation with Mosley was of the might-have-beens of recent history – a lugubrious subject at the best of times, tending to leave the words hanging heavily in the air. Mosley was, of course, a King's man at the time of the Abdication – a mistake which cut him off from his potential working- and middle-class following – and remained convinced that, if Edward had stayed on the throne, war would have been averted. True, the anti-appeasers like Churchill and Duff Cooper were strong in the King's camp but they were not as strong as the anti-war element, including Mosley himself who maintained a clandestine correspondence with the King throughout the crisis. He was fond of repeating what he claimed to be Edward's words to him: 'Every drop of my blood is German.' Certainly Mosley gave advice to Edward on his ill-fated trip to Germany after the Abdication, and I received the strong impression that he had the stenographic report of his conversation with Hitler which is missing from the captured German archives. Mosley was occasionally given to elaborating on this theme in romantic fashion by arguing that an American queen on the throne of Britain would have been a fatal blow to American isolationism, thereby acting as an extra anti-Hitler deterrent. In any case, Mosley added, neither he nor the former King would have been prepared to serve under the Germans in the event of a German victory – the King being bound by his abdication, and Mosley not willing to do . . . and here there was a pause which Diana Mosley filled by adding 'an Adenauer'. It was an interesting intervention – Lady Mosley was given to stating bluntly what her husband often liked to elaborate in more guarded terms – since it implied a total inversion of values or, even more unhappily, a total absence of them – with Adenauer appearing as another variety of Quisling.

On those occasions it was difficult to avoid the impression of Lady Mosley, despite her great charm and sweetness of nature, as a kind of *tricoteuse*. One fidgeted as she talked, not impulsively but in measured tones, of 'Hitler's beautiful hands', his wit, his high intelligence and his deep musical culture. It was not long before she seemed to be equating her own and her husband's hardships in Holloway with those of the concentration camp victims. Of course I believed them both when they denied ever having been anti-semites. Lady Mosley was fond of quoting Lloyd George on the subject: 'Of all the bigotries that savage the human temper, there is none so stupid as the anti-semitic.' Sir Oswald was more disingenuous on the subject, with his argument that it was the Jews who took the war into his camp rather than he into theirs. Yet what neither of them seemed to realise was that their disclaimer of anti-semitism made their case look worse rather than better. It suggests a cynical exploitation by his movement of anti-semitism as an untapped source of popular support. What else was the famous march into the East End about if it was not designed as an intimidatory challenge to the Jews in that area? And what were Sir Oswald's railings at the time about 'the sweeping of the ghettoes of Eastern Europe' intended to do but to add the fuel of his rhetoric to the fiery mischief of the march itself? It is curious that the anti-anti-semitic Mosley and the anti-racialist Mosley should have been responsible for two notorious marches – one into the heavily Jewish East End of London before the War, and one into the heavily black Notting Hill area after the War.

The latter act makes an interesting contrast to Enoch Powell's anti-immigration campaign. It is therefore somewhat revealing that Mosley had a boundless contempt for Powell, variously describing him as 'hysterical' or 'a Victorian figure' or finally and most crushingly as 'a middle-class Alf Garnett'. 'We have nothing in common,' he said once, 'Powell is a man of the extreme right and I am a man of the centre.' He was more impressed by Cecil King, with whom he entered into some kind of political alliance in the early Seventies. They had a common sense of frustration and a common sense of destiny. Both, too, were convinced of imminent disaster. They both agreed on a common programme when disaster struck, which would enable them to form a Cabinet of all-the-talents which would rule under full emergency powers for a limited period of four years, subject only to a periodic parliamentary vote of confidence. The armed forces would be represented in the Administration largely to deal with opposition from 'sectional interests'. The main purpose would be, in Sir Oswald's words, 'to squeeze the wind and

297

water out of the economy'. In the same vein, Sir Oswald talked of 'the old lady [Britain] who has fallen into the ditch and we have to get her up again and brush her down'.

At my last meeting with him only four months ago, Sir Oswald told me: 'We should have told Hitler that he could do what he liked in the East, but not to touch France or move against the West, that if he wanted the Ukraine as far as we were concerned he could have it.' I was somewhat taken aback, for nowhere in his writings does he make this point quite so plainly or brutally. In fact in his autobiography he argues that Hitler, fearing racial contamination, did not really want to build an empire in Eastern Europe. It seemed too late to point this out to him and in any case I had come to talk about another subject. It struck me as odd, however, that so crude a view, not unknown in the blackest reactionary circles in Britain and more especially in France, should in all probability have been his all along. Such a policy would not have averted a world war, and it would only have been feasible for a short period on the backs of a decadent Britain and France. Meanwhile we turned to lighter things: among them Sir Oswald's unstinted admiration for Sir James Goldsmith. For a moment, I wondered whether he saw in him a new Cecil King.

The Spectator, *December 13, 1980*

1981

MITTERRAND: A FLAWED TRIUMPH

The scale of the Socialist victory in the French General Election following its victory in the Presidential one is now on such a scale that it even has some of the Socialist leaders worried. Not only does it remove any alibi for a scaling down of some of the more extravagant promises or even for caution, but the very size of the absolute majority held by the Socialists alone will encourage the kind of factionalism to which Socialist parties are heir. There are already four more or less distinct tendencies within the French Socialist Party of which the far Marxist Left, the CERES group, represents about twelve per cent of the newly elected Socialist deputies. Now Mitterrand has decided to extend this majority to include the Communists by bringing them into the Government.

They will add yet another faction – and this time a highly disciplined one – to an already faction-ridden majority. Mitterrand's decision to bring them in, eagerly backed by the CERES group, is a puzzling one, seemingly largely symbolic for they are needed neither as ballast nor as hostages.

Their support for the time being anyway was assured with or without ministerial posts. Their surrender to the Socialists after their poor showing in the first round of the Presidential elections was unconditional. Their presence in the Government changes nothing: they will stay with the ship as long as it suits them and desert when it suits them. Disarmed for the time being politically, they are also disarmed industrially. Their trade union arm, the CGT, will behave itself not so much because Communists are in the Government, but because it is in too weakened a state to do otherwise.

Mitterrand should know, and no doubt does know, if only from his own most recent experience, that agreements with the

299

Communists are not worth the paper they are written on. In any case, on the terms that are at present being negotiated with them for their eventual entry into the Government, there is nothing that they cannot put a reasonably good face on. Thus, on the issue of Government solidarity and the Government domestic programme, no problems need arise. The foreign issues are trickier but present no insuperable difficulties. They have already committed themselves to support of France's existing alliances and the Common Market, and that leaves only Afghanistan, Poland and the Soviet SS-20 missiles. On the latter, they support the idea that these should be reduced in the context of general disarmament negotiations, on Poland they are already declared opponents of Soviet intervention, and on Afghanistan, without contradicting their previous stand in favour of the Soviet invasion, they can join in the call for a negotiated Soviet withdrawal. They can bow the knee to all these concessions as they have already bowed the knee to Mitterrand in giving him their full support both in the final round of the Presidential elections and in the Parliamentary ones.

Indeed, if there is any hard swallowing to be done, it will be on the Socialist side, not the Communist one. They will have to face the fact that in letting the Communists in, they will be disappointing many of their own supporters who thought that by giving them an absolute majority they were effectively preventing the need for Communist participation, not paving the way for it, and they will have to face the international consequences of such participation. For the past few weeks, the Foreign Minister, M. Cheysson, and M. Mitterrand himself have been heavily engaged in reassuring Washington, Bonn and the Gulf States as to the new French Government's intentions, only to undermine this newly won confidence by including Communists in the Government. The question therefore arises why, in view of the disadvantages and the lack of any real need to do so, Mitterrand is bent on having Communist ministers?

The answer seems to be that he is continuing the long-term strategy which he first forged with the union with the Communists ten years ago. He has already succeeded in largely marginalising the French Communist Party and he wants to carry the process still further. To him, the Communists are not just a party but an important working-class segment of the nation which must be reintegrated into it. To bar them now, when the Socialists are strong and they are weak, is the best way of ensuring their revival. He wants no enemies on the Left, and the best time to make overtures to the Communists is not when they are strong but when they are weak. This is the gamble, and having won his first one – that of reducing the Communists to a junior role in the working class movement – who is to say that Mitterrand will not win the second?

All this indicates that, whatever else the Mitterrand experiment will turn out to be, it will not follow the pattern of a banal Social-Democratic one along West German and former British lines. It will involve France in profound social changes of a kind that will have their effects throughout Europe. Although his success was only made possible first by the split within the former majority and then by the dramatic drop in the Communist vote, the underlying reasons for it are much more profound. They are, ironically enough, largely due to the success of previous regimes, beginning with that of de Gaulle, in carrying out France's second industrial revolution and transforming it into the world's fourth most important trading nation. This has produced a huge wage-earning and salaried class which has found it increasingly difficult to identify itself with the neo-conservatism of its rulers. This sociological change has transformed voting habits throughout the country, giving the Socialists heavy majorities in, for example, such former 'backward' regions as Brittany and Alsace-Lorraine. It is a change which de Gaulle vaguely but strongly felt, hence his championship of what he called 'participation' and regionalisation, notions which his conservative successors derided. The final irony, of course, is that the Left now owes its almost unlimited powers to the Constitution created by de Gaulle and which it fiercely opposed for many years. We are, one feels, on the edge of exciting times, in which once again France will play the role of the great innovator.

The Spectator, *June 27, 1981*

1982

THE POMPIDOU I KNEW

With the publication this week of the late President Pompidou's memoirs, some deep wounds have been reopened and two major mysteries revived.

The first concerns de Gaulle's 'disappearance' at the height of the student riots in May 1968 and the second the alleged involvement of Madame Pompidou in a sex scandal which became known as the Markovic Affair and was used by Pompidou's enemies within the Gaullist camp to discredit him.

Both these matters form the major portion of the book which consists of notes taken by Pompidou at the time and which were entrusted to his widow and who has now authorised their publication.

They are in a very real sense a posthumous revenge by Pompidou on his tormentors, real or imagined, the chief of them being de Gaulle himself.

It so happens that during that period when Pompidou was Prime Minister and then ex-Prime Minister and not yet President, I saw him fairly often alone. I shall never forget his cold fury at the time at the attempts being made as a result of a deliberate campaign to besmirch his wife's reputation by allegations that she had attended disreputable parties organised by film star Alain Delon's bodyguard Markovic who had been found murdered.

The Press had been full for days past concerning 'a highly placed figure' who was compromised in the affair. Everyone knew that this referred to Pompidou – everyone except Pompidou who was the last to learn the truth and the last to learn that both his and his wife's names figured in the Markovic dossier.

What had happened was that a Yugoslav pimp who was in prison on a charge totally unconnected with Markovic's murder had decided to cash in on his fellow Yugoslav's notoriety by claiming that he had been at parties attended by the Pompidous. He insisted on giving evidence to that effect and the evidence, which was later found to be totally baseless, was duly recorded in the dossier.

The Minister of Justice at the time, René Capitant, a notorious Pompidou-hater, brought this to the attention of the General himself who remarked that it seemed to him to be rubbish but that Pompidou should be told. The task, a distasteful one, was entrusted to the man who had succeeded Pompidou as Prime Minister, Couve de Murville.

He baulked at doing so and finally after several days' delay it was a personal friend of Pompidou's, the Minister of the Interior M. Marcellin, who broke the news to Pompidou.

By that time Pompidou was in a towering rage and busily drawing up a blacklist of people he would revenge himself upon when the time came. This needless to say gave a special edge to his own Presidential ambitions. His enemy number one, he decided, was Couve de Murville whom he cut out of public life after he became President.

We now come to the famous 'disappearance'. I write of this rather ruefully for I accepted from Pompidou himself his belief that de Gaulle, on leaving Paris on May 29 to go to his country home at Colombey-les-deux-Eglises, had gone for good.

As a result I confidentially predicted this, only to have my prediction belied some four hours later. De Gaulle did not go to Colombey as he told Pompidou he would do but instead went to General Massu's headquarters in Germany at Baden-Baden.

Meanwhile for two agonising hours his whereabouts remained unknown. What de Gaulle had carried out was a deliberate piece of deception aimed at finding out how the country at large and his ministers in particular would react to his disappearance. Pompidou, however, says that it was Massu who restored his morale and decided him to return to Paris. I doubt this version myself and I am now referring to the notes that I took at the time.

De Gaulle had been involved in several disputes with Pompidou, the most important being whether the best way of meeting the student crisis was to hold a referendum or a general election. De Gaulle wanted a referendum, seeing the dissolution of Parliament while the government enjoyed a majority as a capitulation to the rioters.

Pompidou had warned him twice that if he did not follow his advice to hold elections then it would be best if de Gaulle resigned.

It was at the height of this disagreement that the General announced to everyone's astonishment that he would leave that Wednesday morning for Colombey. Everything was stage-managed to indicate that he was going for good. All his personal belongings and those of Mme de Gaulle were stacked into a car which was to follow them to Colombey.

Even Mme de Gaulle's personal maid, who normally stayed behind if the de Gaulles were leaving only for a weekend, travelled with the baggage. The Presidential party took off by helicopter, one with de Gaulle and Mme de Gaulle and another with the security police and members of de Gaulle's personal bodyguard.

Shortly after take-off, the chief of security at the Elysée, M. Jean Ducoet, noted that they were not following the well-known route to Colombey. He questioned the pilot who told him that his instructions were simply to follow the Presidential helicopter. M. Ducoet then tried to communicate with de Gaulle's pilot who refused all conversation.

The helicopters finally landed at Saint Dizier about 150 miles east of Paris where the President's Caravelle awaited them.

The plane flew them to the Baden-Baden headquarters of the French forces in Germany. General Massu was warned of the General's impending arrival only half an hour before the plane landed. When they finally arrived at the Massu home the comedy continued. Madame de Gaulle, no doubt unwittingly, told the Massus that they would be staying with them for two or three days and there was hasty bedmaking and other preparations to accommodate the surprise guests.

After lunch, during which de Gaulle appeared dispirited and Massu argued fiercely that he should return, de Gaulle suddenly got up and said: 'Well, now we must be on our way to Colombey.'

Other witnesses apart from General Massu – including de Gaulle's old companion from his London days, the French ambassador in London, de Courcel – are convinced that de Gaulle had every intention of returning to Colombey that evening and going back to Paris the following day.

It was from Colombey that de Gaulle issued his statement that he would be staying on as President, that he would retain Pompidou as his Prime Minister and that Parliament would be dissolved and early elections held. It was the end of a psycho-drama.

After the election victory Pompidou was promptly sacked and his resentments understandably mounted. In fact his dismissal had been on the cards for a long time, long before even the events of May, and were only delayed by the fact that Couve had been unable to win a Parliamentary seat.

When he became President, Pompidou had little time and even less taste for revising his notes of the time. The result is a work of a bruised and deeply wounded man who, to the end, nursed his grievances, many of which were justifiable.

Friday, June 18, 1982

SO BANG GOES THE EXOCET EXCUSE

The French Government has now officially denied that French technicians showed the Argentinians how to mount Exocet missiles on Dassault-produced Super Etendard planes thereby helping them to sink the *Sheffield* and the *Atlantic Conveyor* during the Falklands War.

So be it, and no doubt the British Government – for different reasons – will be as content as the French one to let matters rest there.

However, one would feel happier if M. Hervé Colin, the head of the French team providing the usual after-sale service in the Argentine, who confirmed the original allegation, was available for further comment. He has somewhat conveniently gone on holiday without leaving a forwarding address.

Meanwhile, the newspaper *Le Monde* claims that the Argentine now has a stockpile of 100 Exocets, including ten of the type that sunk the *Sheffield*, and a force of fourteen Super Etendards.

This goes well beyond the original contract with the French, signed when Giscard was President, and indicates clearly that the contract was expanded under the present Socialist Government.

Originally the excuse for supplying a Fascist-type regime with arms was that the present French government was obliged to fulfil contracts signed by its predecessor. Now that excuse falls to the ground – and so do Socialist claims that they would apply moral restraints on France's thriving arms trade.

In fact, the situation in that regard is no different to what it was under Giscard except that the smell of hypocrisy is much stronger.

An example of this is provided by the case of South Africa. A great deal is made of the fact that arms exports to that country are banned and this is constantly cited as an example of Socialist virtue in a wicked world. What is overlooked is that the ban was originally imposed by Giscard.

It is amusing now to recall earlier Socialist promises to 'moralise' the arms trade or President Mitterrand's insistence before opening the Paris Air Show last year that all the military planes on display should be disarmed for the duration of his visit.

Another striking example of this hypocrisy is provided by the very terms on which the Dassault aircraft firm was partly nationalised earlier this year. While the major private banks, were totally nationalised, Dassault and the missile manufacturers Matra took on a Government-controlling interest of only fifty-one per cent.

This was done solely so as not to frighten off foreign customers who might have been unhappy at the thought that total nationalisation might lead to changes in policy and on the board.

As for the Exocet, after its successes in the South Atlantic, the queue of prospective purchasers for this missile is becoming of an almost unwieldy length.

It is not generally known that Britain itself has a seven per cent interest in the Exocet and this gives it a considerable advantage – it is thought here that Britain has a stockpile of 300 Exocets. Other favourite customers in the queue are the Italians and the sheikhdoms of the Gulf States.

Clearly in the coming years owning a collection of Exocets will become something of a status symbol among minor powers.

Friday, July 30, 1982

GRACE AND THE MONACO
MATCH-MAKER

To anyone who was present at her marriage to Prince Rainier in Monaco twenty-six years ago, the death this week of the former Grace Kelly must hold a special poignancy.

Memories of the wedding, which with its elaborate preparations stretched over a period of three weeks, fade hard in the memories of its embattled participants, among whom I was one. But through the lingering fog of champagne fumes, what one still recalls very clearly was the prevailing cynicism which the occasion provoked.

Monte Carlo was quickly re-baptised 'Monte Kelly' as Hollywood seemed to complete plans for a take-over of the principality and loud-mouthed film executives were broadly hinting that the whole thing was an elaborate promotion stunt for Miss Kelly's next film after a decent delay of a year or two. After which, of course, the marriage itself would head for the rocks.

Well it didn't work out that way, did it? Grace never made another film and the marriage blossomed into a singularly happy one.

It was interesting to note as the years rolled on that in a place so given to scandal as Monaco no breath of it was ever attached to either Rainier or Grace (it was left to a later generation to rectify this). It also became clear in the process that by this marriage Rainier had not only secured his happiness but also saved his throne.

Matters were not propitious for the survival of the Grimaldi dynasty at the time of the marriage. Only a year before the Prince had been locked in bitter disputes with his twelve-man 'parliament' and had even used the threat of abdication, which would have meant the principality's automatic absorption into France to bring it to heel.

There had also been a bitter quarrel with his step-grandmother, Princess Ghislaine, and her explusion from the palace.

Rainier was reputed to be lonely, shy, insecure and obstinate.

Neglected as a child, he had been packed off to a minor English public school and the misery of the experience continued to warp his personality. As friends he had dubious local cronies and he also had a long-standing mistress in the French film actress, Gisèle Pascal.

The principality itself was at the time a charming backwater and the sloping background to the harbour was dotted with pleasant villas, many of them English-owned. The casino and its hotels provided the principal source of income.

It is amusing to recall that in the early Fifties there was an outcry at the construction of some low, red-painted Coca-Cola warehouses on the harbour front opposite the casino, which were deemed to be an eyesore. There was little then to indicate that this eyesore would soon be overshadowed by a forest of skyscrapers.

As the marriage seemed to guarantee the survival of the principality, so it became an attractive prospect for investment and the building boom came almost simultaneously with the marriage itself.

There had been many claimants to the role of match-maker in the Rainier–Grace Kelly Marriage. I think the principal architect of the marriage was the wordly-wise Irish American priest, Father Tucker, who had been recommended to Rainier to act as his personal chaplain.

It was Father Tucker who persuaded Rainier to break off his romance with Mlle Pascal and it was he, too, who at the height of the domestic crisis persuaded Rainier to undertake a prolonged trip to the United States in the hope that he would come back with an American bride. Certainly, Tucker knew the Kelly family and Grace herself very well.

Grace's last years were, of course, rendered unhappy by her concern for her 26-year-old daughter, Princess Caroline. She had opposed her marriage to Phillipe Junot, the Paris playboy and businessman, but wisely gave it her consent when she saw that it was inevitable.

The stormy marriage broke up after only two years. Now Caroline's affair with Vilas, the Argentinian tennis player, is being recorded in serial-like detail by the picture magazine *Paris-Match*. Now the Caroline problem will be all Rainier's and one wonders how he will cope with that and how he will also cope with the 17-year-old Princess Stephanie, who was with her mother at the time of the fatal car accident. She, too, has recently been showing signs of some of her older sister's unruliness.

Friday, September 17, 1982

MENDÈS-FRANCE: AN ENIGMA

M. Mendès-France held power for seven months and seventeen days in the mid-Fifties and then faded into oblivion, his warnings unheeded, his advice ignored. Yet his death last week received the kind of treatment in the French media reserved for men who have changed the course of history. On the day of his death *Le Monde* devoted three pages to him, including virtually the entire front page, and the next day it did even better with no fewer than eight pages of adulatory articles and tributes to him. He got the front page once again with the banner headline proclaiming in mystic and mystifying terms that 'The scale of the tribute to Mendès-France proved the fame and relevance of Mendèsism'. This hyperbole was best summed up in a full-page cartoon in the weekly *L'Express* which showed the wraith-like figures of de Gaulle and Mendès-France shaking hands above the clouds. All this is puzzling in the extreme – especially the reference to 'Mendèsism', whatever that may be – and suggests that the French Left in praising so lavishly a figure from the past was trying to compensate for a more mundane present.

For not dissimilar reasons the Right, which had covered him with calumny during his political lifetime, now covered him with flowery tributes. Even the Communists, who had most reason to hate him – had he not snubbed them by refusing to accept the premiership in 1954 if his majority depended on communist votes? – joined in the chorus of praise. How is it then, one is tempted to ask, that a man so hugely esteemed had so brief a spell of power and so long an eclipse? Thereby hangs an interesting tale.

Mendès formed his one and only government in 1954 when France was faced with two explosive issues on which decisions could no longer be postponed. The first concerned the war in Indochina which, with the fall of Dien Bien Phu, had taken a

disastrous turn, threatening the survival of the French expeditionary force. The second was the question of joining the European Defence Community (EDC) which would have permitted
the rearming of West Germany. Previous governments had
stalled on both issues but now military events permitted no
stalling on the first and Washington, which threatened to go
ahead with the rearmament of Germany without French approval, permitted no stalling on the second. Unpopular decisions
demand unpopular men and Mendès, very much a loner in the
National Assembly, certainly qualified as such. On hearing his
promise that he would make peace in Indochina within a month,
a relieved Assembly gave him his majority, happy to have found
a scapegoat on whom it could hang the responsibility both for
'betraying' Indochina and rearming West Germany. On the
latter issue, however, he turned his back on his famous axiom 'to
govern is to choose', and left it to a free vote with the government abstaining. EDC was duly defeated to the fury both of
Washington and London. The London anger was particularly
misplaced as Mendès had made it clear that he would support
EDC but only on condition that Britain joined it too.

Meanwhile the Indochinese peace gamble was won and in a
brilliant side-stroke Mendès headed off a revolt in Tunisia by
putting that country on the road to independence. By that time
he had as it were fulfilled his contract and the time had come to
overthrow him, which the Assembly did, its decision only slightly hastened by his attacks on legalised private distillers, his
advocacy of milk as a substitute for wine and his habit of
addressing the nation over the heads of deputies in weekly radio
fireside chats. Mendès could also claim to have been the father of
the French atomic bomb but he always denied paternity for it,
claiming that the atomic commission he set up was restricted
solely for the industrial use of atomic energy. Nevertheless the
forty other members of the commission, which included army
and air force generals, all agree to a man that their task included
both the military and civil use of the atom. A legend has since
developed that Mendès's government was some kind of left-wing
coalition. It was nothing of the sort: it was largely composed of
Gaullists and members of some centre groups like the radicals
and M. Mitterrand's own small Centre Party. Throughout his
period in office Mendès played great court to de Gaulle; but as
the General had already disowned his own followers for forget-
ting that their task was to change the constitution and not to join

coalitions to help the Fourth Republic limp along, he was hardly likely to offer him the public support he needed. In any case one of Mendès's last acts, partly intended to please the General, was the ill-fated one of sending Jacques Soustelle as governor-general to Algeria.

With de Gaulle's return to power in 1958 Mendès's political career effectively ended. The General tried to coax him back – after all, they were wartime associates and greatly respected each other – but Mendès's republican sentiments were too outraged by the circumstances of de Gaulle's return to allow him to accept. Also outraged, one suspects, was his considerable vanity: from then on he became more and more a prisoner himself, a prisoner of his own fantasies concerning the General. In his speech opposing de Gaulle's investiture Mendès said: 'If I thought de Gaulle could restore discipline in the army, preserve democracy and make peace in Algeria I would vote for him.' When de Gaulle did just that Mendès shifted his ground to attacking the Fifth Republic's constitution which he claimed would result inevitably in a dictatorship. Instead, of course, it has led to a peaceful transfer of power to a Socialist president and a Socialist–Communist coalition. Two examples of Mendès's wrong-headedness concerning de Gaulle: he did not believe he would retire if and when defeated in the 1970 referendum and he thought May 1968 would develop 'into a civil war'. His misjudgements began to be accompanied by foolish acts.

He was foolish enough to attend a student rally at the height of the May troubles and thereby, incidentally, break an agreement he had made with Mitterrand that neither would appear at such demonstrations; and he was foolish enough to run in tandem with Gaston Defferre in a presidential election (Defferre would be president and he would be his prime minister). The result was that they got five per cent of the vote and the Communists twenty-one per cent. It was left to Mitterrand, whose connections with socialism were as tenuous as Mendès's own, to make his peace with the constitution and bring the Socialists to power. There was therefore a certain irony in the words Mitterrand used when he greeted him on the steps of the Elysée on the day of victory: 'If it had not been for you, I would not now be here.' As it was this turned out to be Mendès's first and last visit to the Elysée under its new occupant.

The Spectator, *October 30, 1982*

OUT OF THE ICE INTO THE FIRE

Returning to Paris after a week's absence during which France's six-month-long government-decreed price freeze ended, my first shock came when I dropped into my local café of the kind used by office workers for a quick lunch.

The bill for a meal of cold pork, salad, cheese and a glass of wine came to just over £5. The week before last the same meal cost a little under £4. It was all part of a pattern of sharp price increases which, combined with earlier government measures, are aimed to achieve the exact opposite of what France's socialist government first intended – a drop instead of a rise in purchasing power.

In fact, for the first time in thirty years, the French standard of living is dropping and by mid-1983 it is estimated it will have dropped as much as ten per cent below its level at the time of the elections last year.

The grimmest news, however, comes on a more esoteric level and it was contained in an article tucked away on page twenty-eight of *Le Monde* this week and written by the paper's noted financial expert, Paul Fabra.

It concerned the scale of France's present foreign indebtedness. This has been a closely guarded French Treasury secret for some time and the publication of the actual figures by a paper as well disposed to the government as *Le Monde* has caused a considerable stir as well as provoking bitterness in government circles.

M. Fabra estimates France's foreign indebtedness at the moment as being at least 45 billion dollars, which is double what it was in 1981 and this indebtedness is progressing at such a rate that it will soon be treble the 1981 figure.

'The last illusion,' according to him, is that France can go on being bailed-out in this fashion. The French Treasury, he claims, believes that it can go on borrowing abroad for the next two or three years without the conditions being too onerous or too humiliating.

He points out that, given the present climate of caution and uncertainty in banking circles, this is by no means certain. Two factors will sooner or later begin to deter foreign lenders, the first being the spiralling nature of France's indebtedness and the second, that all this borrowing is destined largely not for productive investment but to cover current deficits in the budget and in the nationalised industries and to build up foreign currency reserves to support the franc.

Even if these objections are surmounted Fabra says France will find itself in three or four years with a foreign debt bigger than Brazil's present one.

It may be said, he comments, that what Brazil can permit itself, so can France, but sooner or later these debts will have to be paid off. Then there will be the grave risk that their size and the cost of servicing them will not only become a heavy extra charge on the nation, but insupportable to the industries which are doing much of the borrowing, such as Renault and the nationalised oil company, Elf.

The greatest immediate danger, he points out, is that France will be tempted to reduce its foreign borrowing by resorting to protectionism towards which it has already taken the first steps. This will endanger exports and lead to an even sharper drop in the standard of living than has already become necessary to pay off foreign debtors.

It all leads one to the thought that by the time the next British elections come around Mrs Thatcher will be able to point across the Channel for an example of what she will be warning the British electorate against.

Friday, November 12, 1982

IN THE POPULARITY STAKES, JEAN-PAUL 1, JACK NIL

There was an Australian Labour politician in the Thirties called Ted Lang, who became Premier of New South Wales and who was sometimes compared by his more ardent admirers to Lenin.

Now, oddly enough, France's Minister of Culture is called

Jack (not even Jacques) Lang and his detractors compare him not to Lenin but to a Soviet cultural commissar.

A former provincial lawyer before he became active in the French state-subsidised national theatre, his rise in the Socialist Party has been rapid ever since he caught M. Mitterrand's eye some five years ago.

Their relationship developed into a close family friendship, but even so, it was something of a surprise when, on becoming President, Mitterrand – himself a man of deep culture – appointed him to a post which carries great prestige in France and which under de Gaulle was held by so distinguished a figure as the novelist and art historian André Malraux.

Ever since his appointment, Lang has made himself somewhat notorious by denouncing what he calls 'American cultural imperialism' and using his influence on French television to replace American films with heavy social dramas concerning revolutionary movements in the Third World.

The effect of all this was to lead to a revival of cinema-going and a sharp increase in sales of video recorders.

Now the battle to give the French not what they want but what Lang thinks is good for them has gone a stage further with an open campaign to promote a state-financed film, which is proving a flop, and to denigrate a commercially produced one which is proving a huge success.

The film which has turned out to be a flop is called *A Room in Town* and was financed by French TV. It was produced by Christine Gouze-Renal, a sister-in-law of President Mitterrand and directed by Jacques Demy, who made *The Umbrellas of Cherbourg*.

It is about a strike in the provincial city of Nantes in 1955.

The other film, which will probably be a sensational box office hit – it has been seen by three million people in the three weeks it has been showing in France – is *The Ace of Aces* made by Jean-Paul Belmondo.

The battle opened with full-page advertisements, paid for out of public funds, in which an imposing list of credits express their esteem for the first film and their low opinion of the second.

As one commentator put it, it amounted to 'an expression of frustration that the public should reject what the critics think it ought to like'. In the advertisement the success of Belmondo's film is attributed to its huge publicity budget and not to its entertainment value.

Belmondo has replied to all this in an open letter about what he calls 'this attempt to demolish a competitor because the public like him'.

He goes on: 'These are dangerous practices. They are leading our profession into an anti-democratic framework. How could you be in favour of universal suffrage and deny the French the right to buy the books they like, or to see the films they want. When are they going to ban a candidate because he had effective publicity and his posters were too good?'

The first round, I should say, in this polemic goes clearly to Belmondo.

Friday, November 26, 1982

1983

THE GUILTY HOME TRUTHS THAT BARBIE MAY REVEAL

When will France cease to be haunted by the ghosts of its wartime past?

Suddenly the country has found itself reliving the tragic events of forty years ago and faced with the prospect of reliving them in even more harrowing detail in some eighteen months' time when Klaus Barbie finally comes to trial.

And harrowing it will be, not only because of the nature of Barbie's crimes – the world has long been familiar with the catalogue of Nazi horrors – but because of French complicity in them.

It could not, after all, be otherwise – for Barbie operated in Lyons in the unoccupied zone of France and was dependent at every level of his activities on the co-operation of French officials, French police and French informers.

There are hopes that this aspect of the case against Barbie can be kept out of the trial by insistence on the strict terms of reference laid before the court. These will be based on charges relating to crimes against humanity – such as mass deportation – and not war crimes, for which Barbie has already been tried in his absence.

These hopes are likely to turn out to be illusory if only because of the nature of the beast. Barbie is not merely a policeman with a taste for torture. He is also an astute political animal.

He is hardly likely to forego this last opportunity of creating as much mischief and embarrassment for his captors as possible. There will also be some in France who will be able to help him in this task, feeling this to be also their moment for revenge.

Already, for example, apart from potential witnesses there

are one or two lawyers of the extreme right straining at the leash to leap to his defence.

People of France who are claiming that this will be in some way an exemplary trial which will exorcise the ghosts of the past and provide a useful history lesson to the present generation are, it seems to me, and to many others, being very naive indeed. The lesson is likely to be a recital of how shamefully many of their forebears behaved at the time.

Barbie's capacity to do damage is considerable. He has in his time bribed too many people, tortured too many people and 'turned' too many members of the Resistance not to be able to smear a wide range of people across a wide political spectrum.

The fact that he will also lie and distort liberally does not lessen but enhances the damage his evidence will do.

He will lie and distort with all the greater recklessness knowing that many of those he will smear are dead and that many who were in the Resistance are now bitter political enemies.

It will be a final irony if Barbie succeeds in reviving ancient quarrels within the Resistance or in turning his trial into a bitter quarrel among the French themselves.

All this is not speculation, for in fact the tenor of Barbie's defence is already known to the French authorities. For example, officials of the French Ministry of Justice interviewed Barbie at length as far back as 1948, when he was being used as an informant by the Americans and was under their protection.

Furthermore, as recently as four years ago, a French journalist interviewed Barbie in Bolivia, where he indicated the line he would take if he should be questioned regarding the torture and murder of Jean Moulin, the head of the French Resistance movement, in 1943.

Moulin's arrest, his prolonged interrogation under torture and finally his death constitute Barbie's chief claim to notoriety.

Moulin was captured while attending a highly secret meeting of the Resistance chiefs in a villa in a Lyons suburb. How Barbie got wind of this meeting has always been a major mystery in the French Resistance movement.

In 1948, the novelist René Hardy – who led a major Resistance group engaged in rail sabotage – came under suspicion because he had attended the meeting and had made his get-away under suspicious circumstances. He was arrested, charged with having betrayed Moulin, and subsequently acquitted.

Two years later a *wagon-lit* attendant said that he recognised

Hardy as the man the Gestapo removed from a night train at a wayside station.

His evidence, which Hardy did not deny, created a sensation because Hardy had never revealed to his companions that he had ever been questioned by the Gestapo. He was re-arrested and acquitted a second time.

In his 1978 interview Barbie claims to have obtained his information regarding Moulin's movements from Hardy and then goes on to say that there was a political motive behind the betrayal. He claimed that Moulin was a 'crypto-Communist' and that the Gaullists decided to get rid of him because of the danger he represented as a possible Communist take-over of the Resistance movement.

The story was balderdash, but it gives a good indication of the kind of exploitation that Barbie in court will no doubt make of the Moulin capture.

Despite the fact that historians have made mincemeat of this theory – and despite the fact that the Communists themselves have never exploited it – there are many Frenchmen eager to discredit the Resistance, who firmly believe in its truth.

It is on these divisions among the French themselves, especially in matters relating to the War, which Barbie can play on with dangerous and even devastating effect.

Friday, February 11, 1983

SO MUCH FOR THE OLD PALS' ACT

President Mitterrand's spectacular reaction of expelling forty-seven diplomats and officials should go a long way towards finally clearing him of suspicions at home and abroad that the presence of Communists in his Government would limit his freedom of action in relation to the Soviet Union.

He has, in fact, right from the start, taken a tougher line with Moscow and by contrast a more co-operative one with his Western allies – and especially Washington – than any of his Conservative predecessors.

The special relationship with the Russians which de Gaulle

forged and so lovingly cultivated has disappeared from sight. It is only recently, for example, after two years in office, that the French Foreign Minister, Claude Cheysson, paid his first visit to Moscow, a chilly affair which resulted in little more than an examination of current trade figures between the two countries.

Overshadowing all this in importance, however, is M. Mitterrand's steadfast support for the installation of American missiles on the Continent which he has carried to the point of intervening directly in the recent West German elections, an intervention which helped considerably in Chancellor Kohl's victory.

Yet the misgivings regarding the presence of four Communist Ministers in the government continued to linger on, with Washington worried about security and possible leaks to the Russians and domestic opinion increasingly perturbed by the opportunities being offered to the Communists to infiltrate the administration.

Oddly, Americans seem to have overestimated the dangers of a Communist presence in the government; Russians seem to have overestimated the possibilities this offered to them. It was this overestimation by the Russians which finally decided the President to take action, and in the most dramatic manner.

He was infuriated – as a spokesman for him made clear – that the Russians, by the scale of their espionage operations in France, appeared to regard this country as a kind of 'soft under-belly' of Western Europe.

The decision to expel the Russians in such numbers and in one fell swoop was therefore a political decision of the highest importance. It goes a long way to ensuring that Franco-Russian relations remain at freezing-point for quite a long time to come.

Inevitably, too, it will have important domestic repercussions. If President Mitterrand wanted deliberately to rid himself of his Communist Ministers, he could not have gone about it in a better way. Obviously the Communists cannot regard this as an issue on which to resign without laying themselves open to the charge of supporting Soviet espionage and thereby proving that they have a higher loyalty to Moscow.

They will have to accept this latest humiliation – the most bitter so far – as they have accepted earlier ones at Mitterrand's hands.

They will, however, be bent on revenge – and the opportunity for this will come with the application of the government's new and tough austerity measures. Outwardly they have accepted them, but they are already beginning to have reservations in Parliament and, more importantly, in the trade union federation, which they control – the CGT.

This will be their main arm in the war they are now bound to wage against Mitterrand.

If that happens, they will certainly be bundled out of the government. Their departure will provide Mitterrand with an opportunity for which he is hankering to broaden his government towards the Centre. It is an objective which he cannot fulfil while he has Communist Ministers.

Friday, April 8, 1983

WILD WORDS – AND A WHIFF
OF TEAR GAS

There is a change, a whiff of May 1968, in the Paris air these days.

The past week, for example, has seen the first massive student demonstrations since that fateful month fifteen years ago and on one particular late afternoon police were battling law students, medical students and farmers at three different points on the Left Bank.

They were reproducing scenes from another decade with such perfection that they must have had a rejuvenating effect on elderly spectators. I know that sitting yesterday evening in a terrace café on the corner of the Boulevard St Germain and the Boulevard Raspail – which provided then as now a perfect view of the action – the scene had this effect on me.

Nothing was missing – there were some freshly uprooted paving stones, even a smell of tear gas.

Understandably, these scenes are being greeted with ill-concealed and even unconcealed delight by the French Right, which particularly relishes the idea that a Socialist Government may be as effectively destabilised by student riots in 1983 as was General de Gaulle's in 1968.

Such a notion seems widely far-fetched at the moment yet the Socialists themselves are disturbed by the situation, bearing in mind no doubt how quickly things got out of hand on that previous May. Now, as then, concessions to the students can encourage other sectional interests to take to the streets or the huge mass of unorganised workers to take strike action.

There have even been suggestions from some Socialists that the students are being actively encouraged by the Opposition. Even if this were true, I doubt if that would have much effect because of the overwhelmingly Left-wing sympathies of the students themselves.

In any case, the student grievances are solidly based and are basically similar to those which fuelled the 1968 riots.

France is the only country in the Western world which does not practise selection for entry into its universities. As a result, the process of elimination begins after and not before enrolment. This takes the form of tough examinations which as many as forty per cent fail in the first year.

It is this addition of a still further tough exam at the end of an extended seven-year course which has touched off the present revolt in the medical and law faculties.

To revert to the present dangers, these are not likely to materialise into anything dramatic as yet, though there is enough inflammable material around not to rule out such a possibility.

The real danger of an 'explosion of discontent' will come in the autumn, according to a surprising number of eminent local commentators and politicians on both sides. Among those who seriously consider such a possibility is the normally cautious former President Giscard.

For the moment, the major Opposition leader Jacques Chirac is keeping his own counsel and the former Prime Minister Raymond Barre has issued a warning to the Opposition 'not to blow on the flames'.

However, as the political correspondent of *Le Monde* points out, 'Others will be tempted not only to blow on the flames but to pour oil on them.' One of these is the Conservative organ *Le Figaro* which came out this week with a banner headline over five columns: 'It's the revolt'.

It must be admitted that for those who see the revolt as either coming in the autumn or being already here the signs are encouraging and threaten to become more so.

By November we will have the first results of the austerity plan launched by the Government a month ago and the predictions are deeply pessimistic.

There will be a sharp drop in purchasing power, a rise in inflation into double figures and a 200,000 increase in unemployment.

The Finance Minister Jacques Delors is under heavy fire from his own followers and many not only predict that he will fail but they make little secret of the fact that their own hope is that he will do so.

It would appear, therefore, if current signs are to be trusted, that Britain, West Germany and the United States will be emerging from the depression just as France will be mired in that economic bog, we in Britain know so well, known as 'stagflation'.

Meanwhile, the political atmosphere is becoming increasingly poisonous. For example, the No. 2 in the French Socialist Party, Jean Poperen, has accused the Opposition of preparing a *coup d'état* against President Mitterrand rather in the manner of the one that deposed President Allende in Chile. These are wild words indeed and M. Poperen accompanies them with a declaration to the effect that 'a class war exists and it is up to us to wage it'.

These are hardly words to encourage French businessmen to heed M. Delors' appeals to them to co-operate with the Government.

Matters are made worse by the fact that Parliamentary elections are still three years off and there is speculation that to head off another May 1968 – if it comes and whenever it comes – M. Mitterrand may, like de Gaulle before him, be forced to hold early parliamentary elections.

In all this the President is something of a puzzle. Seen as a strong man abroad, he is increasingly being seen as a weak one at home.

A distinguished political writer, Raymond Aron, claimed this week that M. Mitterrand seemed to be confused about the role of the President under the existing Constitution and to confuse it with the largely decorative one of the President under the previous one.

The President nowadays, writes M. Aron, is in fact the chief executive and unless he takes prompt and firm decisions on virtually all matters the machinery of government simply seizes up. He added that the President was being indecisive on many key issues of domestic policy and tended to take the advice of the last person he spoke to.

Friday, April 29, 1983

CITY UNDER SIEGE

L ike the rain and the cold, the demonstrations that have plagued Paris for the past four weeks simply won't go away. On the contrary, they appear to be growing in volume and variety, with here and there a spark or two igniting strikes, an ominous sign that the unrest may spread from students, shop-keepers and farmers to the working class.

The Socialist government has responded to all this by laying on a most imposing show of force since May 1968, all the more imposing because unlike the events of fifteen years ago the demonstrations of recent weeks have on the whole been peace-able.

There have, of course, been scenes of violence organised by groups of toughs now labelled 'extreme Right' instead of the previous 'extreme Left'. These can be quickly isolated and their ringleaders arrested. There have been, too, instances of police brutality but this time it is the Right which is denouncing them and the Left which is maintaining a dignified silence.

Meanwhile, the show of mechanised and armed police force is maintained on a scale which astonishes tourists and gives Paris the air of an occupied city.

As such, this show of force is in danger of becoming counter-productive; instead of reassuring citizens, it frightens them, instead of calming them, it angers them. In short, the police's very presence in such numbers so ostentatiously displayed with all their frightening gear, is in itself becoming a provocation.

Interesting enough, this was the view taken by President Mitterrand himself when, as leader of the Opposition, he called for the withdrawal of the riot police from the Latin Quarter in May, 1968.

Possibly true then, it is certainly true now in the much calmer atmosphere of May, 1983.

All French governments over-react to the slightest smell of trouble in the streets but one would have thought a Socialist government would have been slower to do so if only because its leading members have so often denounced over-reaction in the past.

I thought at first that the reason why the government were overdoing things was conditioned by the area in which I live on the Left Bank. It houses within a radius of half a mile no fewer than seven ministries including such focal points for demonstrators as the Ministries of Labour, Agriculture and Education, to say nothing of the Prime Minister's residence, Matignon.

This is so choked with black-clad CRS riot police and their vehicles as to give one the impression of living under a state of siege.

However, driving in late one evening from Charles de Gaulle airport through deserted streets, one was able to see large concentrations of CRS at all key points and especially at the Alma and Concorde bridges. Outlined against a clear sky, in a state of full alert and at some points standing sixteen-deep, they looked like Martians defending freshly conquered territory.

By the time I got home it was less of a shock to find that I had to get through a throng of CRS to reach my own doorway. All this raises the question as to why the government is so obviously exaggerating the dangers it may be facing.

The most obvious explanation is the one that gives credence to the view expressed by some of its members that there is some kind of Right-wing plot afoot to overthrow it. Thereby, it would mobilise the waning enthusiasm of its supporters. If so, it is a dangerous gambit. I see that one of the demonstrations scheduled for this week is called by the Trotskyists and its declared aim is 'to sweep the Fascists off the streets'.

It may not be long before the Communists, who are hard up for a cause, try to get in on this act.

If so, the merry month of May may well end up in serious trouble.

Friday, May 20, 1983

WHY THE FRENCH ARE FEELING
OUT OF IT

The French are puzzled and even a little peeved that France has not featured more in the course of the present British General Election campaign.

Sam White's Paris

It is, after all, now two years since France elected a Socialist President and a Socialist Government and this, it is felt here, has produced results which might have been discussed during the campaign.

On reflection, however, it is easy to see why neither side in Britain has wished to make much or even anything of what has been going on across the Channel.

Take the Labour Party first. It would, I imagine, have dearly loved to point to Socialist France as an example of the rewards its own strikingly similar policies would bring to Britain.

But as the French Socialists are now in full retreat from the selfsame policies, this is hardly the moment to hold them up as models.

As for the Tories, one has the impression that international good manners have inhibited them from fully exploiting the evident failures of President Mitterand's government and, by corollary, Mr Foot's remedies for Britain's ills.

Mrs Thatcher's own relations with President Mitterrand are excellent and he has come as a welcome relief from his icy and pedantic predecessor. Why put that personal relationship in jeopardy by dwelling on the French domestic scene?

Furthermore, Socialism in France has not only produced a more agreeable opposite number in Paris but has also weakened the exclusive Franco–German partnership so much resented in Whitehall in the past.

Altogether, a Socialist France – or the model of it presented by M. Mitterrand – is not unwelcome to Mrs Thatcher, not only for the reasons already advanced but for the extra bonus that it has reduced the competitiveness of a major trade rival.

Meanwhile, Mrs Thatcher's seeming ascendancy in this election is being watched with awe by Opposition leaders here. Some are already claiming to be drawing useful political lessons from it for the future.

And no one here has failed to notice the contrast between Mrs Thatcher's elated air after the Williamsburg Conference and M. Mitterrand's distinctly dejected appearance.

After only a token resistance he signed a communiqué giving total victory to the monetarists on the other side of the Atlantic and on the other side of the Channel: he contented himself with a vaguely worded promise of some future monetary conference to reform the present international monetary order which he attacked shortly before leaving Paris.

Back home, the President is facing a sea of troubles. A major revolt against his leadership and policies has broken out within his own Socialist Party while his Communist allies are up in arms against the defence document he signed at Williamsburg, which to all intents and purposes makes France once again a member of NATO.

Here is what the French equivalent of the *New Statesman, Le Nouvel Observateur*, writes this week: 'We have now reached the point where we must seriously ask if the present Government will be able to survive until the end of its term in three years' time. It may well be that the President will have to resort to early elections in order to be able to cope with the situation.'

It is tempting to conclude that the kind of collapse the British Socialists are experiencing in Opposition is already threatening the French Socialists in Government. It is both tempting and not far off the mark.

Friday, June 3, 1983

INDEX

Sam White's Paris